SO-BAX-661

Acclaim for Randy Poe's
Skydog: The Duane Allman Story

"Thorough and enthralling."

—*Guitar Player* magazine

"This is a well-researched, respectful, and mercifully non-sensationalistic bio of an essential figure who straddles genres and musical ideologies to leave us a body of work that seems to grow in richness and meaning as time goes on."

—*Living Blues* magazine

"Author Randy Poe takes a scholarly look at this architect of Southern rock, piecing together the story of an artist whose brief career was influential enough to spawn a whole genre of popular music."

—*Blues Revue* magazine

"Well-written and researched . . . Allman's passion for music oozes off every page."

—*Classic Rock* magazine

"With an exhaustive discography plus many wonderful archival photos, *Skydog* is a highly valuable and quite poignant look at one of the finest guitarists in modern music history."

—*Nashville City Paper*

"Author Randy Poe is from the South, and he brings an understanding to the music and life of Allman that's respectful, insightful, yet surprisingly honest. Duane's significance as a musician, his too-short life, and his inspiring force are given the full treatment they deserve."

—*Harp* magazine

"*Skydog: The Duane Allman Story* is a fast-paced read full of essential detail."

—*All About Jazz*

"Poe does a fine job of detailing Duane Allman's life, making *Skydog* a good choice for those wishing to learn more about one of the greatest slide guitarists of all time."

—*Dirty Linen* magazine

Skydog

The Duane Allman Story

Randy Poe

Foreword by Billy F Gibbons

Backbeat Books

An Imprint of Hal Leonard Corporation
New York

Backbeat Books
An Imprint of Hal Leonard Corporation
7777 West Bluemound Road
Milwaukee, WI 53213

Trade Book Division Editorial Offices
19 West 21st Street, New York, NY 10010

Originally published in hardcover in 2006 by Backbeat Books
Revised paperback edition published in 2008 by Backbeat Books

Printed in the United States of America

Text Design and Composition by Leigh McLellan Design
Front Cover Design by Richard Leeds—BigWigDesign.com
Back Cover Design by Clare Cerullo
Front Cover Photo by Jim Marshall

The Library of Congress has cataloged the hardcover edition as follows:
Poe, Randy, 1955-
  Skydog : the Duane Allman story / by Randy Poe ; foreword by Billy F. Gibbons.
    p. cm.
  Includes bibliographical references (p. 293) and index.
  ISBN-13: 978-0-87930-891-9 (alk. paper)
  ISBN-10: 0-87930-891-5 (alk. paper)
  1. Allman, Duane, 1946-1971. 2. Rock musicians-United States-Biography. 3. Allman Brothers Band. I. Title.

  ML419.A565 P63
. 787.87'166092--dc22
  [B]
                              2006023613

ISBN 978-0-87930-939-8

www.backbeatbooks.com

For
Bill Ector, Joe Bell, and John Lynskey,
Keepers of the flame

With special thanks to
Bert Holman and Kirk West,
Keepers of the backstage passes

Contents

Foreword

by Billy F Gibbons

Duane Allman . . . the master of slitherin' 'round with sound on his slide mo-chine. Killer guitarist and Southern gent who knew how to make a six-string sting with his personally branded savvy and swagger. What a blast! What a character . . . what a gifted kind of guy. Let's hit it. . . .

I met Duane at the same time I formed the ZZ Top band, lookin' 'round some of the same corners everybody was . . . checkin' somehow and someway to embrace a bit of that spirit of this phenomenon now respectfully called "The Blues." Quite the challenge . . . not only as interpreters, but as players and soothsayers of the mystical art form. Duane had it and had it down . . . his guitar-slingin' slide work remains to be enjoyed, time after time . . . even in these contemporary times . . . through his association with his bandmates on record.

This work is a labor of love and a compliment to Duane Allman. And why not . . . ? Duane's unorthodox attack with his ever-present glass Coricidin bottle wrapped around his favorite finger wrung whips, flips, chunks, and chips of licks and chops that became super-suited for leanin' hard into whatever was on the deck. That doesn't mean there were spaces left unturned . . . there were plenty . . . all combining timing with such taste that the legacy of his performances stands solid as rock, with grace . . . as does that ferocious command of delivery Duane brought forth whenever he felt like it.

My initial encounter with the Allman Brothers Band—Duane, Gregg, Dickey, Butch, Jaimoe, and Berry—occurred way down in New Orleans for a big-time billing night with the ABB and ZZ Top, along with Canned Heat and Quicksilver Messenger Service at Don Fox's famed brick and wood-framed turn-of-the-century waterfront cotton warehouse, aptly named The Warehouse. The booking, scheduled to cover the two-night weekend, invited a quick and hasty dash into the Crescent City in advance of the opening night, as ZZ and the Brothers had been given privilege to come in early and stay overnight inside "the room" . . . a giant warm open room with a wide sturdy stage, an un-sturdy catwalk bridge overhead to what served as dressing rooms, and two tiny, box-like balcony spaces to crash in. Just enough for a headcount of a scant few. Yet, in those meager and humble beginning days, no one was about to complain as Mr. Willie's house cuisine "speciality" (Mr. Red Beans and Creole Rice's Gumbo), simmerin' directly below, could be had by lowering a bucket-on-rope affair and hoisting it up backstage before show time.

That fateful opening night endeared me with Duane and all our bandmates forever as the evening's dusk turned dourly dark with the approach of a nasty, unexpected hurricane. Yeah . . . you know the ones . . . the ones that whip up on you without warning and wail unmercifully through what seems like forever . . . especially when the roof departs the premises overhead and a huddle of guys, guitars, and a few uninitiated gals gather under the only remaining vestige of shelter. Duane calmly smiled and said, "Billy G, let's you, me, and the fellas rip a version of 'One Way Out,' 'cuz this may be it, Bruthuh . . . !" We was soaked, scared, and loaded. Yet, after a scathing rain-wracked howl of a night . . . the show somehow went on. I won't forget it, nor will I forget the enthusiasm of that first wicked night . . . rugged, rockin', ragged, and definitely righteous. Everybody smoked and everyone was toked. Uh . . . make that stoked.

So let's get on wit' it. You've spent the dime, now take some time with this creation that paints a picture of this charismatic character of the slide guitar. Duane will do the rest. He stands as one of the very best.

Prologue

When he and his sister were still quite young—he was 9, she was 13—there was no place on the planet more fun than Daytona Beach, Florida, in the summertime.

It didn't matter that the only motel their parents could afford to stay in had no air conditioning. There were tiny slat windows that opened with a hand crank to let in the cool ocean breeze.

The stuff that *did* matter was the sand, the salt air, the saltier water, the pier, and the boardwalk with its long stretch of souvenir shops, food stands, and pinball arcades.

They were just children, but since they were on vacation their parents let them stay out later than usual. It was the early 1960s—back in the days when a couple of kids could still run around outside after sundown without a worry in the world.

As they stood there, looking out at the vast ocean, the boy and his sister suddenly heard loud, blistering rock & roll coming from the big building halfway down the pier.

Their father was a minister—their mother a high school English teacher. In their sheltered Northern Alabama/Southern Baptist upbringing, one of the things the siblings had never encountered prior to that warm Florida evening was genuine, *live* rock & roll.

Slowly, hesitantly, they walked down the pier toward the music. Afraid to venture too near a room filled with such unquestionable iniquity, they got as close to the building as they dared.

Suddenly, the lead guitar began to wail—playing slow, bluesy licks that mesmerized them both. Ungodly was much too weak a word to describe the music they were hearing.

The girl giggled. The boy listened intently, hanging on every note. For him, it was a life-changing experience that he would still remember with total clarity some four decades later.

The girl was my sister. I was the boy. The guitar player was Duane Allman.

CHAPTER ONE

Where It All Begins

"The first stuff I heard was Hank Williams and Flatt & Scruggs
on my grandma's old 78 player." — D.A.

The blues, along with country, gospel, and jazz, originated in the south-eastern United States—an area of the country once rife with the op-pressed and disenfranchised. Few among the population of the Old South escaped adversity in one form or another, whether it was the hardship of slavery suffered by Africans brought to the region to work as field hands; the death and displacement caused by the battles fought to rid the territory of Native Americans; or the indignities inflicted by the carpetbaggers, who infil-trated from the North after the Civil War with the sole objective of profiting from the defeat of the Confederacy.

The harshness of such oppression produced intense emotions, and from those emotions came great art. Thus, at the beginning of the 20th century, the emotional music of the blues emanating from the South came to be heard by a young composer named W. C. Handy.

While waiting for an overdue train to arrive at the Tutwiler, Mississippi, station, Handy had fallen asleep, only to be awakened by a wandering musi-cian who sat down next to him and began to sing. The performer, an African-American man in tattered clothes, moaned the lyrics of a song about going "where the Southern crosses the Yellow Dog." The line referred to two rail-roads: the Southern and the Yazoo Delta. It was Handy's introduction to the blues—a genre he would almost single-handedly popularize over the course of the next decade.

The musician in the train station that day—his name lost to history—had accompanied himself on guitar as he sang about the Yellow Dog. As enamored as Handy was of the lyrics, he was equally fascinated by the sound the guitar made as the singer slid a pocketknife up and down the strings. Handy later wrote in his autobiography, *Father of the Blues*, that it was "the weirdest music I had ever heard."

Born in Florence, Alabama—one of the four towns that make up the area known as Muscle Shoals—Handy was so moved by the music he heard in the Tutwiler train station that he soon began composing works in a similar vein. Between 1912 and 1917, he wrote four of his most famous songs: "Memphis Blues," "Beale Street Blues," "St. Louis Blues," and "Yellow Dog Blues." "St. Louis Blues" would become one of the most recorded songs of the first half of the century, earning Handy the title Father of the Blues, while "Yellow Dog Blues" (in a tradition that continues to the present day) lifted the line "where the Southern crosses the Yellow Dog" from the unknown blues singer in Tutwiler.

The 1920s became the decade of such classic female blues singers as Sippie Wallace, Ida Cox, Victoria Spivey, Ma Rainey, and perhaps the best-known female blues singer of all time, Bessie Smith—whose many hits recorded before her untimely death included Handy's "St. Louis Blues," featuring Louis Armstrong on trumpet.

As the audience for the music grew, record labels sent talent scouts to the South to find more blues singers. What the scouts discovered was a host of performers who had continued to focus on the very sound that had so affected Handy—a guitar being played with various implements used as a slide. Charley Patton and Blind Willie Johnson both used a knife. Son House broke a bottle and slid its neck along the strings. Willie Wilson's slide of choice was a medicine bottle on his little finger. The list of accomplished slide guitarists from the South also included "Statesboro Blues" composer Blind Willie McTell, Kokomo Arnold, Barbecue Bob, Blind Boy Fuller, Bukka White, and the man from whom all modern blues music has emerged—Robert Johnson.

Looking to escape from low-paying field labor, many blues musicians took to the highways leading out of Mississippi, Alabama, and Georgia, heading north to seek success in Memphis, Kansas City, Chicago, and other urban areas. One of the best known of the Mississippi-born blues musicians, McKinley Morganfield, aka Muddy Waters, left the Magnolia State for Chicago in 1943. Although Alan Lomax had made some field recordings of Waters in 1941, the great bluesman's first recording session in a real studio took place in Chicago in 1946.

That same year, on November 20th, Howard Duane Allman was born in Nashville, Tennessee. The first son of Willis and Geraldine Allman, Duane arrived just over a year after the end of World War II.

Duane's father and his Uncle Howard were both army men. Willis had joined first, in 1937, and he eventually talked his younger brother into enlisting as well. Just as the blues musicians had moved north to escape working in the fields, Willis had joined the army to escape a similar fate.

Given the job of signing up new soldiers, Willis traveled throughout the South. While on a recruiting mission in Rocky Mount, North Carolina, he met Geraldine Robbins. Just prior to the onset of the war, Willis and Geraldine were married. Soon after, the U.S. Army sent Willis and Howard to Europe—and the brothers would eventually be among the thousands of Allied soldiers who landed on the beaches of Normandy on June 6, 1944: "D-Day."

With the war (but not the Army) behind them, both brothers returned to the States to work as recruiters in Nashville. Willis and Geraldine made their home on Westbrook Avenue, just a few miles southwest of the Ryman Auditorium— home of the Grand Ole Opry.

In the years between the two world wars, when Willis and his brothers, Howard and David, were still kids, they had listened to the Grand Ole Opry on the radio. Raised on a farm in Dickson County, Tennessee—less than 50 miles from Nashville—the three boys and their parents, John and Myrtle Allman, would spend their Saturday nights with the dial tuned to Nashville's 50,000-watt station, WSM. The sounds of Roy Acuff and Bill Monroe came in loud and clear.

In the Depression-era days of the rural South, particularly before the proliferation of record players, radio was one of the few sources for musical entertainment. The only alternative for the Allman family—and many others—was to make the music themselves. Duane's grandfather, John, was a singer in a barbershop quartet, while John's brother, Walton, was proficient on banjo, guitar, and mandolin. Willis was a good singer, too. By the time Duane came along, music had played an important part in his family's lives for several generations.

Just over a year after Duane's birth, on December 8, 1947, his brother Gregory Lenoir Allman was born. In 1949, the family of four moved to Fort Story, an army base in Virginia Beach, Virginia.

That Christmas, Geraldine and the kids went to visit her folks in North Carolina for the holidays. Willis was unable to go because he was required to remain on duty at the base. On December 26, Allman and Second Lieutenant Robert Buchanan went out for some post-Christmas relaxation at a bar in Norfolk. While there, they were approached by a fellow veteran—previously unknown to them—named Michael Green. The three men had drinks at the bar, and later headed to another watering hole. When Allman and Buchanan decided to call it a night, Green asked to be dropped off at yet another bar, so the three vets hopped into Buchanan's car.

Michael Green, sitting in the back seat, suddenly pulled out a gun and ordered Buchanan to drive to a desolate area outside of town. After robbing both men of the few dollars in their pockets, he began leading them toward the nearby woods. After Green told the two men to lie down, Willis Allman made a play for Green's gun. When Green pulled the trigger, Allman and Buchanan ran—Allman going one direction while Buchanan went the other. As Buchanan ran, he heard the pistol go off again.

Willis Allman was later found a short distance from where the chase had begun. Shot in the chest, he had died at the scene. The soldier who had survived the fierce battle on the beaches of Normandy had been murdered in East Ocean View, Virginia, by a fellow veteran.

Not long after Willis's death, Geraldine's in-laws took her and the two boys into their home. Duane—who had celebrated his third birthday only a month before his father was murdered—would spend the next few years living with his mother, his little brother, and his grandparents in Nashville.

Gregg's memories of those days are a combination of an idyllic childhood and the mischievousness of his older brother. "We were middle-middle-class, but it was great," he recalls. "That was in the '50s. We had the soda shops and the movies for ten cents. Oh man, things were so simple back then. We'd go on the golf course—there was this creek running through it—and we caught these little tiny fishes with a million bones in 'em. We caught 'em on pieces of bacon.

"We did a million things, man. Duane hung me one time from this tree. He learned to make a damn hangman's noose at a very young age—13 wraps and the whole bit, you know? So he ties it to the limb of this tree and puts the other end around my neck and pulls it up nice and snug. And then he says, 'Hey, Mom made some cookies. Let's go get some!' He takes off running and, of course, I'm running right behind him—until I run out of rope. I was starting to turn kinda blue when they finally came out and got the rope off me. He pretty much whipped my ass every day of my life when we were little."

Shortly after Willis died, Geraldine had found secretarial work. But she eventually chose to attend college in an effort to get a degree in a field that promised better wages. She decided to become an accountant, attending school with the help of the military benefits provided to her as a soldier's widow.

At the time, Duane and Gregg were attending Parmer School in the Belle Meade section of Nashville. But when Geraldine discovered that her late husband's military benefits included a break in the tuition at Castle Heights Military Academy (CHMA), she decided to send her boys there while she finished her own education. CHMA was in Lebanon, Tennessee—less than 30 miles east of Nashville—but it might as well have been a thousand miles away as far as the brothers were concerned.

When they arrived at Castle Heights in the fall of 1955, Duane and Gregg entered a world neither could have imagined: barracks, uniforms, and a daily disciplined regimen unlike anything they had experienced thus far in their young lives. Duane entered in the fourth grade; Gregg was one year behind him. Although they didn't room together, both boys were housed at Hooker Hall—Gregg on the top floor, Duane on the first.

As a former CHMA student explains, Duane and Gregg were "down in what they called the goober school, which was basically the elementary school. It was in another section of the campus. The goobers had a little bit different uniform, and they were more like little kids. When you got to the ninth grade, you were no longer a goober—you were a cadet. You were up with the big guys."

A single photo of a group of "goober school" kids perfectly captures the Allman boys' reaction to the circumstances into which they had been thrust.

The year is 1956. Gregg, in the second row, looks downright morose. His head is tilted down, as are the corners of his mouth. Duane, on the opposite end of the third row, has a devilish smirk on his face. His hat is cocked to one side, his right eye completely covered by its brim.

Having grown up with music in the house, the brothers decided they should play an instrument. "We wanted to get into the school band," says Gregg. "We both wanted to play trumpet, but we lost interest in it. My mother always called it her folly because back then it was $200 for a trumpet—that was quite a bit."

Decades later, several schoolmates posted their memories of Duane and Gregg's days at the school on a Web site dedicated to CHMA. There's an account of one student who got caught with the Allmans as the three boys were returning from an area known as the "butt hole," where they had been smoking Lucky Strikes that Duane had somehow managed to procure. The result was several hours spent in the Hooker study hall. Another alumnus tells of a talent show in which Duane and Gregg performed a little number called "The CHMA Blues." Although it might have been a hit with their fellow students, one faculty member was less impressed, summoning them to his office and awarding them with demerits for their performance.

After the boys had spent two years at Castle Heights, Geraldine gave them a reprieve. Now that she was a certified public accountant, Mrs. Allman was going to start a new career in a new state. The family was moving to Daytona Beach, Florida—and Duane and Gregg couldn't have been more ready.

CHAPTER TWO

A Guitar & a Motorcycle, Part 1

"The cat that actually taught me how to play is Jim Shepley—old 'Lightning Fingers'—the first, number one, taking-care-of-business man in Daytona Beach, Florida." — D.A.

The **Allmans' new house** at 100 Van Avenue in Daytona Beach sat on a peninsula between the Halifax River and the Atlantic Ocean. Duane was still in the South, but it must have seemed like a different world compared to the one he had just left when, in 1957, the boy found himself—just as the ads say—surrounded by water, sand, sun, and fun.

The first big car race was still two years away when the Allmans made their move to Florida. Long before the Daytona 500 came along, the town's premier racing event had been the Daytona 200, but the vehicles flying along at full throttle weren't racecars—they were motorcycles.

The Daytona 200 was celebrating its 20th anniversary the year Duane and his family arrived. Although the race had begun in another area of town, by 1957 it was held near Ponce Inlet, just south of Duane's house. If you were a boy living in Daytona Beach in the late 1950s, a serious admiration of motorcycles and the men who rode them was practically unavoidable. Duane Allman was no exception. It would be a few years before he could have a motorcycle of his own—but he knew the day would come.

Duane and Gregg enjoyed their first summer in Daytona, went to school in the fall, and then began an annual pilgrimage back to Nashville to spend a few weeks with their grandmother during the summer. It was on one of those visits that Gregg discovered the guitar.

"Our grandmother lived in this house in the projects, and there was this retarded guy that lived across the street," says Gregg. "He was a couple of quarts low. One day I came outside and looked over, and he was painting his car with house paint with a big brush—I mean, the tires, the chrome, everything.

"This guy had an old Bell Tone guitar—the strings were about an inch high off the neck. It was just leaning against the porch. I went up there, and I was just *fascinated* by it. I said, 'Can you play it?' He said, 'Sure.' He played 'Comin' Around the Mountain When She Comes,' and so I thought, 'Well, if this guy can play, I can.' So I asked him if he'd teach me how to play. He taught me that one song—and that did it. I was hooked."

When Gregg got back to Daytona, he had to have a guitar of his own. His mother suggested that he get a job to pay for it, so he took on a paper route. When the big day finally came for him to purchase his very own Sears Silvertone, he discovered he was 95 cents short. After a dejected Gregg returned home with the sad news, his mother gave him the money he needed. The next day he had the guitar in his hands.

By this time, Duane had acquired a motorcycle. Gregg later told the writer Alan Paul that it was "a tiny little Harley 165—one of those little ones where you mix the gas with the oil. He drove the damned thing into the ground—just rode it until it fell apart—and one day he brought it home in a bag."

And there was Gregg with his brand new Sears Silvertone. "He looks at my guitar and says, 'Now what you got there, baby brother?' I go, 'Now all right, Duane, that's mine.' He would slip into my room and play it. I swear to God, we had more fights over that guitar than you'd believe."

With Duane's motorcycle in pieces, the guitar became his new obsession. Soon, Geraldine had no choice but to get Duane a guitar of his own. "Then not only was there peace in the family," says Gregg, "but we started playing together. I had shown him how to play at the beginning, then he started showing me some licks, and we would just help each other out—that's how we learned."

Both Duane and Gregg were born left-handed—but unlike Albert King, Jimi Hendrix, and other southpaws who chose to pick with their left hand and handle the fretwork with their right, the brothers both taught themselves to play right-handed.

Although Gregg showed his brother some basic chord changes, there was another player in town who helped to take the young guitarist to the next level. "Duane had a friend named Jim Shepley who was a couple of years older and had started a couple of years before," Gregg recalls. "He turned us on to Jimmy Reed records. He had a bunch of those hot licks down, and I thought, 'Man, this guy is something else!' And so he sat with Duane all the time."

Jim and Duane had met in a Daytona Beach pool hall not long after the Allmans moved to town. Duane Allman, all of 11 years old at the time, had marched up to Shepley (age 14) and introduced himself. "He saw me and came over and started talking," Shepley wrote in a piece for *Guitar Player* magazine. "I learned that he had just moved down from Tennessee with his mother and his brother."

Shepley attributes Duane's gravitation toward him, in part, to the loss of his father at such an early age. "Duane's father had been killed . . . so if he looked up to someone a little older than him, he kind of latched onto him." But Duane would discover another reason to latch onto Shepley—those Jimmy Reed licks. "Duane had never really heard [them]," Shepley wrote, "and he flipped out and immediately wanted me to show him all that stuff."

Reed's simple blues style—referred to by one critic as "primitive, to say the least"—was essentially Blues Guitar 101. It was the perfect starting point for Duane. "From the first day I showed him Jimmy Reed licks," noted Shepley, "Duane knew that he only wanted to be one thing: a rock & roll star."

Another event took place during one of the boys' summer trips to Nashville that would escalate Duane's musical ambitions even further. "The first rock & roll show that me and my brother ever went to was headed up by Jackie Wilson," says Gregg. "B.B. King was also on that show, and Johnny Taylor—all these incredible people. We were way up in the cheap seats."

It was then and there that Duane Allman saw his future. "Little brother," he said to Gregg, "we've got to get into this."

After Duane and Gregg returned to Daytona, their woodshedding picked up several notches. And, by the end of 1960, the boys had their first electric guitars: Gregg got a Fender Musicmaster, and shortly thereafter ("to keep us from fighting," says Gregg), their mother bought Duane a cherry-red 1959 Gibson Les Paul Junior.

Now both teenagers, Duane and Gregg began playing their new electric guitars in local groups, beginning with a Daytona Beach YMCA ensemble called the Y Teens. Then they struck out on their own. "When we formed our first band in 1963, most of the people in it had played the blues or rhythm & blues, or a rock & roll variation of it," says Gregg. "The music made you move and everybody liked it—and we just kind of migrated towards it. The band was called the Shufflers. I played lead guitar and Duane sang."

But soon the guitar became an obsession for Duane, having such an effect on his schoolwork that he found himself being sent back to Castle Heights. Although Gregg would eventually graduate from Daytona Beach's Seabreeze High School in 1965, both of the brothers bounced in and out of CHMA between 1961 and 1964. Duane's eventual departure from formal education wasn't a matter of his deciding to leave on a specific day, never to return. He had simply lost interest in going to school with any regularity once he discovered the guitar.

For at least a few months in the latter part of 1963, Duane and Gregg were both going to CHMA at the same time. Mike Johnstone, a fellow guitarist, was also at Castle Heights that year. "I had started playing in bars, underage, and playing whenever I could at school dances and stuff, and doing all the activities that go along with that—like drinking and just being a fuck-up in general," Johnstone says. "My dad was concerned, so he said, 'I'm gonna send you to Castle Heights. I think this is the best bet for you at the moment—you need to be going where there's a little more discipline. And you can bring your guitar.'

"So I said, 'Okay, I'll do it.' I didn't really want to, but I went. The first day I was there, there were very few people in the dormitories because I was a day or two early. Now, at that time, there was a popular song on the radio called 'Memphis'—an instrumental by Lonnie Mack. It was the best guitar playing I'd ever heard. All the guitar players were going, 'How could anybody ever play as good as that? That's the new bar. That's how good you have to be now.' And when I got to the school, I heard this song wafting down the hall."

Johnstone thought he was hearing "Memphis" on a radio in someone's dorm room—until he realized that the music kept starting and stopping.

"I followed the sound," he continues, "and it was coming out of this room one floor below me. I knocked, and a guy comes to the door. It was Duane

Allman—a redheaded guy with a guitar hanging around his neck. He had it plugged into an old amp, and he was playing the song just as good as Lonnie Mack. So I thought, 'Well, shit! I gotta make friends with this guy.' I went in and sat down, and we hit it off right away. He told me he had a brother who was at the school, and he had a guitar too."

Duane took Gregg's guitar out of the case and handed it to Johnstone. "Gregg didn't play keys in those days, just guitar. I told Duane that I had a guitar and an amp—and that I had a bass. He said, 'You have a bass? Nobody has a bass! We need a bass player.'"

Duane had already rounded up a drummer and a sax player, so with Johnstone on bass he had a band. "We rehearsed down at the auditorium there at the school and played school dances. We did what I call black rock & roll—the early R&B things: Bobby 'Blue' Bland and Ray Charles and James Brown. I remember we played 'Stormy Monday.' I was coming out of surf music—that was my deal. I got started listening to Chet Atkins, which led me to the Ventures. Duane was into that, too, but he was more into B.B. King and things like that."

Duane was also developing his ability to lead a band. According to Johnstone, Allman would "kick the ball along, keep the thing moving. I've been to a lot of rehearsals and been in bands that didn't know how to do that. The average person may not even appreciate what a bandleader does. The good ones, they don't demand respect—they *command* respect. There's a difference. He wasn't a bully or anything; he just knew exactly what he wanted to do. He was a leader."

Mike Johnstone was one of many who would find that Duane was not only a natural leader but a natural teacher, always eager to pass along what he knew to anyone willing to learn. Johnstone recalls one occasion when he asked Allman about a chord he was playing. "He said, 'That's a 9th chord.' I said, 'Where would you use it?' And he goes, 'Well, let's say you're going to do a turnaround . . . .' And I go, 'What's a turnaround?' He sort of taught me all those things."

But the real eye-opener for the young musician was discovering Allman's work ethic. "Duane had a great record collection, and he brought it with him. The rooms all had two bunk beds, a desk for two people to sit side-by-side and do their homework, and a closet that two guys split. You had two pairs of pants, two coats, two shirts, three pairs of socks, and two pairs of shoes in there. Everything else, you had to fit in somehow. If you had a guitar case under your bed, that was okay. If you had a record player or a radio, that was okay. To have a record collection in your footlocker, taking up space you could have used for other things—that was sort of a hardship.

"Duane had one of those little record players that looks like a suitcase. The speaker's in front, the top opens up, and the turntable's inside. He would sit there and play along with a B.B. King record. When he got to something he wanted to learn, he would stop the record. He was barefooted, and he would put his foot inside the record player and stop the record with his toe—the turntable would still be spinning underneath the record—and he would play until he learned the lick. Then he would let the record go. When it got to the next lick, he would stop it with his toe again. He would do that all the way through the record, then flip it over to the other side, and when he was done with that side, he would flip it back over and do it all again. He'd do that for hours.

"He was the first guy I ever saw practice that much—who was that organized. And it was like, 'Okay, now I see what it takes. I see how the guy got that good.' That was an inspiration for me from then on. If you want to be good, that's what you've gotta do—the record collection, the homework, the research, the practice routine, and all that kind of stuff."

It was that very kind of stuff that caused Duane's second stay at Castle Heights to be brief. "He didn't last too long," says Johnstone. "Somewhere in the middle of that year, he either went AWOL or got kicked out or both. He was just gone one day."

Another of Duane's CHMA classmates, Lamar Hill, recalls that Allman—as per military custom—went by his first name during those days. "Howard was not very sociable," he says, "but he was a nice guy when he chose to be. He spent most of his free time in his room playing guitar—imagine that! I would guess that he was not close to many people while he was at Castle Heights. I have no recollection of him being involved in any athletics or being a member of any of the campus organizations."

Ray White, another Castle Heights student, says, "Colonel Hale, one of the teachers and the eventual headmaster, told me that one evening when he was making his rounds during CQ—call to quarters—he heard the Allmans playing their guitars. He went in to tell them they should apply themselves to their studies, as they likely wouldn't make much money playing music."

Johnstone says, "I have a yearbook that has my picture on one page, and on the opposite page there's Gregg. Duane wasn't in the yearbook because he was gone before the pictures were taken. But he was there earlier that year. On the day that President Kennedy got shot, I was hanging out with Duane. He was there then."

Duane had made it to the photo shoot for the 1961–62 *Adjutant* (the CHMA yearbook), but before the end of the next school year he was gone. He ended up back at Seabreeze High in Daytona Beach, but his days there were no more productive than his final brief stay at Castle Heights.

Whenever he was in Daytona Beach, Duane continued to hang out with Jim Shepley. And by the middle of his teen years, he was already beginning to show a tendency toward living on the edge. Perhaps part of the reason for his actions was the loss of his father at such an early age. But if Shepley was a kind of father-figure for Allman, Duane had no problem sharing his on-the-edge lifestyle with his older friend. Nor did Jim Shepley—still a teenager himself—show any outward signs of wanting to act as an authority figure to Allman.

One of Duane's close calls came on the night he and Shepley ascended to the top of an unfinished apartment building. On the roof there was a large Christmas tree that Duane proceeded to climb. When he reached its summit, the tree began to tilt—leaving Allman hanging more than a hundred feet in the air. Like Harold Lloyd dangling from the hands of a clock atop a skyscraper in the movie *Safety Last*, Duane somehow managed to survive this death-defying act.

It was also in Daytona—and with Shepley—that Duane first dabbled in booze and drugs. They drank beer together, as well as buying pot on the black side of town. Allman also sniffed glue—Testors being his brand of choice. "It was like, let's get high and go play music," says Shepley. "And that's what we did."

They also managed to get in trouble with the law. When Shepley had a minor accident, bumping the back of a sheriff's car, an inebriated Allman spilled out of Shepley's automobile, yelling at the officer as he staggered to his feet. "What the hell you want, you son of a bitch?" demanded Duane—to which he added, "I'm gonna kick your ass. I know the mayor of this town!" Not surprisingly, Shepley and Allman were carted off to jail for a brief stay.

Allman had already destroyed one motorcycle by this time, and his unsafe driving habits showed no signs of improving. "Duane was one of those people you meet in your life that you know is not going to make it to 30," says one of his Seabreeze High classmates. "He was as self-destructive as anybody I ever knew. I can remember him driving motorcycles really recklessly. You do things when you're a kid that you'd never do when you're older—but he'd take it *way* past that."

Another classmate says, "He was looking for excitement. I mean, if we'd had hang gliding and bungee jumping and the stuff we have today, he would've probably done it all. His motorcycle stuff, I think, was just another way for him to get some kind of separation between the things that he thought were drudgery in life—school and responsibility and stuff—and feeling free like a bird. He was always looking for the big push, the big thing, the excitement."

Fortunately for Allman's physical well-being, playing and listening to music took up a lot of the time when he might have been tempting fate. In Duane's calmer moments, he and Gregg listened to the radio—just as two generations of Allmans before them had done. But the brothers weren't interested in the Grand Ole Opry. They tuned instead to 1510 AM.

"We listened to WLAC radio a lot," Duane later told Ellen Mandel of *Good Times* magazine. "They played some James Carr, some Roosevelt Sykes." WLAC also played Jimmy Reed, Muddy Waters, Etta James, Chuck Berry, Howlin' Wolf, and a lot of other black recording artists. Duane referred to the disc jockeys at the Nashville-based station as "a bunch of crazy old drunk guys playing rhythm & blues records."

Whether they were drunk or sober, the most popular voices on WLAC belonged to Gene Nobles, Bill "Hoss" Allen, and John Richbourg—known to his audience as John R. In 1992, not long after both Nobles and Richbourg had died, Allen told a reporter that he and his fellow jocks "initiated a new sound to white kids who probably never would have heard it if it had not been for the power of WLAC."

All three were white men who intentionally sounded black—both in their vocal delivery and in the slang they used. Although Duane's accent would always be that of a Southern-born, Southern-bred Caucasian, he became fluent in the black slang he picked up by listening to WLAC. (In a 1970 radio interview, Duane would say of bandmate Dickey Betts, "He is just as bad as there is, man," prompting a listener to call into the show and ask why Duane would have Dickey in the band if he was so "bad." The black slang meaning of the word wouldn't reach the white public at large until much later.)

The deejays at WLAC wielded a lot of power, primarily due to the fact that at night the 50,000-watt station frequently could be heard all the way from Canada to Jamaica. As Duane said, they would "take that good stuff and get it to you, no matter where you live."

These men were on the air not just to play records but to sell them via mail order on behalf on their sponsors: John R's show was sponsored by Ernie's Record Mart, while Gene Nobles' was backed by Randy's Record Shop. (Hoss Allen would later take over the Randy's Record Shop show when Nobles retired.) All three men were instrumental in spreading the sound of R&B throughout much of the eastern half of the U.S.

Between spinning records, Richbourg's patter consisted of bits like this: "This is John R, honey, way down south here in Dixie; 1510 on the dial—the Soul Center—on the air 24 hours a day every*where*." And when they weren't plugging records, the WLAC deejays were selling Royal Crown Hair Dressing and "live baby chicks delivered right to your door!"

Duane was enthralled by the whole mystique of late-night radio shows selling hairdressing, baby chicks, and R&B records, while broadcasting sounds that most kids in the South were forbidden to listen to by their horrified parents. But Duane was doing a lot more than just listening to R&B on the radio. Thanks to Jim Shepley's gig with an integrated band, Allman was going to see black musicians perform *live*.

"There was a place in Daytona at the pier," recalls fellow Daytona Beach musician Sylvan Wells. "It had a big dance hall right in the middle of it—still does. That was the place where everybody tried to hang out. Everybody'd go there and sit on the sides of the pier leading to the dance hall. At the bottom of the pier, where it joined the mainland, was a nightclub that had a band that was half-black, half-white. The guitar player was Jim Shepley.

"The Ocean Pier would book black acts, so the musicians would hang out there. I saw Hank Ballard & the Midnighters at the Ocean Pier in 1959 or 1960. You would see all kinds of people. As a musician, you could go to any of the black clubs, and you were treated with respect and invited to come in as long as you wanted to sit in and play. So it wasn't unusual at all for the white musicians to run around with the black musicians. There may have been segregation on the street, but it didn't exist among the musicians."

Shepley's band at the pier was technically an all-white group called the House Rockers, but the members of the vocal group they backed up—the Untils—were all black, resulting in a unique but acceptable form of integration. Occasionally, Gregg or Duane would sub for Shepley. "They only needed one guitar player," says Gregg, "so we switched off."

As Duane and Gregg took turns playing in the House Rockers, they were moving more and more into the world of R&B. But at the same time, on the other side of the Atlantic, a major musical change was afoot—a change that would affect music of just about every genre. If Duane's dream really was to become a rock & roll star as Shepley said, he was about to find out just how big rock & roll stars could be.

CHAPTER THREE

The Escorts

*"Daytona Beach, Florida—a place that is not
very conducive to musical growth."* — D.A.

In **1964 the Beatles** came to America. On the evening of February 9th, they performed five songs on the *Ed Sullivan Show* while more than 73 million people around the country tuned in. The four lads from Liverpool wore strange suits with collarless jackets, had hair longer than any man most folks had seen, and featured an instrumental lineup that would affect thousands of young musicians.

Duane had played in bands since shortly after he had taken up the guitar, but the Beatles showed him The Way: a lead guitarist, a rhythm guitarist, a bass player, and a drummer. And so, in early 1964, Duane began putting together his first proper rock & roll band.

"Duane and I were in the same class at Seabreeze High School," recalls bass player Van Harrison. "Back in those days, Daytona Beach was kind of a small town—there wasn't a hell of a lot to do, so we were all trying to form bands. Quite a few of us were messing around with the idea.

"I had been playing guitar with a band and didn't like the way we sounded. We needed a fuller sound, so I said, 'We ought to get some bass going here.' Nobody else wanted to do it, so I said, 'I'll do it.' Then I heard Duane play at some high school function. I was impressed with how he played, so I went up and started talking to him about what the possibilities were and what we could do."

Harrison came into Allman's life at an opportune moment: bass guitar players were like left-handed pitchers—vital, but always hard to find. Duane already had his brother to play rhythm guitar and do some of the singing, and he had found a drummer named Maynard Portwood. "Maynard was a great-sounding drummer," recalls Harrison. "He was not real spectacular, but the beats that he had—they had a lot of emotional feeling. Although he was missing most of his front teeth."

With Harrison on bass, Duane's rock & roll band was complete. "We said, 'Okay, we're gonna do the popular stuff and see what kind of jobs we can get,'" says Harrison. "Duane was an interesting personality. The band would work on something until we got it right. If we didn't have it right, we wouldn't do it. But Duane would also experiment and try things that really stretched us. He wasn't playing slide guitar then, but he was always looking for that unique sound—that different sound. We tried a lot of the Beatles stuff. We did some of the four-part harmony that was going on at that time. Hell, I wasn't that good of a singer, but we could pull it off sometimes.

"After a while we were about the best group around, I think. And then we started getting more and more into the blues. We liked the simplicity, but we also liked the idea that you could go off and improvise on these things, and let your own emotions and passions show in the sounds that you made.

"There were a lot of little high school dance clubs and teenybopper clubs around the east coast of Florida that were operated by local people—and across the state, in Orlando and up in the college towns. We would play a lot of those things. We were always trying to get the equipment and the instruments that we wanted so we didn't look like a bunch of redneck backwoods guys. That was a struggle—getting the money to get good stuff. I don't think we ever got it while I was there, but we had a good time."

Although Duane and Gregg wanted to call the band the Allman Joys, they ended up naming it the Escorts to appease Harrison and Portwood. Van Harrison remembers it this way: "I said, 'Look, if you call it the Allman Joys, we're going to feel left out.' So Duane said, 'We'll try something else for a while.' But he didn't like the Escorts—he thought it was kind of a wimpy, stupid name, and I have to agree with him. But that's what we had."

Neither Duane nor Harrison confined himself to playing in the Escorts. "I joined the union and put my name out as a bass player," says Harrison. "I got hired by some black bands. I played up at the Paradise Inn, a black club over by Bethune-Cookman College. Duane and I both played there—we would play together, or sometimes we'd play separately.

"Duane had a sense of social justice. We were spending time with black musicians, and in those days that's not the kind of thing that regular white Southern boys did. We got taken down verbally for doing that a few times. We went into some restaurants where they didn't want us to bring our black friends in with us. One time we almost had a confrontation. I forget if it was Duane or me who told 'em to shove it up their ass. These were the friends that we had and these were the guys we were working with. It was normal for us."

There was another Daytona Beach band called the Nightcrawlers, and in 1964 the Escorts and the Nightcrawlers were, by most accounts, the best-known rock & roll bands in town. But the Nightcrawlers got a leg up on the Escorts when they found a guy named Lee Hazen who could get their music down on tape. "I had a recording setup at my cottage in Ormond Beach," says Hazen.

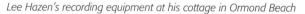

Lee Hazen's recording equipment at his cottage in Ormond Beach

"It was an old servant's quarters behind a large home on John Anderson Drive. It had a living room, a kitchen/eating area in back that used to be a screened-in porch, a bedroom, and a bath. I had a huge hi-fi system set up in the living room and kept adding on to it with recording in mind. Once I had built a custom mixer, I started recording bands in the back room. The Nightcrawlers were first, and the Escorts were second."

"Lee was a little older than the rest of us," says Sylvan Wells, who played guitar in the Nightcrawlers. "I think he was probably 23, 24, and we were all 19. Lee wanted to be a recording engineer. He had bought all kinds of tape recorders and microphones, and had basically gutted his kitchen and put up egg crates all over the place. He invited us and the Allmans to use his place to rehearse [in exchange for] recording us. And he would let us drink, so it was a no-brainer. We would use the place to rehearse, and Lee would practice recording us."

One of the Nightcrawlers' songs that Hazen got down on tape was an original called "Cry." "At that time," says Wells, "the Allmans were much better musicians than we were, but we were writing our own material. Lee started recording us, and then one night we heard 'Cry' on the radio. Lee had taken it upon himself to give it to a deejay, and the next thing we know, the record is Number 1 in Daytona. Shortly thereafter, record companies are calling, trying to find out who it is.

"Duane and Gregg were not happy that we were getting the breaks and they weren't. I mean, we were still friends, but there was a tension, really, from then on, because we were starting to release records, touring, leaving town, and they knew that we had no intention of continuing—that when we finished junior college, we were going to break up and go our separate ways. Rob Rouse and I were the leaders of the band, and we had already made that decision.

"Gregg never dealt with our success very well. Duane, on the other hand, was much more philosophical about it. I can remember him saying to Gregg at some point, 'Hey, don't be upset. Figure out what they're doing, and we'll do it better.' Duane was the driving force—always."

Hazen reports that the Nightcrawlers' next effort, "The Little Black Egg," became a regional hit. Originally released on Hazen's own label, Lee Records, it would eventually be re-released by Kapp Records in late 1966 and climb onto the national pop charts for a month in early 1967.

Duane's band had also been hard at work at Hazen's homemade studio. "The Escorts wanted to make a tape that they could play to club owners," says Hazen. "Sort of a preview of their sound. So, on two different days, we recorded. All were cover songs, as they didn't have any original material."

The first Escorts session consisted of some 15 songs including "Mr. Moonlight," "Don't Let the Sun Catch You Crying," "Pretty Woman," "That Boy," "Love Potion #9," "You've Lost That Lovin' Feelin'," and "Ferry Cross the Mersey." Clearly, the British Invasion had made a major impression on the Allmans. Duane sang the lead vocals on about half the songs; Gregg handled the vocals on most of the others, with Duane, Gregg, and Van doing three-part harmonies on the Beatles' "That Boy."

"I've had several conversations with Gregg about the tapes," says Joe Bell of *Hittin' the Note*, a magazine that specializes in the music of the Allman Brothers Band and like-minded acts. "Gregg said that, early on, Duane was doing most of the singing. As things evolved over time, Gregg gradually took on that role. Evidently Duane knew that Gregg was going to be a singer before Gregg did himself and encouraged him in that direction. As his little brother grew more confident in his own voice, Duane continued to improve his singing through his fingers. However, it's so much fun to hear Duane sing on the Escorts tapes. It kind of reminds me of an amateur singer—you know, he has the feel and he has the passion, but he doesn't quite have the voice. But it's wonderful to hear him because he puts his all into it. It also makes him a little more human. He was this Guitar God, but his singing was human."

The recordings the Escorts made at Hazen's studio paid off, getting the band an ongoing engagement at the premier gathering place for the kids of Daytona Beach—the Martinique Club. "Main Street of Daytona is where the pool halls were and where all the kids generally hung out," says Wells. "There were two pool halls—you'd always see Shepley and Duane in them during the day. Everybody hung out down there. The Martinique was kind of the marquee place to play. It was a huge success—a huge draw. All the musicians would hang out there. Duane and Gregg played there a lot."

Along with the tapes Hazen was cutting at his home studio, he also made a live recording of the biggest Daytona Beach rock & roll event of 1965. The Beach Boys had come to town, and the opening acts were the Nightcrawlers and the Escorts. The venue was a local ballpark. That night, April 17th, Duane

Four Escorts and a Nightcrawler— (L–R) Van Harrison, Tommy Ruger, Gregg (in sunglasses), Duane, and Maynard Portwood on the day of the Beach Boys' concert

introduced his band as "the Escorts combo from here in town." Once again, he and Gregg split the vocal duties. The opening acts literally shared the stage: the Escorts would play a song, followed by the Nightcrawlers doing a number, and then back to the Escorts. By the time their joint set ended, there was no doubt about which group had the better lead guitarist.

More than 40 years later, Van Harrison still laughs when he recalls sharing the stage with the Escorts' biggest rivals: "Sylvan and I have been friends for years, but that night I thought he sounded like shit. Sylvan always had this idea of 'just drive it hard and play it loud and everybody will love it.' I remember talking to Gregg [while the Nightcrawlers were playing], and he said something along the lines of, 'God, those guys sound terrible.'"

Having opened for the Beach Boys—the most successful American rock & roll band of the early 1960s—the Nightcrawlers and the Escorts had secured their places on the local scene. But Duane wanted more—and he saw that evening as a ticket to greater things. "I remember it being a big deal," Harrison says. "Duane said, 'Man, if this works out, we can make it big. We can go on the road. We can do this, we can do that. . . .' I didn't say a lot because I wanted to keep playing, but I remember thinking, 'There's no way in hell I can go on the road except for weekend things. Maybe I can sneak away on a Thursday and do a couple of nights.' I was still in school. Duane had left school by that time."

Sylvan Wells was Duane's classmate at Seabreeze High. "My best recollection is that he quit after his junior year," he says. In the end, Duane simply chose to walk away from school—if not to the disappointment of his family, then certainly to the chagrin of Van Harrison. "I sat him down and said, 'Hey man, this is stupid. You're going to ruin your life,'" Harrison says. "We had a lot of those discussions. Duane was one of these guys who could've made an A in anything he wanted. He was a good writer—very articulate and very smart. But Duane said, 'Look, this school shit isn't my thing. I don't need it. I can write. I can spell. I can read. What are they gonna teach me that I don't already know how to do?'

"I was trying to finish high school and get into college," says Harrison. "I wanted to be an engineer, and I think somewhere along the way that was what resulted in our separation. My goal was to become a professional, which I did. Their goal was to become musicians, which they did."

Another factor that may have contributed to the bass player's departure from the band was his experience with what he refers to as Duane's "dark side." "He seemed to want to experience life very fast," says Harrison. "Sometimes I used to think, even at that age, 'This guy's going to burn himself out. I hope he doesn't burn me out with him.' We would go out and get a bottle of whiskey

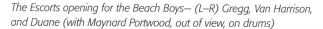

The Escorts opening for the Beach Boys— (L–R) Gregg, Van Harrison, and Duane (with Maynard Portwood, out of view, on drums)

and some other stuff, and go off and have a good time before I was old enough to do that kind of stuff.

"Duane had what I would call a conflicting personality. He had this highly responsible attitude towards how good we had to be and how hard we had to practice. He and Gregg practiced all the time together since they were brothers, and when we got together we'd practice hard—we did it over and over again 'til we got stuff right and it sounded *good*. But on the other hand, he had this lack of conviction. He would disappear. He would go off when we were supposed to do something or be somewhere, and we wouldn't know where the hell he was."

Harrison illustrates that tendency with this story: "Bud Asher was kind of a big guy around town. He owned a hotel and was a football coach, and he used to have these big concerts at Easter time down on the beach. We had a gig one time at [Asher's] Safari Inn for, I think, three or four nights. That was a big deal back then. It paid well, it gave us lots of exposure, and the crowds were huge—and Duane disappears. So it's Gregg and Maynard and me trying to pull off this stuff as best we can, and then Duane shows up about the second night. He walks up with his arms around two girls we never saw before and says, 'You guys don't sound bad!' I remember Gregg turning ten shades of red and being about as pissed off as I ever saw him."

The demo tape the Escorts had made at Hazen's studio in an effort to secure gigs had accomplished that goal, but the band decided to go back in later that year to lay down some more tracks. By the time of their second recording session, Van Harrison was gone—replaced on bass by Bob Keller—and the Escorts were now calling themselves the Allman Joys. ("They had to quit using the name 'The Escorts,'" says Hazen, "because there was another band with that name.")

Duane showed off his guitar chops at the session on two instrumentals, "Cryin' Time" and Lonnie Mack's "Memphis," the showpiece song he had mastered at Castle Heights Military Academy. The Allman Joys recorded a dozen songs that day, with Duane once again handling the lead vocals on about half the numbers, including "She's About a Mover" and "Hitch Hike." New member Bob Keller took the lead on the Rolling Stones' "The Last Time," but it was Gregg who gave a foretaste of things to come when he sang the Bobby "Blue" Bland hit "Turn on Your Love Light."

CHAPTER FOUR

The Allman Joys

*"He listened to the tapes and said, 'You cats better look
for a day gig—you're the worst I ever heard.'"* — D.A.

Despite the popularity of the Nightcrawlers, the Allman Joys were still
the biggest draw at the Martinique. It was there that Duane and Gregg
would frequently hang out, even on their nights off. And it was there
that they would first come face to face with a drummer by the name of Butch
Trucks.

Born in Jacksonville, Florida, on May 11, 1947, Claude Hudson "Butch"
Trucks Jr. began playing drums in the eighth grade. "The band director gave
three of us sticks and said, 'Play me something,'" Trucks told Kevin Spangler
and Ron Currens in an interview for *Hittin' the Note*. "Everybody else got
trombones and trumpets and stuff like that. He told me to play something
with the sticks, and I just kind of played a long roll. He said, 'Whoa, you ever
played, boy?' I said, 'No,' and he said, 'Well, *you're* playing drums!'"

Butch auditioned for the high school band the following year, and, he recalls,
the director "immediately made me first chair, which pissed off all the seniors."
That was nice—but to be cool in Jacksonville in the early 1960s, you had to be in
a rock & roll band. For Butch, however, there was a slight problem: "My family
was one of the pillars of the North Jacksonville Baptist Church. My parents were
never gonna buy me a set of drums because they were Southern Baptists, and

a set of drums—you had to take them to a place where people actually danced. And worse than that, they might drink at some of those places."

Butch continued to work on his parents, until "in the 11th grade, after enough pressure, they finally got me a set of drums as long as I promised never to play in a place where they served liquor. My first band was the Vikings, and that was really neat because I was in the 11th grade and earning my own money. Then, in the 12th grade, I was with a band called the Echoes. That was when the Beatles came out, and we were a Beatles copy band. And I also played with the Jacksonville Symphony Orchestra for a while, with a little offshoot called the Jacksonville Symphonette. We'd play on Friday nights down at the Prudential Center. I played tympani."

There were two other young musicians in Butch's neighborhood, David Brown and Scott Boyer. "David and Butch and I all went to Englewood High School in Jacksonville," recalls Boyer. "We were all in the Key Club together. We put together a musical thing to play at one of the Key Club conventions, doing [the Dave Brubeck Quartet's] 'Take Five.' I played upright bass and David played sax and Butch played drums, and one of the other guys played the keyboard part."

The three may have been playing together on that occasion, but, Butch recalls, "We hated each other's guts. Scott was this little nerdy violin player, and David Brown was playing saxophone in my main rival band on the other side of town, so we'd always just *really* dig at each other."

Their attitudes toward one another changed dramatically after high school graduation. "I went off to college," says Butch, "to Florida State, where I majored in staying out of Vietnam. We wound up on the same floor of the same dorm at FSU. David decided to get a bass, thinking there wasn't much of a career in playing saxophone because the days of the big horn bands were kind of dying, with the Beatles and that kind of thing [becoming popular]. And then the Byrds came out with their first album and it *changed our lives.*"

"I'd been playing coffee houses and stuff like that," says Boyer. "I knew all these Bob Dylan songs. It was around then that the Byrds came in, and the Lovin' Spoonful. So David approached me with the idea of the three of us getting together and me gettin' an electric guitar, and they'd back me up on bass and drums, and we'd make some money off this folk-rock thing. That was pretty much how it all got started."

"We started a band called the Bitter Ind.," says Butch. ("It was I-n-d period—meaning 'Independents'," explains Boyer. The name also played off the well-known New York City club called the Bitter End.) "We did three-part harmony and played all the fraternity parties; ceased going to class and grew the first long hair at Florida State."

At the end of the school year, the Bitter Ind. moved on. "We decided to go to Daytona and hit it big," says Butch. "All summer long it was a real happening place, with a lot of clubs and places to play. So we auditioned at all the clubs in Daytona Beach and everybody loved us, but every club owner said the same thing: 'You can't dance to the music.'"

Eventually, though, the Bitter Ind. managed to get hired for a night at the Martinique. "We started playing our set and in comes—some *presence*," recalls Butch. "You'd a thought the Beatles just came in. I mean, it was like the Red Sea parting—people letting them come in and sit down. It was very obvious that there were some *personages* in the audience. . . . It turned out to be the Allman Joys—Duane and Gregg Allman."

Duane was impressed with what he heard. "He walks up to us," says Butch, "and starts saying, 'You guys are great, man! Where'd you come from?' and on and on and on. And so we gave him the sob story about how we'd been there for ten days trying to get a job and we're broke—got nothing—and he says, 'Well, come on, man, you can stay with us.' So we hung out for a couple of days, and then Scott and David and I decided that we just weren't gonna do anything in Daytona, so we went back to Jacksonville."

Not long after the Bitter Ind. returned home, Butch got a phone call from Duane. "They were playing downtown at this place called the Beachcomber, a little late-night club in downtown Jacksonville," he says. "They needed a drummer and wanted to know if I'd come down and play."

Butch happily agreed to sit in. For the first time, Duane, Gregg, and Butch—almost three years before they would become one-half of the Allman Brothers Band—played together on the same stage. The evening was not only a precursor to that future development but a turning point for the Bitter Ind.

"It turned out the guy who managed the club was a huge Bob Dylan fan," says Butch. "Now, the Allman Joys had about three or four more weeks on this job at the Beachcomber. So Duane said, 'Well, why don't y'all audition, and if they like y'all, then y'all can just finish up our gig here.' So we played for this guy and he loved us, and we wound up working there for another year or year and a half."

By the summer of 1965, Gregg had graduated from high school and was free to hit the road—at least until it was time for him to go to college in the fall. The Allman Joys were playing steady gigs at the Martinique and other places in and around Daytona, but Duane had much bigger plans in his head. To grow in popularity, the band would have to reach a wider audience. It would have to start traveling around the country. To get gigs outside of Florida, the Allman Joys would need more than just the tape of songs they had recorded at Lee Hazen's. They'd also need a booking agent and that all-important publicity still.

In one of the earliest in a long line of publicity photos for the Allman Joys, Duane and Gregg—holding their guitars—flank Bob Keller, who's balancing his Fender Precision Bass upside down, with its headstock on the floor. Sitting in front of the other three musicians is Maynard Portwood—drumsticks in hand and snare drum resting on his knee. All four are wearing collarless suits, white shirts, and ties—outfits practically identical to the ones worn by the Beatles on the picture sleeve of the single for "I Want to Hold Your Hand."

The band got their first out-of-town gigs through an Atlanta-based company called Allied Artists. Later the group would switch to 1-Nighters, a booking agency in Nashville. During their travels, the Allman Joys would meet and become friends with a host of other Southern musicians looking to make it in the rock & roll world—groups like Dirty John & the Nightcaps and the 5 Men-Its. As would turn out to be the case with the Allman Joys, these two bands—and many others like them around the Southeast—consisted of members who would eventually, in one form or another, achieve the success they were looking for.

Bill Connell, who succeeded Maynard Portwood in the Allman Joys' drum chair in 1966, explains one branch of the Southern-band family tree: "I started with Paul Hornsby in a little group called the Pacers back in about '63. The Pacers broke up and splintered into two bands, one of which turned out to be the 5 Men-Its. The other turned out to be Dirty John & the Nightcaps. That was Johnny Townsend's band.

"So Paul and I split from the Pacers," continues Connell. "He went with the 5 Men-Its, and I went with Dirty John & the Nightcaps. That was Tippy

Armstrong and Johnny; the 5 Men-Its were Paul Hornsby, Eddie Hinton, Johnny Sandlin, Fred Styles, and Paul Ballinger."

The work for these Southern proto-bands was often not glamorous. "We did what you call the chitlin' circuit," says Gregg Allman. "In Mobile, Alabama, at the Stork Club, we worked seven nights a week, six sets a night, 45 minutes a set. There were four of us, and we made $444 a week."

In fact, the Allman Joys' first official road gig began at the Stork Club. During the band's stay in Mobile, they met Dirty John & the Nightcaps. "We were playing Dauphin Island, and we went into Mobile one night," says Townsend. "We had a night off, so we stopped by the Stork Club and saw these guys with long hair playing their asses off—playing Yardbirds songs! We were playing some of the English stuff, but not like these guys were playing it. We were all just amazed."

Connell remembers the story slightly differently: "In Mobile one night there was a big R&B concert with Otis Redding, Sam & Dave, Billy Stewart, Joe Tex—everybody. I was playing Dauphin Island with Dirty John & the Nightcaps, and the Allman Joys were playing the Stork Club. Johnny Townsend, Tippy Armstrong, and I went to this R&B concert, and the only other white people we saw were Duane and Gregg—that's how we met. They came out to Dauphin Island and saw us do a Sunday matinee, and we came back in and saw them do a Monday night show, because they were doing six nights a week, and we got to know each other."

Not long after disbanding Dirty John & the Nightcaps (at which point Bill Connell took Johnny Sandlin's place as the drummer for the 5 Men-Its), Townsend headed off to the University of Alabama. During his sophomore year there, Townsend got a call from a friend and fellow musician named Johnny Wyker. Wyker was forming a new band and wanted Townsend to be a part of it, telling him it would be a perfect way to help finance his education. Townsend agreed to join as long as Wyker would agree to include Tippy Armstrong in the lineup. The band continued to grow until it became a seven-piece ensemble, resulting in an obvious name: the Magnificent Seven. In short order, the Magnificent Seven got a contract with Columbia Records, was rechristened the Rubber Band, and Johnny Townsend's college days came to an abrupt end.

Maynard Portwood had been Duane's drummer since even before the Escorts were formed, but by January 1966 Allman had decided it was time for a change.

"The Allman Joys stole our drummer, Bill Connell," recalls Paul Hornsby. By this time, the 5 Men-Its were actually only four: Eddie Hinton on guitar; Hornsby, who played both Hammond organ and guitar; bass player Mabron McKinney; and, depending on the day, either Bill Connell or Johnny Sandlin on drums. "One would play for a few months and drop out, and the other one would come in—and then the same story," says Hornsby. "They'd swap back and forth."

"My senior year in high school," says Connell, "Duane called me from New York, in January, and said, 'We want to get rid of our drummer, and we'd really like for you to come play with us.' My father was an old retired army major, and he wanted to see me finish school. I said, 'Duane, I really need to finish high school.' He said, 'I understand. Gregg wanted to do that too.' He said, 'I tell you what: The night you graduate, there'll be a plane ticket for you. Come to New York and start playing.'"

As soon as Connell received his diploma, he was gone: "I walked off the stage on Friday night in Tuscaloosa, Alabama, went to the airport, and the ticket was there. I was 17 years old and that blew me away—that somebody really came through with a promise like that. So I flew to New York and joined those guys.

"When I first got there, it was culture shock. Of course, I wore my little Alabama Sunday School suit on the plane up there. The plane pulled into JFK, and there were about 50 of the weirdest people I'd ever seen in my life with signs that read 'Welcome Bill.' Alabama hadn't been exposed to the hippie thing yet. I got off in my Sunday School suit, and here were 50 Greenwich Village hippies welcoming me. It was a bizarre ride for the next few months.

"I started playing with them at this club, Trude Heller's, in Greenwich Village. They had already played there a couple of times. After Gregg graduated from high school in '65, they had gone up to New York and gotten some gigs. As a matter of fact, we worked several of those big Village clubs."

By 1966, it was becoming obvious that Gregg wasn't going to be heading off to college. In the fall of 1965, Duane had managed to convince his brother to give the Allman Joys another year. Reluctantly, Gregg agreed to put his goal of becoming a dentist on hold a little longer.

Although Gregg would never enter the dental profession, he and Duane found themselves confronted with a tooth-related problem they could no longer ignore. Duane had put in the call to Connell not because the band needed a drummer with better musical skills; in truth, it was because they needed a drummer with better teeth.

"Maynard didn't have any teeth," says Connell. "They were all kind of rotted out. Duane and Gregg had given Maynard five or six hundred dollars—which was a lot, back then—to get his teeth fixed. And he went and blew it on something else. It was like, 'That's it. We can't make it with a man with no teeth during this Beatles thing,' so that's why they got rid of him and asked me to come. That's how I got hired. I had good teeth. I must've played okay, too."

Connell's arrival wasn't the only change in the band. By the time the new drummer arrived in New York, Mike Alexander had replaced Bob Keller on bass. More important, Gregg's primary instrument had become a Vox Continental portable organ.

The Allman Joys were constantly on the road, occasionally playing in the same towns as their Southern brethren. "When I was with the Rubber Band," says Townsend, "we hung around with those guys, and they told us unbelievable stories. They were very, very streetwise at that age, and it amazed us because we were like little Southern Baptist sissies. But every time we played in the same area, they would come see us—and we'd go see them."

"We played the old rock & roll circuit," Connell says. "We played St. Louis and Nashville—the whole 'east of the Mississippi' circuit, when I was with them." Duane recalled those days in 1970, telling disc jockey Ed Shane, "There's a garbage circuit of the South, man, that you work at and you make about $150 a week and eat pills and drink—it's a bad trip!"

When it came to rock & roll and R&B in Duane's old hometown of Nashville, *the* place to play was the Briar Patch, at the corner of Fifth Avenue South and Lea Avenue. And the Allman Joys' gigs at the Briar Patch in the summer of 1966 would bring Duane and the band their first genuine shot at the Big Time. The group's first week of shows was promoted in local ads as a "Limited Engagement"—although the longer the Allman Joys stayed in Nashville that summer, the less limited their Briar Patch gigs became.

It was during the band's initial run at the Briar Patch that John D. Loudermilk came into their lives. Primarily known as a country songwriter, Loudermilk had a knack for creating the kind of songs that crossed over into the pop charts, including "A Rose and a Baby Ruth" and "Abilene" for George Hamilton IV; "Waterloo," a huge hit for Stonewall Jackson; and the seminal "Tobacco Road," originally a hit for the Nashville Teens in 1964, but eventually covered by everyone from the Animals to Jefferson Airplane to Junior Wells to Lou Rawls.

Loudermilk was not only a revered songwriter, recording artist, and record producer; he also had a talent for finding talent—or, in the case of the Allman Joys, a talent for listening when someone else found an act they thought he should hear. "George Hamilton IV had seen them," Loudermilk recalls. "He called me and said, 'You might enjoy hearing these guys and consider producing them.' He was knocked out with them. So I went to the Briar Patch to hear them, and *I* was knocked out with them."

Mightily impressed with the Allman Joys' musicianship, Loudermilk decided to give the band the ultimate test—a lesson he'd learned from Elvis Presley's manager: "Tom Parker told me one time how to check out an artist. He said, 'You turn your back to the artist. You know what he looks like onstage. Just turn around and watch the audience. You can see the emotion in their faces, and you can tell about how much they'll pay to continue having that emotion.' He was a genius at doing that—that and fucking up people's lives that he managed. But he knew what he was talking about there, so I went to the Briar Patch and did just that. The kids were going crazy."

John D. met with the band and encouraged them to hang out in Nashville as much as possible for the foreseeable future. He sent his wife and kids to Myrtle Beach for a long vacation and brought the Allman Joys to his place outside of town. "They moved out to the house for part of the summer," says Loudermilk. "We lived out in the country on some acreage in Brentwood. I told 'em, 'Well, what you need to do is start writing your own songs.' They were doing Beatles' stuff, you know. They said, 'We don't know if we can do it.' I said, 'Sure you can.' I wrote a lot of stuff with 'em, but I never took any of the writer credit or anything—just kind of showin' 'em, you know. They were quick to learn, and they listened to me. So we practiced. We had the best time—sittin' around talking and philosophizing. See, I was a little bit older than them, so they listened very carefully and they learned real quickly."

According to Loudermilk, the Allman Joys managed to keep themselves entertained via various means when they weren't writing songs or rehearsing: "These kids were doing some drugs, you know, and I didn't want to get involved with that. And they brought little girls that were *way* underage out to the house—scared the hell out of me!"

Loudermilk did his best to get the top producers in Nashville excited about the band. "I tried to get all the guys I knew to go see them—like Owen Bradley and Chet Atkins. There were several other producers, and none of 'em saw it, you know? They went over [to the Briar Patch] with me, but nobody was knocked out with 'em." Finally, Loudermilk decided to simply finance the recording project himself—but not before having the band sign contracts with him for management, production, recording, and publishing.

Owen Bradley, one of the most respected record producers in Nashville, had just completed building the now-legendary Bradley's Barn recording studio just outside of town. Although Bradley had no interest in producing the Allman Joys, he was happy to rent studio time to Loudermilk. On the resultant tapes, the Allman Joys' sound is a mix of the Beatles, Animals, Booker T. & the MGs, and Mitch Ryder & the Detroit Wheels—with a Southern-accented singer and a lead guitarist clearly obsessed with his fuzz box. The sessions at the Barn included songs written by Loudermilk, Roy Acuff Jr., Robert Johnson, Willie Dixon, Oscar Hammerstein and Jerome Kern, and Gregg Allman. But it's a pretty huge leap from "Crossroads" to "Old Man River," and no matter how impressive the band was performing live at the Briar Patch and a hundred other clubs, it's obvious from the Bradley Barn recordings that the Allman Joys were still searching—still trying to find their own unique sound.

Unfortunately, the biggest sound they made during the sessions was not exactly what Loudermilk had in mind. "They shot off a pistol in the studio," he says. "It was the very first session at Bradley's Barn. I think they had seen the pistols in my car. I have always carried two pistols in my car—one for me and one for my wife. If you break down, somebody's gotta stay with the car and somebody's gotta go after help, and so both need to be protected, you know. So they brought one of the little pistols into the studio. They shot a hole in the roof, and Owen Bradley called me about two weeks later and said, 'Man, it's raining and the water's coming right through this hole.' I don't remember if I fixed the hole or if I paid to have it fixed or what. It just became part of the myth."

Among the tracks produced by Loudermilk that August were "Spoonful" and "You Deserve Each Other." Buddy Killen, owner of Dial Records, agreed to release the two sides as a single the following month. Dial had a distribution deal

with Atlantic Records and had already been responsible for a number of hits by soul singer Joe Tex, but the world wasn't quite ready for an up-tempo, fuzztone-blasting version of the old Willie Dixon blues tune about "that spoonful."

After the Bradley Barn sessions and the release of the single, Loudermilk decided it was time to concentrate on songwriting again. Killen acquired the tracks Loudermilk had produced, and then brought in producer John Hurley to work further with the band. As the Allman Joys' producers changed, so did their bass player.

"The Allman Joys," explains Connell, "went from Bob Keller on bass and Maynard Portwood on drums to Mike Alexander as the bass player and me as the drummer, and then back to Keller on bass. Then Keller just walked away one day. We had met Ralph Ballinger in St. Louis—he was playing in a group up there—so they called him when Bob left, and Ralph came on."

After Duane Allman's death, most of the pre-Allman Brothers Band record-ings he had played on were released in one form or another. Among them was an album containing a dozen of the Allman Joys sides produced by Loudermilk

Fourth Allman Joys lineup— (L–R) Bill Connell, Gregg, Duane, and returning bass player Bob Keller

and Hurley, entitled *Early Allman, Featuring Duane and Gregg Allman*. The musicians' credits on the back of that album have been in dispute since the LP's release in 1973. The sole bass player listed is Ralph Ballinger, although Connell recalls that Mike Alexander and Bob Keller both played on Allman Joys sessions as well. The sole drummer listed on the album is Tommy Amato.

When the Allman Brothers Band boxed set, *Dreams*, was released in 1989, the Allman Joys tracks credited the bass player as Bob Keller and the drummer as Maynard Portwood. Understandably, none of this sits well with Bill Connell. "I recorded that whole album," he says. "We did some of it with John Loudermilk out at Bradley's Barn, and then back in town at RCA, and also at Buddy Killen's studio. When that got released later—all those tunes from Bradley's Barn and Killen's place and RCA—I was not credited on *any* of that. The reason Tommy Amato got listed, I guess, was he was *the* session drummer in Nashville at that time. I can remember one three- or four-day period when we were playing in Nashville when, boy, I had the worst flu that I had ever had in my life and couldn't play. I just could not play. Tommy Amato came in and played three or four nights for me at the Briar Patch, but he didn't play on any of those cuts."

After their lengthy stay in Nashville, the Allman Joys were back on the road in late 1966. On November 25, they played the Fort Brandon Armory in Tuscaloosa. The promotional poster billed it as a "Gigantic Show and Dance" featuring the Allman Joys "playing their smash hit 'Spoonful' on Dial Records." In attendance that night was a young keyboard player named Chuck Leavell. A friend of Paul Hornsby's, Leavell was impressed with the band's look and sound. Duane's fuzztone guitar licks were cool, but Leavell also dug Gregg's gravely voice and that Vox organ.

Despite the hopeful reference to the Allman Joys' "smash hit" on the poster for the armory show, the single of "Spoonful" achieved only modest regional sales, and it failed to generate enough interest to make Buddy Killen want to release the album—or even another single. In the liner notes for *Early Allmans* some seven years later, Killen was quoted as saying, "Nobody really understood what Duane and Gregg were about at the time. Eventually I gave them their release." Although it was probably a slight exaggeration on Allman's part, Duane later recalled Killen's sendoff this way: "He listened to the tapes and said, 'No, man, you cats better look for a day gig—you're the worst I ever heard.'" Needless to say, the Allman Joys didn't take that advice.

After Killen passed on the Allman Joys, Loudermilk recalls, "Duane came to me and said, 'Man, I don't know what we're gonna do.' I said, 'You ain't going to get nothing done here. You ain't gonna get anybody to listen to you here. I can tell you what to do—get your ass out of here and get to the Coast, man!'"

Due to a series of events no one could have predicted, within a matter of months after Loudermilk's suggestion Duane and Gregg did, in fact, get their asses to the Coast.

CHAPTER FIVE

Like Sands Through the Hour Glass

"I was living in L.A. and said, 'Boy, the band business stinks!'" — D.A.

With the **Allman Joys'** short-lived recording career on Dial Records over, the band stayed on the road, grinding out the usual club-circuit gigs generally available to a group of accomplished musicians with a booking agent and a several-months-old single that had been a regional hit.

Not having had the Allman Joys' experience of being discovered and signed to a label, the 5 Men-Its had solved the whole record-making issue by going to a place called Fame Studios in Muscle Shoals, Alabama. There they cut a few tunes, had them pressed into singles, and got some regional airplay of their own.

"We were a weekend college band," Paul Hornsby says. "The Allmans were the first full-time professional musicians I knew that played every night—and that's all they did. They were a touring band, playing clubs. After they got our drummer, Bill Connell, Johnny Sandlin rejoined the 5 Men-Its, and the Allman Joys talked us into signing with the agency they were signed to, 1-Nighters out of Nashville, and going on the road. So we started playing the same club circuit that they played, following each other all over Kentucky, Indiana, Illinois, Iowa—whatever part of the country you want to call that."

By the time they joined the club circuit, the 5 Men-Its had been a four-piece band for some time—so they became, simply, the Men-Its. As with the Allman

Joys, the Men-Its had a tough time keeping their band together. In early 1967, they lost a key member when guitarist Eddie Hinton departed to go to Muscle Shoals and become a session player. "When Eddie left the group," says Hornsby, "we garaged it for two or three weeks, trying to put something together. We found Pete Carr, and he rehearsed with us. I think we did maybe two gigs with Pete in the Men-Its."

Guitarist Pete Carr was a fellow Daytona Beach musician whose life would frequently intersect with Duane's. Born in 1950, Pete always seemed to be the "kid" of the Daytona music community. "I had seen Duane and Gregg play at the Daytona Beach Island Recreation Center," says Carr. "Their name was the Escorts at the time. I couldn't have been more than 14. I was playing guitar and learning in my bedroom, listening to records."

Too shy to speak to the Allmans that day, Pete eventually built up enough confidence to introduce himself when the occasion arose. "I think I was 15 when I met Duane and Gregg," he recalls. "I talked to them for the first time at the Martinique Club." By this time, the band was calling itself the Allman Joys. "I had my guitar with me, and I introduced myself when the band took a break. I asked Gregg to show me some guitar lines, and he said, 'That's my brother Duane's department.' At that point I introduced myself to Duane Allman. That meeting began a friendship that lasted until Duane's death."

When Hinton left the Men-Its, the Allmans suggested their young friend as a replacement. "I was 16 when Duane and Gregg told me about this band in Alabama that needed a guitar player," says Carr. "That's when I went up [to Decatur] to join the 5 Men-Its." (It should be noted that the precise date of the 5 Men-Its' name change—as well as whether it was spelled Men-Its, Men-its, or Minutes—is remembered differently by different members of the band. In an interview with writer Bill Ector, Hornsby explained the origin of the band's name: "[When we were starting out] we got this gig in Panama City, where this old redneck woman ran the place. She hired us for a night, and when she asked us our name, someone said, 'Hell, we've been hired for five minutes and we don't even have a name for ourselves.' Someone else said, 'Hey, that's it! We're the 5 Men-Its!'" Later, after the band had been a quartet for a while, the decision was made to drop the "5." Four decades later, the various versions of the name have become interchangeable among the band's former members.)

Almost simultaneous with Hinton's split from the 5 Men-Its, the Allman Joys disintegrated, with drummer Bill Connell going into the Navy and bass player Ralph Ballinger—as Connell describes it—no longer wanting to do "the road thing." Connell tells his story: "One week in March, the 5 Men-Its and the Allman Joys ended up at my parents' house in Tuscaloosa, Alabama. Sometimes we would lay over for a couple of days until we had to be in Peoria or wherever. We all just flopped and slept anywhere—couches, whatever—but my parents were okay with that because my father had been in a road orchestra in the '30s, and they used to travel all around. I guess that's why he was open to what I was doing.

"From my sophomore year in high school, we were all fearful of getting out of school and having to go to Vietnam because of the draft. Back then there was no lottery number selection. If you had one eye and one foot and could aim, you went and that was it. Hornsby got out on a 4F for severe asthma, I think. But Tippy Armstrong had to go in, and it really screwed him up, which I think led to his [eventual] suicide. There were several of us that had to go. There was no out. If you're not in college, you're gone.

"Gregg and I had been dodging the draft for about a year, but that week when we were at my parents' house, I got my draft notice. I had no choice. I mean, it was either go in the infantry or try to find another way out. My father had been a major in the Army, and he knew a commander in the Navy who found me a billet in the Navy. That's when I left the Allman Joys."

The Allman Joys' leader quickly turned to Paul Hornsby with a proposal: "Duane came up to me and asked, 'Why don't we join forces?' " Under the circumstances, the decision was easy—but there was no room in the merger for the Men-Its' new lead guitarist. "When we joined up with the Allmans," says Hornsby, "Pete fell by the wayside." ("I was just a kid," says Carr. "They had no need for three guitar players in the band, so I left and traveled around Alabama, meeting some great musicians.")

The new band—Duane, Gregg, Paul Hornsby, Johnny Sandlin, and Mabron McKinney—began rehearsing, getting to know each other's material. Hornsby remembers how it went: "We did all of the R&B covers and a lot of the British covers—Yardbirds' stuff like 'Over Under Sideways Down.' Both the Allman Joys and the 5 Men-Its had done that, so we kept that in the repertoire. And, of course, 'Turn on Your Love Light'; that was sort of a standard song that a lot of Southern bands played at that time. One song that was held over from the 5 Men-Its was 'Dimples.' Eddie Hinton and I had done double guitar, twin guitar harmony, on that. Then Duane and I did the same parts. In the Allman Brothers Band, Duane and Dickey did the same parts—same arrangement. That was a song that was inherited by one band from another. 'Stormy Monday Blues'—both bands had always played that song, and now it's thought of as an Allman Brothers song. We had that song back then."

With the set list coming together, the band headed out for four weeks' work in St. Louis. "We didn't even have a name yet," says Hornsby. "I think we might have kicked the name Almanac around, but I don't know that I ever saw that name in print. We might have even played a gig or two as the Allman Joys."

Nitty Gritty Dirt Band member Jimmie Fadden says Mabron McKinney bumped into the Dirt Band at the St. Louis airport. "Mabron said, 'Hey, are you guys in a band?'" recalls Fadden. "He guessed we were a band because we had long hair. So when we said we were, Mabron said, 'I'm in a band, too! You've gotta come hear us play tonight.'" At that point, the Dirt Band was a fledgling act touring behind their first single, "Buy for Me the Rain." That evening, the Nitty Gritty Dirt Band—along with their manager, Bill McEuen—went to St. Louis's gaslight district to hear McKinney and his bandmates—whatever they were calling themselves.

Bill McEuen was so impressed with what he heard that he was convinced he had discovered the next Rolling Stones. His brother John, a member of the Dirt Band, recalls that encounter: "We ran into the Allmans on the road in 1967, around the end of March. My brother Bill told them: 'Come on out to L.A. and I'll be glad to manage you.'"

Having nothing else on their agenda, the band headed for the West Coast. "They showed up the next month in L.A. and moved into the Nitty Gritty Dirt Band house in Beechwood Canyon," says John. "It was a four-floor house, and they kind of took over the first floor for about five or six weeks."

Duane was in Los Angeles—the entertainment capital of the world, where he could play his music at the host of venues the city had to offer. He'd be able to share his music with the world once a record deal was in place. No more "garbage circuit of the South." At least, that was the plan.

The band signed a management deal with Bill McEuen, and on June 15, 1967, they got the record deal he had promised them. "Liberty Records signed 'em," says John. It was decided that Dallas Smith would produce their first album, "because he was a staff producer, and my brother had worked with him getting the Dirt Band there."

Liberty was the label of rock & roll legend Eddie Cochran of "Summertime Blues" fame. Johnny Burnette—one-third of the Rock & Roll Trio, the band that popularized "Train Kept A-Rollin'"—had been on Liberty with hits like "You're Sixteen." The Rivingtons were on Liberty, too—they were the four black guys who sang "Papa Oom Mow Mow" and "Bird Is the Word," only to be ripped off by a white surf band from Minneapolis who stuck the two songs together and called it "Surfin' Bird."

This was the Big Time in the Big City—but the band was still trying to find its way musically. On the road they had been performing songs by other artists for the most part. Liberty Records, of course, would require original material—or at least songs that hadn't already been hits. Paul Hornsby says, "We had not been together long enough to have a repertoire of original songs. We got the band together, rehearsed, got enough songs to play a club gig, and played for a month. Then we went to L.A. and got signed. We didn't have a lot of original stuff to choose from, and Gregg had not started writing all that much at that time."

Liberty wasn't sure what they had. "They were like a rock & roll version of the Dirt Band, in the sense that they had several different styles that hadn't quite coalesced into one," says John McEuen. And there was still the nagging question of "who *are* they?" The group was happy to go with the name Allman Joys again, but the label decided that the candy-bar name didn't really capture the proper rock & roll image. "The record business being what it was in that time period," says McEuen, "'Allman Joys' didn't quite sound right to them. And it probably wasn't right."

So the Allman Joys became the Hour Glass.* And, after what must have seemed like a lifetime of trying to reach this moment, it looked like their

---

*Although the band's name has often appeared in print as a single word—even on some Hour Glass reissues—the label copy for all of the band's original recordings consistently listed the group's name as the Hour Glass.

dream would finally come true. Soon, however, it began to take on nightmar-ish overtones.

Liberty Records did, indeed, have a rich history of rock & roll icons like Eddie Cochran and Johnny Burnette. It was also the home of the Sunset Strings, the Johnny Mann Singers, Trombones Unlimited, novelty acts like the Chip-munks, and even (believe it or not) the Van Nuys First Baptist Church Choir. What it *didn't* have on its roster in 1967 was a longhaired, retro-clothes-wearing, semi-blue-eyed soul, semi-psychedelic-sounding rock band. Never mind that this wasn't exactly the look or sound Duane and the guys had in mind. The Hour Glass was going to be the band to fill a gap in the Liberty roster—whether they liked it or not.

Having signed a recording contract that gave the band no artistic control, the Hour Glass found themselves in the studio with a collection of mostly for-gettable songs by otherwise great songwriters, under the direction of producer Dallas Smith, who had produced the Nitty Gritty Dirt Band's debut album on Liberty.

According to John McEuen, Smith—who had also been working with saccharine-coated pop singer Bobby Vee—was "definitely a formulaic producer. I don't think [he was the type of producer who] had an ear for great music, as much as there was a lot of great music in that era that couldn't be buried, no matter who you were. In the case of the Hour Glass, I don't think they'd developed enough to push through a few cool things yet. Nor were they of the mindset where they could force control and say, 'Well, this is the way we're do-ing it.' It's their first real record deal. They're young. 'Oh, he wants us to record this song. We'd rather do this other one, but I guess we gotta do it. . . .' They hadn't gotten to that stage yet where they could say, '*This* is what we do.'"

There's little question that the Nitty Gritty Dirt Band qualifies as one of the finest bands of their era—an era that continues to the present day. Three years after their debut on Liberty, they would record an album called *Uncle Charlie & His Dog Teddy* (not a Dallas Smith production, by the way), which would include "Mr. Bojangles," a song that would become an instant classic. But the Dirt Band was about as musically close to the Hour Glass as the Van Nuys First Baptist Church Choir.

Smith knew the Hour Glass musicians were from the South. He knew they had been playing blues covers. And he could hear the soulful qualities in Gregg's voice. Therefore, he referred to them as a "Motown band." One can only ponder what Duane Allman must have thought the first time he heard that phrase.

The Hour Glass years were long before the days of cassettes or CD-Rs. The demos they listened to were acetates—45s cut on a lathe that could be played a handful of times before the needle wore them out. The band went through a box of acetates and picked out several by songwriters with familiar names—Goffin & King, Curtis Mayfield, and Del Shannon among them. The songs might as well have been by Irving Berlin or John Philip Sousa.

"When we got signed, we had to have an album," says Hornsby, "so they threw a bunch of demos at us. We were just naïve Southern boys—we wanted to please everybody, so we did just about anything they told us to do. They suggested that we cut a lot of bad songs, unfortunately. They assured us that that was 'the shit,' you know. So we did it, and none of the material reflected what the group did live. We hated the songs so bad that very few of 'em we ever played live."

Listening to the first Hour Glass LP today, one can only wonder how bad the demos must have been that they chose to leave in the box. Of the 11 songs the band recorded, among them were two by the successful team of Gerry Goffin and Carole King, a Curtis Mayfield number, and a Jackson Browne song called "Cast Off All My Fears." The only concession made by the producer and the record label was to let the band cut one of Gregg's old Allman Joys compositions, "Got to Get Away"—but not before making sure that Metric Music, Liberty's music publishing arm, got the publishing rights.

Gregg had to write John D. Loudermilk and ask to be released from the publishing deal he had signed in Nashville. "I wrote him back," says Loudermilk. "I turned Gregg's letter over and wrote on the back, 'You are released from all of the contracts we have without any payment or anything to me. I just want to see you guys make it.' I tore up the contracts. I'd been held back in my career by contracts, and I didn't want to do it to them."

"People listen to the first album," says McEuen, "and they ask, 'How come they didn't sound like the Allman Brothers?' In that era of recording, the control of the artistic end was as far away from the artist as it could be—and Dallas Smith is a case in point. When he was producing the first Dirt Band album, one of our cuts was an instrumental I'd written, and he walks up to me and says, 'Okay, we're ready for that instrumental. Let's get this over with. I hate this song.' So that's the record producer relating to the artist."

The first Hour Glass album was doomed before a note was laid down, and the realization of this inevitability hit Duane harder than any of the other members of the band. As Paul Hornsby said, most of the Hour Glass just wanted to please everybody. Duane Allman, on the other hand, had spent a lifetime not worrying about pleasing authority figures. His vision was to make the music he wanted to make. As far as Duane was concerned, he *was* the authority figure. From the beginning, he and Dallas Smith—rather than collaborating—were making an album in spite of each other.

John McEuen was brought in on August 10, 1967, to play on a song called "Silently," co-written by Del Shannon. (Not surprisingly, Metric Music owned the copyright on that one, too. The Hour Glass probably chose to record it for no other reason than the fact that it was written by someone whose name they actually recognized.) Right away, McEuen saw the effect the whole process was having on Duane. "The thing that I remember, sadly, was seeing Duane come in the studio so high that he could hardly wear his guitar. I thought, 'Oh my God, this is too bad. This is an example of Southern Comfort meeting Southern California.' He could barely open his guitar case."

Dallas Smith recorded the basic tracks with the band. Then he added background singers. Then he added horns. Then he pushed Gregg's voice way up front in the mix. Needless to say, this wasn't the band members' vision of what their sound was supposed to be. In fact, the album sounds like a mid-'60s Gregg Allman solo project—a collection of mediocre songs with a good singer being backed by a group of competent musicians. There is no way to listen to the 11 tracks on *Hour Glass* and think, "band"—least of all, "Southern blues-rock band."

The cause of Duane's frustration in the studio becomes apparent from the very first song. In fact, his initial guitar solo doesn't come until "Cast Off All My Fears," some four cuts into the record. He pops up again a couple of songs later, playing a brief lead line over the fade of "No Easy Way Out." In the few other spots where he can be heard at all, Duane's playing seems totally out of place—proof that the band was completely off the course he had tried to set for it. The liner notes described *Hour Glass* as everything "from rhythm and blues to driving psychedelic beats . . . reeking of soul." In other words, an album consisting of a hodge-podge of genres performed by a band being pulled in various musical directions by a producer with no apparent focus.

But when they played live—that was a different story. Onstage they were the *real* Hour Glass. They played torrid blues-rock, the kind of stuff that had gotten the crowds on their feet in Missouri and Alabama and Georgia and Florida. Hour Glass opened for the Doors at the Hullabaloo and tore the place apart. They had a steady gig at the Whisky a Go Go. Audiences loved what they heard and came back for more.

"When they opened at the Whisky a Go Go, I was standing in the front row," says Johnny Townsend. "There was a big buzz about the group. People—pretty much a lot of the Hollywood elite in the music world—were there that night to see them just burn the stage. Frightened people to death, really: 'What the hell is this? These guys are fucking killers!'"

"We played there probably more than any other band they ever had," says Hornsby. "We were a favorite, if I could be so bold to say it. We drew well and we drew a lot of big people. People who were in bigger bands would always come hear us play. Man, we'd look out there and we'd see 'most anybody sitting in our audience. We started having jam sessions when we'd play there—that was a novel thing at the time. And we'd invite a lot of our friends from other bands to sit in and jam with us. So we'd have anybody from Paul Butterfield to Janis Joplin to Steve Stills, Neil Young, Buddy Miles, Eric Burdon—just to name a few who were regular attendees who would wind up jamming with us."

Remembering those performances, John McEuen says, "It was obvious that this Duane Allman guy was either transported from a different age or he was going to be a leading commentator on the guitar for our age. When they came out here, it was in that nascent stage—but it became obvious that he was a guitar player of unusual abilities."

The band's song selection was a lot more adventurous than the dreck on their album. "When the Hour Glass opened for the Dirt Band at the Hullabaloo," recalls McEuen, "their first song was 'Norwegian Wood,' as an instrumental, played by Duane on electric sitar. And then somewhere in the middle of the show, I remember seeing Duane throw his guitar up so high it disappeared." "He would toss his guitar straight up in the air," says fellow Dirt Band member Jeff Hanna, "and then he'd take a step forward and his guitar would land on the stage right behind him. It was pretty dramatic stuff." "And they'd close their set with 'Buckaroo,' the Buck Owens theme song," says McEuen. "Now, if this isn't somebody looking for a space to occupy, I don't know who is. They'd also be doing things like 'Try a Little Tenderness.' One night at the Whisky they were playing when all of Three Dog Night came in and just sat there watching them." (When the first Three Dog Night album arrived, there was "Try a Little Tenderness"— with, according to McEuen, the Hour Glass's "exact same arrangement.")

Hour Glass was released in October, along with the single "Nothing But Tears"—an apt enough title under the circumstances. On the cover, the band's name is splashed across the top in a predictably psychedelic typeface. And then there's the photo: Gregg, Johnny, Paul, Duane, and Mabron, wearing attire that is virtually indescribable. Gregg and Duane's clothing is actually pretty close to what you'd expect rock stars to be wearing on an album cover in 1967, but the rest of the band . . . Johnny Sandlin has on a uniform that looks like a reject from the *Sgt. Pepper* cover; Paul Hornsby is wearing a ghastly necklace of faux saber-tooth tiger fangs; and Mabron McKinney has been forced to don a tux, cape, white gloves, and a top hat. And did I mention that the photo is *upside down?*

At least they had the live gigs to fall back on. The Hour Glass opened for the biggest acts of the day: Big Brother & the Holding Company, Jefferson Airplane, the Animals—they even did three shows with Buffalo Springfield at

The ridiculous cover of the Hour Glass's first album—an unfortunate beginning to the band's ill-fated tenure on Liberty Records

the Fillmore in San Francisco. But the label put restrictions on their live work, further cramping the band's style.

Although the Liberty Records brass didn't mind the Hour Glass playing major shows out of town, they decided to nix the constant gigging in Los Angeles. "They didn't want us to be overexposed," says Hornsby. "They felt like it would cheapen the band if we played so much right in L.A. They wanted to 'leave 'em wanting a little bit more.' But our only income was live gigs, because we weren't selling records. We were always in debt. We were borrowing money from the management, which didn't do us any good.

"We did play a lot of big gigs with a lot of big acts. We played San Francisco occasionally—we played two or three times at the Fillmore and we played the Avalon Ballroom. We did a lot of festivals and a lot of local TV. Sometimes we would get booked in some of the outlying areas, outside of the immediate L.A. area, where nobody really knew us and we could actually make some eatin' money. The Whisky and the Fillmore and all were prestigious gigs, but they weren't big-paying gigs because a lot of bands would play for the exposure value more than anything. So we could play there and brag about it, but we didn't have any money to take home."

By the end of 1967, Liberty Records was ready for the Hour Glass to go to work on its second album. But by then, Mabron McKinney had already left. Duane might have been the brains of the outfit, but McKinney was smart enough to realize the Hour Glass was just marking time.

CHAPTER SIX

Power of Love

"You have to utilize what's inside you to create what you want to create. If it doesn't come out pure, it's no good." — D.A.

The **Hour Glass's** first album and first single had come and gone with little fanfare, but after opening for Buffalo Springfield at the Fillmore in San Francisco on December 21–23, 1967, the band felt that things were starting to go their way. Sure, the money was small, but the prestige of playing at one of Bill Graham's venues meant a lot. The band's reputation as a live act was continuing to grow despite the fact the gigs had been cut back by the label. And it was clear from the jam sessions at the Whisky that many successful artists truly respected their musicianship. Things seemed to be coming together, and the Liberty execs believed that a second album might propel the band to a high level of success.

Before recording of the second album could begin, there was the matter of replacing Mabron McKinney on bass. Duane went with familiarity, calling on Bob Keller, who had already done two stints with the Allman Joys. As it turned out, the third time was not the proverbial charm. "He lasted a month," says Paul Hornsby, "and then disappeared before a gig."

In an interview with Michael Buffalo Smith for *Gritz* magazine, Johnny Sandlin recalled, "We were thinking he might have killed himself or something. We lived right across the street from where that HOLLYWOOD sign is. You see it in all the movies. We thought he may have gone up there and jumped or something. I don't think we heard from him for about six months. We didn't know if he was alive or dead or what."

Just before Keller's disappearing act, Pete Carr had come out to visit the band in L.A. In those days, Duane was known as the Dog; Sandlin was called the Duck; and Carr had his own, less fortunate, animal nickname. "We always called him Beaver," says Hornsby. "It was 30 minutes before a gig at the Whisky and suddenly there's no bass player. We said, 'All right, Beaver, come with us. You're going to be our bass player tonight.' He said, 'Man, I'm a *guitar* player!' I said, 'Yeah, but you're gonna play bass tonight.' He said, 'Well, I'll try it.' He'd never played bass in his life. He played the gig, and he was our bass player until the end of the group."

With Pete Carr on board, the band went into the studio in January 1968 and recorded their entire second album within a month. This time, there was one major concession on Liberty's part that appeared—at first—to be a huge victory for the group. "We got to pick our own material," says Carr. "We even did some of our Southern friends' songs."

The "Southern friends" were Dan Penn, Dewey Lyndon "Spooner" Oldham, Marlin Greene, and the 5 Men-Its' former singer-guitarist, Eddie Hinton. The two Hinton/Greene tunes recorded by the Hour Glass were "Home for the Summer" and "Down in Texas"—the latter being the strongest song on the album. The Penn/Oldham number, "Power of Love," would also become the LP's title, as well as the single. Penn, Oldham, Hinton, and Greene were all based in Muscle Shoals, Alabama, where the 5 Men-Its had done their first recording, and where quite a few important Southern soul records had been cut by that time.

"By the second album we also had a few feeble original tunes," says Hornsby. Gregg was a long way from becoming the crafter of great songs that he would later prove to be, but at least there was one member of the band who had something original to bring to the table. The Hour Glass ended up recording seven of the younger Allman's compositions for *Power of Love*. Although most of the songs had been written since the move to L.A., the band was forced to dip into the back catalog for "Changing of the Guard," which the Allman Joys had cut at Bradley's Barn two years earlier.

Publicity shot of the Hour Glass in its final incarnation—Duane in front; Pete Carr leaning on fireplug; back row: (L–R) Johnny Sandlin, Gregg, and Paul Hornsby

The remaining tracks were a cover of Solomon Burke's 1962 hit, "I'm Hanging Up My Heart for You," and their instrumental version of the Beatles' "Norwegian Wood," featuring Duane on electric sitar—the piece John McEuen recalls as the band's opening number at their live gigs.

And so the battle of control over song selection had been won. That particular skirmish, however, had little to do with the outcome of the overall war. To Duane's chagrin, Dallas Smith was once again put in charge of producing the record. As unpleasant as the band's experience had been with Smith while working on the first album, this time it just got uglier.

Duane had led the band from the beginning, just as he had done with the Escorts and the Allman Joys. Onstage, he was the man in charge. Now, once more, Duane had to listen to Bobby Vee's record producer tell him what *his* band should sound like. Duane could put up a brave front. He was always the most confident man in the room. But when the guitarist realized that he would be expected to adhere to the wishes and whims of Dallas Smith one more time, he solved the problem by mentally removing himself from the process. Eventually, he removed himself physically as well.

"During the cutting of the second album, Duane was constantly at odds with the producer," says Hornsby. "They didn't get along at *all*. You didn't tell Duane what to do. Duane had to be in control. He had no respect for Dallas Smith whatsoever. In fact, on more than one of the sessions he was pretty out of his mind. I mean, one session I remember we had to shut it down because Duane kind of got out of control. You know everybody has those moments from time to time—or most people do. But, unfortunately, it was hindering our album, you know?

"During that second album, Duane would quit the band every other day. And right in the middle of the album—we already had the basic tracks cut—he quit and flew to Daytona. Some of that was fighting the producer, but he was having some personal problems, too. I can't remember what it was all about, but he quit. And there we were. We didn't know what we were going to do. The focal point of the band had quit in the middle of an album."

"I remember being with Duane outside the studio and him throwing down a beer can and leaving as our manager was trying to talk to him," says Carr.

The immediate solution was to take advantage of having serendipitously hired a lead guitarist to play bass. "We started putting Duane's guitar parts on with Pete Carr doing them, just to complete the album," says Hornsby. "Pete was a good guitar player, but there was nobody like Duane."

"I played lead guitar on 'I Still Want Your Love,'" says Carr. "Duane had left, and they asked me to fill in, so I did. It was a quick guitar take, so it was nothing great, with no preparation."

"Somewhere near the end [of recording the album]," says Hornsby, "Duane comes back." When the record was finished, Duane had played lead on everything but "I Still Want Your Love." Allman's evaluation of Carr's playing on the song was less than complimentary. "Duane and I were in our apartment after we had gotten a dub of the record. Duane got mad, saying 'That sucks!' I tried to calm him down, saying something like, 'I know it's not good. You would have done much better.' Truth being, he *could* have done better, and I know I could have done better than I did."

Whether leaving before finishing the album was solely because of problems back home or not, only Duane really knew. It was clear to all involved that he was miserable with the way the sessions were going. Due to the undeniably vast improvement of the second album over the first, it's difficult to grasp Duane's immense frustration. At least things were pointing in the right direction.

"To this day, I think Gregg did some of his best singing on those albums, as young as he was," says Carr. And perhaps he has hit the nail on the head: Dallas Smith's focus was clearly still on Gregg. It would become even more obvious that this was Liberty Records' intention when the finished album was released. On the front cover, Gregg is the center of attention in the photograph of the band. Duane is to his left, looking at least a foot and a half shorter. Because we see Duane only from the chest up, it's impossible to tell if he's sitting on a stool while Gregg is standing, or if it's just a matter of camera angle. The rest of the band stands behind the brothers, looking at something off to their left and appearing to be no more than bystanders who accidentally walked into the middle of the photo shoot.

The emphasis on Gregg becomes even more obvious on the back cover. There's a line drawing of the heads of the Hour Glass members, with Gregg's in the forefront and nearly twice the size of any of the other four. The liner notes, written by Neil Young (then of Buffalo Springfield), tell of Gregg leading the band through the recording of "To Things Before" (about which, Hornsby now says, "I can't even remember how that one goes"). The members of the Hour Glass might have considered Duane to be "the focal point," as Hornsby puts it, but Dallas Smith and Liberty Records clearly had other ideas.

In March, the album and its single, "Power of Love" b/w "I Still Want Your Love," were released. The public paid little notice. "Power of Love" is a good song, but if the album had a hit single crying out to be released to the record buying public of 1968, it was Hinton and Greene's "Down in Texas." However, it was not to be.

At least you can hear the Hour Glass playing as a band this time around, even with the record company's emphasis on Gregg. The feel of *Power of Love* is much looser than the previous record. It also more closely represents what the Hour Glass was about—with the emphasis on "more." Even Duane must have been pleased with his guitar work on "I'm Hanging Up My Heart for You"—but that's only one out of the 12 tracks. Overall, the songs are simply too weak for a band this strong. And, strangely enough, the one piece that was a key part of the band's live set—the instrumental of "Norwegian Wood"—just doesn't work within the context of the album.

Years later, when United Artists reissued both Hour Glass albums as a two-record set, Ben Edmonds wrote in the liner notes, "The music on these two records is not very good. This is not to say that the music is necessarily *that* bad." It's a perfect summation of the Hour Glass's output on Liberty Records.

CHAPTER SEVEN

The Epiphany

"You just slide a bottle up and down 'til what you want out of it comes out. You just slide away at it 'til you've got it down." — D.A.

Duane was crazy—which helps," says Paul Hornsby. "He was always nine steps ahead of himself and everybody else. He was just a real hyper guy. He was the kind of guy that you felt had something to say. He was always on the cutting edge of everything—from the clothes he wore to the music he played to the books he read. When he said something, everybody listened. When you heard him say something, some of it might be bullshit, but it was always *interesting* bullshit.

"He was the kind of guy who could walk into a room and he had that charisma about him that caused everybody to notice him. Of course, in those early days, shoulder-length reddish-blond hair itself was quite a striking thing. Coming out of Alabama or Florida at that time, you would tend to notice somebody like that anyway. But he was noticed when we got to L.A., too."

The charisma seemed to come naturally for Allman, but he was not one to simply rely on personal charm to get him to the next phase of his musical career. Just as in the early days when he would stop the turntable with his toe to learn a new lick, Duane Allman was absolutely driven to become an even better musician than he already was. "I think the guitar was just an extension of himself," says Hornsby. "If you ever saw him sitting down, he had a guitar across his lap and a book in his hand. So he was either reading or playing guitar—always. You never, ever saw him without a guitar in his hand unless he was walking down the street."

When Johnny Townsend moved to Los Angeles in 1968, he spent the first few weeks living with Duane and Gregg in their apartment. While there, Townsend got a first-hand look at what Duane's work ethic was all about. "I think they'd just finished their second album on Liberty. I remember a night sitting around the apartment and seeing Duane just lying over on the couch, playing his guitar. It was like seeing Sonny Rollins when he used to play out on the Williamsburg Bridge. It was just like that. Duane would fall asleep at three or four o'clock in the morning, still playing his guitar—still had it around his neck.

"He'd wake up in the morning and go take a whiz, still have his guitar around his neck—careful not to pee on the strap. Make his coffee and he'd still be playing. I'd never seen anybody that dedicated. Sure, he had some natural talent, but it was like Michael Jordan. He worked harder than anybody else on the floor to get where he was. That was the thing I always admired and respected about him—he had that dogged determination: 'I'm going to be the best.'"

As unpleasant as recording the two Hour Glass albums had been, the time Duane spent in Los Angeles in 1967 and 1968 literally changed his life. He might not have been able to play live as much as he wanted to, but not being able to gig gave him the opportunity to go out and catch other bands. And seeing one particular act so enlightened Allman that it would do no less than revolutionize his whole concept of how to play the guitar.

"We loved Taj Mahal," says Paul Hornsby. "We went out to see his band at a club that was called the Golden Bear, I believe." Pete Carr recalls the profound effect that night had on Duane: "We went to see Taj Mahal, and he had Jesse Ed Davis with him. They did 'Statesboro Blues,' and Davis played slide guitar on it. After hearing that, Duane started practicing slide all the time."

Jesse Edwin Davis III was a full-blooded Kiowa Indian. He would go on to work with such luminaries as Eric Clapton, John Lennon, Albert King, and Willie Nelson, among others. But in 1968, he was the lead guitarist in Taj Mahal's band. "He made quite an impression on Duane," says Hornsby. "From the first time that we saw them, we picked up 'Statesboro Blues.' Taj was doing that, and from then on we claimed that song. That was the first song that

Duane played slide on in the Hour Glass. Of course, now when you think of 'Statesboro Blues,' you think of the Allman Brothers' version, but Taj was doing it before them. We pretty much did the same arrangement as Taj."

Everyone who was there at the time agrees that this was the moment of the Epiphany—the Magi had come bearing the gift, and Duane was there to receive it. On the down side, everyone also agrees that Duane's learning experience took its toll on the assembled.

"He drove us crazy," says Hornsby. "There's nothing in the world worse than hearing somebody learn how to play slide guitar, unless it's hearing somebody learn how to play the fiddle. I used to complain to Duane. Every time you'd see him, he was playing that damn slide—just driving you crazy."

Duane later recalled the torment he was inflicting on the other members of the Hour Glass: "I got me a [Coricidin] bottle and went in the house for about three weeks. I said, 'Hey man, we've got to learn the songs—the blues—to play onstage. I love this. This is a gas!' So we started doing it, and for a while it was everybody looking at me and thinking, 'Oh no! He's getting ready to do it again!' Everybody just lowered their heads—start it off fast and get it over with.

"But then I got a little better at it. . . ." It is a sentence that will go down as one of the great understatements of all time.

CHAPTER EIGHT

The Hour Glass in Muscle Shoals

"You have to be right up front and be true to yourself and other people around you—true as you can be." — D.A.

After *Power of Love* was released in March 1968, the Hour Glass went on the road. "We were on a 'promotional tour' for a brand-new album we didn't like," says Paul Hornsby. "But we felt that if we could record in Muscle Shoals, they would be the people that would understand our music. We didn't feel like Liberty Records knew how to cut us—and it's obvious now that it was true."

Hornsby and Sandlin suggested that the band go to Rick Hall's Fame Studios in Muscle Shoals. "I'd worked at Fame Studios since I was in high school," Sandlin told interviewer Dave Kyle. "Rick had used me . . . on some sessions in the early '60s. I'd been around the studio and I knew it always sounded great, so I kept telling the guys that we needed to go to Fame."

"Johnny Sandlin was from Decatur, and he knew all about the Muscle Shoals studios," says Pete Carr. "Duane, Gregg, and I really had no experience with Fame before then. From the first day I met Johnny, he played me recordings he loved coming out of Fame. He thought it was the best place around and loved the music they did there."

The songs that had been cut at Muscle Shoals included hits by Percy Sledge, Aretha Franklin, Wilson Pickett, Clarence Carter, and other R&B and soul acts.

Even Joe Tex—the Allman Joys' Dial Records label mate—had recorded the soul classic "Hold What You've Got" at Fame.

Luckily, the *Power of Love* tour included a gig in St. Louis that, in the words of Johnny Sandlin, "actually paid pretty good for a change." After that, Hornsby says, "We pooled our money and went to the Shoals to cut a few tracks, with Eddie Hinton helping us. That's where our heroes were. We liked the music that was coming out of Muscle Shoals. They knew our style of music, and they knew how to record us. They got a much better sound for what we were trying to do."

The Hour Glass arrived at Fame in April, ready to record a handful of songs that had become staples of their live act. The decision by the band to take matters into their own hands was a bold move, and Duane's frustration from his lack of control over the L.A. recordings was assuaged as soon as the sessions got under way. Gregg, on the other hand, wasn't as confident about the proceedings.

Johnny Wyker—the songwriter-guitarist who had formed the Magnificent Seven with Johnny Townsend and Tippy Armstrong—was there when the Hour Glass recorded at Fame. "The thing I remember the most is spending a lot of time in conversations with Gregg about whether the music was any good," says Wyker. I'd say, 'Gregg, do you like it?' He said 'yes' every time I asked, but then they'd do the next song and we'd go through his doubts all over again. Maybe Gregg had been in L.A. too long. I think I could be more objective about the music than he could at the time. I just told him, 'If you love it, stick to it!'"

Among the songs they recorded were a Gregg Allman original called "Been Gone Too Long," one written by a pre-NRBQ Al Anderson entitled "No Good to Cry," and a medley of three tunes popularized by B.B. King. Despite Gregg's doubts, these three tracks were all eventually released. The "B.B. King Medley" would be the first to appear, in 1972, given the leadoff spot on a double-album compilation of recordings featuring Duane Allman entitled *An Anthology*. "Been Gone Too Long" would be included on its follow-up, *An Anthology, Volume II*, and "No Good to Cry" would finally show up more than 20 years later on the Allman Brothers Band boxed set, *Dreams*, where it would be mistitled "Ain't No Good to Cry." (Unfortunately for Al Anderson, the credits would say "writer unknown.")

Of the tracks laid down at Fame, it is the "B.B. King Medley" that not only best shows off the Hour Glass's blues-based Southern sound but is a clear precursor to what was to come less than a year later when Duane would put together the Allman Brothers Band. Time and again, the Allman Brothers would turn to classic blues songs, with Duane's B.B. King-influenced lead guitar work and Gregg's blues-drenched vocals leading the charge. The Hour Glass was on the right track, but Duane was yet to find the perfect combination of musicians to capture the sound in his head.

The three songs in the "B.B. King Medley" are "Sweet Little Angel," "It's My Own Fault," and "How Blue Can You Get?" They are all from King's *Live at the Regal*, recorded on November 21, 1964, at the Regal Theatre in Chicago. The blues legend's second album for ABC Records, *Live at the Regal* is still hailed today as the greatest live blues album of all time. Although B.B. didn't play the songs as a medley, he did perform "Sweet Little Angel," "It's My Own Fault," and "How Blue Can You Get?" in that order on that night in Chicago. Duane, well versed in B.B.'s music, realized the potential of merging the three songs.

Gregg's "Been Gone Too Long" is better than any of his originals that had appeared on the Hour Glass's two Liberty albums, and it served as a kind of bridge between the Hour Glass of L.A. and the Hour Glass as the members of the band intended for it to sound. "We just liked the sound we got at Fame better, and we felt better recording there," says Pete Carr. "None of us had been real comfortable with the sound we got in L.A., or with the overall approach to the recording process there."

Best of all, perhaps, the band had made all the music themselves—no tacked-on horns or background vocalists as on the first album; no Dallas Smith to get in the way. "Eddie Hinton helped on the recordings," says Carr, "along with Jimmy Johnson. I remember Jimmy coming out and asking me to pick my bass a little further back towards the bridge so I would get a little more definition in my sound. But neither of them were what I would call real producers of the tapes. I would say that we, the group, were—if you could say there was a real producer at all. We just cut some songs the way we wanted to. But the people at Fame were a great help."

Jimmy Johnson engineered the Hour Glass recordings. Eddie Hinton— who, by this time, was playing lead guitar on sessions at Fame and another studio in town—contributed suggestions. Johnny Wyker was there, too, giving Gregg moral support. When the session was over, Johnson, Hinton, Wyker, and everyone in the band felt that something special had been captured that day. Now all the band had to do was finish the tour, return to Los Angeles, and let Dallas Smith and the Liberty Records execs hear exactly what the Hour Glass was all about—a Southern band playing blues-fueled rock. The group left Muscle Shoals, tapes in hand, confident that the third album would finally be the one to get them over the hump and on their way to the kind of recognition they deserved.

CHAPTER NINE

How Blue Can You Get?

*"A good damn band of misled cats was what
it was." — D.A.*

The reaction by the folks at Liberty wasn't pretty. "I remember being in Dallas's office in L.A. when we played the tapes," says Pete Carr. "He didn't like them, and we were all upset about him being so close-minded. Dallas was a pop producer, and the tapes cut at Fame were *not* pop hit-type songs in his mind."

Paul Hornsby cuts to the chase: "Dallas Smith hated it. We played it for him and he thought it was horrendous stuff." By showing they were capable of overseeing their own sessions while recording at a studio other than the one owned by Liberty, Hornsby says, the band was "cutting Dallas Smith out of the picture. I can see why he turned it down, because that would have ended his involvement with the band. I don't know why he would care that much, really, except that his ego might have been crushed. I don't think he was ever that big a fan of the group in the first place. We weren't fans of his, so it wasn't exactly a match made in heaven."

"You could tell he wanted to have control if he was to be the producer, and I can see why," says Carr. "But we could have come up with radio-oriented music at Fame, along with more bluesy, earthy music, if we were allowed to go back and record more there. We could have been an American/Southern/early Rolling Stones-type of group—but *better* in a way."

"We were signed to Liberty, so we were kind of at a stalemate," says Hornsby. "It weighed heavily on Duane, you know—him more so than the rest of us. I would have been happy to stay in L.A. and play forever. But Duane was sick of the label, and he wanted to come back to the South where he could be—I think I'm quoting him on this—'a big fish in a small pond.'"

But even after two years in California, having jammed with the likes of Paul Butterfield and Buddy Miles at the Whisky and opened for acts like Buffalo Springfield and the Animals at the Fillmore, returning to the South didn't result in the "big fish" homecoming that Duane anticipated. "We left L.A. to come back down South and try it again," Hornsby recalls, "and when we came back—boy, it was like stark realism slapped us upside of the head. Every time we played in California it was like, man, we were just blowing everybody away. I mean—I pity any band that we opened for out there because we brought the house down.

"And here we were back in the South playing these damn small clubs where we'd all started out—and they were wanting to hear, you know, a live jukebox, basically. We were trying to do our 'L.A. Big-Time Rock & Roll Thing,' and they wanted to hear 'Midnight Hour' and 'Mustang Sally.' We didn't get the respect that we had gotten in L.A. It wasn't what Duane had remembered, you know? Everybody was so down and depressed that it just fell apart. Within three weeks after coming back, we were *kaput*."

The Hour Glass went back to play a familiar club in Nashville, the Briar Patch, "and then Duane went and had a falling out with the owner," says Hornsby. The Hour Glass were now *personae non gratae* at the very club that had been the setting for Duane's first real break in the music business. The whole band had to be wondering if things could get any worse.

They could. The final blow came at a gig in Mobile, Alabama. "They wanted to bill us as the Allman Joys because that's what everybody remembered," Hornsby recalls. "I said, 'Well, we're not the Allman Joys. We're the Hour Glass.' But they insisted on using that name and that didn't help our morale a bit. After that gig, we folded."

For Duane, it had been a serious case of way too much valuable time wasted. His summation of the Hour Glass experience came down to a single sentence: "A good damn band of misled cats was what it was."

And then the misled cats went their separate ways. By June, Gregg was back in Los Angeles, recording a semi-R&B version of the Tammy Wynette country hit "D-I-V-O-R-C-E" with studio musicians. It was released later that month, credited to "GREG ALLMAN & The Hour Glass." It made no more noise than the two previous singles, and Gregg was soon back in Daytona with his brother.

In 1967, while the Hour Glass was recording in L.A., Butch Trucks had been doing some recording of his own with Scott Boyer and David Brown. The three-member lineup had remained the same, but settling on what to call themselves was a different matter altogether. "After the Bitter Ind. we became the Tiffany System," says Boyer. "We recorded at Bradley's Barn. It was during the flower power era—the Strawberry Alarm Clock and all that. So we called ourselves the Tiffany System and had these paisley suits. After that, when we went to Miami to do the album down there, we became the 31st of February.

"We were trying to come up with a name. Somebody suggested the 29th of February. Somebody else said the 30th, and then Bradley Shapiro, who was our producer, said, 'Well, how about the 31st?' We all looked at him like he was nuts and said, 'Yeah, whatever.' So, the band actually had three names—same guys in every band—except for a while, in the 31st of February, Duane and Gregg played with us. That was the last year the band was together."

Prior to Duane and Gregg's brief stay with the band, the 31st of February had managed to secure a deal with Vanguard Records, the preeminent folk music label of the era. "We were working through some people in Miami," Boyer recalls. "Henry Stone owned Tone Distributors down there, which was basically a record distribution warehouse that took up an entire block in Hialeah. He was in partnership with Steve Alaimo. They were our record company liaisons. They placed us on Vanguard, and Brad Shapiro produced the first album. We recorded it at Criteria."

The 31st of February was released to no critical acclaim whatsoever. The album's failure to catch on with the public was enough to make the trio decide to become a quartet by adding an electric lead guitar to the mix. "We had just hired this guitar player and were coming through Daytona," Butch Trucks says, "and we ran into Duane and Gregg. They had just split up with the Hour Glass, and they said, 'You wanna join forces?' So we said, 'Hell yes!'"

We fired that poor little guy we'd just hired four days earlier, and put a band together with Duane and Gregg. We went to Miami and recorded a whole bunch of songs with Duane and Gregg, and started playing shows around the Southeast—really good stuff. I mean, with what we had, and the way Duane was playing and the way Gregg was singing, that was a smokin'-ass band!"

"We cut some demos to get a budget to do a second album," says Boyer. "Those were the ones that had the original version of 'Melissa' and some other good stuff, too. We'd hang around the office [of Tone Distributors] drinking coffee and schmoozing with the secretaries, and I think they put this studio upstairs just to get us out of their hair. They said, 'Y'all go stay up there. Do anything you want.'

"It was a little studio—I think it had been a storage room at one point. We had a key, and we could pretty much go there and work anytime we wanted to. We did a lot of stuff up there. I imagine at least half the stuff we did got bulk-erased later on. It's a shame, because there was some stuff we did there that never saw the light of day. Some of it sucked, but some of it wasn't bad."

The 31st of February's recording sessions for their second album started in early September 1968. Among the songs the quintet cut were "Nobody Knows You When You're Down and Out" and Gregg Allman's "Melissa." John McEuen recalls Duane learning "Nobody Knows You When You're Down and Out" during his days with the Hour Glass: "My brother Bill was into traditional blues. Duane had never heard of Scrapper Blackwell, who was this old black guy who hadn't played guitar in 30 years until somebody rediscovered him. Bill showed Duane 'Down and Out' by playing it for him on the guitar. And then he played Duane the record [*Mr. Scrapper's Blues*, Bluesville, 1962]." The old blues tune became part of the 31st of February's repertoire, and it was a song Duane would return to when he joined forces with Eric Clapton for *Layla and Other Assorted Love Songs* two years later.

"Melissa" was Gregg's sole original contribution to the recording project. He had started writing the song in 1967. "I was pretty lonely, and I dreamed up this perfect woman for me—you know, the perfect mate," he says. "So I wrote the song, but I didn't have a name for her. I was in the grocery store—a place that I don't go very often—and there was this cute little girl running away from her mother down the aisle, and her mother was yelling, 'Melissa, come back here.' So I thought, 'That'd do it.' So I named it 'Melissa.'"

Steve Alaimo—singing star of the afternoon TV show *Where the Action Is* in the mid-1960s—produced the tracks and is credited as Gregg's co-writer on "Melissa." More important, on this track Duane got the chance to show off his slide guitar skills on tape for the first time. Duane also plays more straight lead guitar on these tapes than on either of the Hour Glass LPs.

Unlike much of the Hour Glass's recorded material, the 31st of February tapes sound like a *band*. And Gregg's voice has greatly matured—he comes off more soulful, more sincere. In places, the group evokes the Allman Brothers Band—which isn't too surprising, as it included half of the original Allman Brothers lineup.

According to Butch Trucks, during the sessions Gregg had some phone conversations with Bill McEuen. "Gregg's telling us that he's getting some gigs booked for us in California so we can go out there and play—that kind of thing." Then the band decided to take a break from recording and head home. Duane and Butch took a slight detour so Butch could see a girlfriend in Wauchula, Florida, before going on to Daytona Beach. Unwittingly, they had given Gregg the opening he needed to make his escape back to the West Coast.

"He went out there after selling Steve Alaimo 'Melissa' and two other songs," says Boyer. "I remember him coming to me and saying, 'Well, look— Steve Alaimo will buy 'Melissa' and 'Well I Know' and 'God Rest His Soul.' He did that in order to buy a plane ticket to California.'"

"I remember us sitting in the living room at 100 Van Avenue," Butch Trucks told *Hittin' the Note*. "The phone rings and it's Gregg, and he's telling Duane that he's gonna be doing a solo thing out in California—that this McEuen guy will let Duane and the rest of them out of their Hour Glass contract if Gregg will stay and do this solo thing. . . . Duane was *so mad* at Gregg that night. Good God!"

Liberty Records had already shown its hand three months earlier when it released "D-I-V-O-R-C-E," singling out Gregg's name in the credits (even if it was misspelled). It was Gregg they had really wanted—maybe from the outset. And it was a temptation he simply couldn't resist.

"I've always heard that Gregg was forced to return," says Paul Hornsby, "but I doubt that they had to twist his arm very much. I think he really liked it. He liked the personal attention they were giving him. I mean—*I* would have. Can't blame him for that."

For a brief moment, it looked as if things might actually come together again on the West Coast. Boyer remembers what happened: "Gregg called us and said, 'Y'all should just come out here. Our manager's gonna book us ten thousand dollars' worth of gigs.' I had a friend who had just gotten back from Vietnam. He had a Volkswagen bug and was ready to travel the country. I remember having a discussion with Butch and David and Duane, and saying, 'Okay, well, we're all going to California.' I got in that Volkswagen with my friend, and we traveled across the country. The others were going to fly out and meet us, but for some reason they never did.

"When I got out there, I went to have a meeting with Bill McEuen. He said, 'Well, look—you're welcome to come in and audition for a job in Gregg's band if you want, but really all we need is Gregg. He's got star quality on his own. We're looking to market him as a solo artist.' There were no gigs. There was nothing—so my friend and I turned around and came back."

Even though Duane had decided not to go back to L.A. (which turned out to be a wise decision), over the past few years he had spent as much or more time on the road than off. By the late 1960s, "home" was still 100 Van Avenue, Daytona Beach—but it was primarily a stopping-off point between various other destinations. Duane didn't seem capable of staying still. Years later, Bobby Whitlock would recall Duane's pattern during Whitlock's days with Delaney & Bonnie & Friends. "He was intermittently in and out of our lives," says Whitlock. "He would pop in when we were in hotels here and there. He would just float in and float out."

After the demise of the Hour Glass, Duane was intermittently popping in and out of a lot of places. One of the towns he frequented, less than a hundred miles from home, was Jacksonville, Florida. Jacksonville had plenty of night-spots where live music was being played. There was also Willow Branch Park, home to Sunday jam sessions in which the musicians from various local bands would get together and play for free. One of those local bands was called the Second Coming.

The Second Coming had started out in the Tampa area as the Blues Messengers. The members were Dickey Betts and Larry "Rhino" Rheinhart on guitars, Dale Betts on keyboards and vocals, Berry Oakley on bass, and John Meeks on drums.

Forrest Richard "Dickey" Betts was born on December 12, 1943, in West Palm Beach, Florida. "I was subjected to music from my earliest recollections," Betts told interviewer Kirsten West. "All my uncles and my dad played music, and we would have jam sessions on Saturday night at the house." When they weren't playing music themselves, they listened to the radio. As was the case with Duane at his grandparents' house, there was one particular show that made an impression on young Dickey. "The Grand Ole Opry was a big item. . . . I have early recollections of a radio sitting in the kitchen window, with the curtains blowin', and Hank Williams and Lefty Frizzell and those people."

Betts started playing the ukulele before he was in the first grade, and he says he never considered any occupation besides making music. "When somebody said, 'What are you going to do when you grow up?'. . . I said, 'I'm gonna play on the Grand Ole Opry.'"

The Opry isn't known for its ukulele players, so Dickey tried mandolin and banjo before discovering, as a teenager, that the guitar was definitely his instrument. Just as Duane had done, Dickey had begun to borrow his brother's guitar and "kind of play around" with it. One night, while standing in his backyard, Dickey heard a band playing somewhere nearby. He followed the sound across an open field until he came upon a group of musicians rehearsing in a carport. The guitarist was a local player named Jimmy Paramore. But Jimmy wasn't just playing the guitar—he was playing the *blues*.

Although he retained his love for country music, Dickey was soon paying close attention to the music of B.B. King, Freddie King, Albert King, and other blues and R&B guitarists. "I used to listen to Chuck Berry almost religiously," he says. "I used to wear out his records getting licks off them. I would learn, say, the lead, note-for-note, from 'Roll Over Beethoven.' When I would go and play with a band, they would do something like 'Whole Lotta Shakin'' and I didn't know how to play my own stuff from inside me, so I'd play the lead I had learned from 'Roll Over.' I had all these leads that I'd learned from different 12-bar blues, and I'd switch them around. Then I started cutting them in half and piecing them together, and then, before I knew it, I was making up stuff of my own and adding that to my repertoire."

One of Dickey's early bands had an unusual, though steady, gig. "It was in a fair called World of Mirth Shows. We had one of those sideshows on the midway—it was called Teen Beat. This guy would bring out our band and tell all these lies about us to the people. We were pretty good, though, and we had a good show. By this time I had been studying Chuck Berry a lot. We did all these Chuck Berry walks, you know, and splits. I'd get on my amp and jump off it into a split, you know, playin'. And I was a cute little 16-year-old kid."

After the World of Mirth no longer seemed all that mirthful, Dickey decided to form his own band. Over the next few years, he says, he "kept running into" Berry Oakley and a harmonica player named Thom Doucette.

Reese Wynans, a keyboard player from Sarasota, Florida, became acquainted with both Betts and Oakley during the late 1960s. "I knew them well from my days in Sarasota," Reese recalls. "Berry played in one of the bands I was in down there called the Bittersweet. Dickey had a band called the Soul Children—Dickey and Dale, Dickey's then-girlfriend, and Larry Rheinhart—that played the same circuit that I played, so they knew me from that circuit." Eventually, Berry Oakley joined forces with the members of the Soul Children, and the Blues Messengers were born—sort of.

Unfortunately, the band—now based in Tampa—had a drummer who just wasn't in the same league with the rest of the players. Realizing the problem, Dale (by this time Mrs. Betts) told Dickey, Berry, and Larry about John Meeks, a drummer she had once lived with in a communal house on 14th Street in Atlanta near a place called Piedmont Park. As luck would have it, they discovered that Meeks was now living in Sarasota, only 60 miles away. Dickey, Dale, and Berry drove to Sarasota and convinced the drummer to come up to Tampa and sit in. Meeks did, got the job, and moved into the big house the Blues Messengers shared near Tampa Bay.

When Dale had met John Meeks in Atlanta, he was playing drums at a disco called the Scene, a trendy nightspot of the flashing-dance-floor variety. A disc jockey would play records while Meeks played along with whatever 45 the DJ was spinning. Later, after Meeks had joined the Blues Messengers, a couple of guys in suits showed up at their steady gig in Tampa. They told the band they were going to open a branch of the Scene in Jacksonville. This time, though, there would be a live band.

The businessmen promised the Blues Messengers that the pay would be more than what they were making; that they would have a hot new club to play in; and that they would have free living accommodations. There was only one change the suits required: the name of the band would have to be the Second Coming. Although John Meeks once said he had no idea why the owners of the Scene insisted on the name change, one look at Berry Oakley on the back cover of the Allman Brothers' first album—robed arms outstretched as he stands behind (and seems to hover above) the other band members—is probably the only clue one needs.

Raymond Berry Oakley III was born on April 4, 1948, in Chicago. He began playing guitar at the age of 12. Being born and raised in Chicago, Berry had access to radio stations there that featured blues tunes by local musicians like Muddy Waters, Howlin' Wolf, and other greats who recorded for Chicago-based Chess Records.

Oakley was an excellent lead guitarist, playing in several bands while in high school. His setup of choice while in a group called the Shanes was a forest green Stratocaster plugged into a Sears Silvertone 2×12 amp. The Shanes opened for the Byrds, among other acts of note—a good indication that the group wasn't your average high school garage band. During Berry's senior year, he discovered that Tommy Roe's backing band—the Roemans—were about to lose their bass player. By 1965, Roe had already scored a chart-topping, million-selling record called "Sheila," as well as the Top 10 hit "Everybody." Berry jumped at the chance to audition, practiced on a friend's bass guitar for a couple of weeks, and nabbed the job.

Berry became good friends with Mike Callahan, the Roemans' combination soundman/bus driver, as the band toured the country. Callahan recalls that Roe fired both of them "for picking up this bad habit of stuffing towels around the threshold." It's a good bet they weren't canned for smoking Lucky Strikes in their hotel room.

In the meantime, Oakley's family had moved south to Sarasota, living on Siesta Key. Berry went to visit them and discovered a real music scene had developed around Sarasota and Bradenton, including the aforementioned Soul Children, which begat the Blues Messengers, which begat the Second Coming. They needed a bass player, so he joined the band. Now consisting of Dickey, Dale, Larry Rheinhart, Berry Oakley, and John Meeks, the Second Coming made the move to Jacksonville and the Scene.

And then Dale discovered she was pregnant. The band needed someone to sub for her, so Reese Wynans got the call. "Dale Betts, Dickey's wife at that time, was their keyboard player," he says. "They wanted somebody to fill in for her, so I did it. I moved up to Jacksonville, and after she had the baby she returned as the singer only. So I guess I stole her job.

"The Second Coming played six nights a week at the Scene. Our repertoire was about half rock and half blues. Dickey played most of the blues, and Larry Rheinhart did most of the rock. We had a few originals, but mostly we were a cover band. I recall Dickey singing that Paul Butterfield tune 'Born in Chicago.' He also sang 'Born Under a Bad Sign.' Berry Oakley sang 'Oh Pretty Woman' and 'Hoochie Coochie Man.' Larry Rheinhart did a bunch of Hendrix covers—things like 'Fire' and 'Manic Depression'—and Dale sang some Jefferson Airplane tunes.

"The Scene was kind of a psychedelic club—it had flashing strips of colored lights on the dance floor and liquid projection screens on the walls. It also had a quiet lounge with a glass wall where you could sit and watch the band and the dancers and everything. Behind the stage, there was a winding stairway that went down to our dressing room. The guy who owned the club also put us up in some apartments, so it was kind of a package deal. When we started with the band, we were living in the apartments. Then we moved to the Green House over on Riverside Avenue."

When the Second Coming started their gig at the Scene, the Hour Glass—although down to its last few grains of sand—was still together. Berry's wife, Linda, who had seen Duane and Gregg performing during the Allman Joys days, dragged her husband with her to see the Hour Glass when they came to town. "The Hour Glass was playing the Comic Book Club in Jacksonville, and I talked Berry into going," Linda Oakley told writer John Ogden. "He went not expecting too much." But Berry was knocked out by Duane's guitar playing, and the two ended up talking late into the evening about their mutual musical influences.

John Meeks remembers a former waitress at the original Scene in Atlanta mentioning two brothers from her hometown of Daytona Beach—one was an incredible guitar player and the other had an unbelievably soulful voice. The waitress had moved back to Daytona Beach to help her mother run the motor scooter rental concession there. When she discovered that Meeks was now playing at the Scene in Jacksonville, she brought Duane and Gregg up to the club with her, and the two of them sat in with the Second Coming. By this time the Hour Glass was history, and Duane and Gregg were hanging out with Butch Trucks and the 31st of February.

But soon after—with Gregg having returned to L.A.—the 31st of February was floundering and the remaining members of the Hour Glass had scattered. Johnny Sandlin was playing on sessions at Henry Stone's place—the same studio where the 31st of February had been recording. Pete Carr hung out in Daytona Beach for a while, occasionally seeing Duane around town, but then he headed south to play on sessions with Sandlin. Paul Hornsby returned to Tuscaloosa, where he put together a band called South Camp featuring a teenaged keyboard player named Chuck Leavell—the kid who had been so impressed with the Allman Joys at Fort Brandon Armory a couple of years earlier.

And there sat Duane Allman—the guy with all the drive and energy in the world; the guitarist who wanted more than anything to be able to take the music he heard in his head and play it for anyone who would listen; the man who was the *leader* of the band—with no band, no audience, no plan.

He had already experienced the studio scene in Muscle Shoals. Eddie Hinton had been up there for quite a while making a go of it as a session musician. If Allman couldn't form a band that would stay together, maybe it was time to go it alone as a rogue guitarist for hire. As always, Duane Allman was restless—so he decided it was time to move on.

CHAPTER TEN

The Road to Fame

*"Any session is as creative as you make it. Like when I
worked with Wilson Pickett in Muscle Shoals, I suggested
he cut 'Hey Jude.' He ended up using my arrangement
and it worked out just fine." — D.A.*

Muscle Shoals is a small spot in the northwest corner of Alabama. It includes a town by that name along with the hamlets of Sheffield, Tuscumbia, and Florence—the last being the birthplace of W. C. Handy. Within this quartet of tiny road-map dots along the Tennessee River, a visceral version of Southern soul was captured on tape in a handful of local recording studios during the 1960s. The special genre of music cut there during that decade would come to be known as the Muscle Shoals Sound.

Rick Hall's Fame Studios in Muscle Shoals was the first to produce nationally charting records, beginning in 1962 with Arthur Alexander's "You Better Move On." A couple of years later, Jimmy Hughes went to Fame Studios and scored a Top 20 hit with "Steal Away." Then, in early 1966, a local hospital orderly named Percy Sledge recorded a song called "When a Man Loves a Woman" at Quin Ivy's studio in Sheffield. All hell was about to break loose in the Shoals.

Quin Ivy and his partner, Marlin Greene (who would later write "Down in Texas" and "Home for the Summer" with Eddie Hinton for the Hour Glass), knew they had produced something special, but they had no clue what to do with it. Ivy says, "I called Rick Hall and said, 'I've got a song I'd like you to hear, and I'd like you to help me place it with a record company if you think it's good enough.'"

"So I said, 'Fine. Bring it on up,'" remembers Hall. "He brought it up and played it for me. He said, 'What do you think?' I said, 'An absolute smash.' He said, 'You really think so?' I said, 'I really think so.' He said, 'Well, will you help me place it?' I said, 'I sure will.'

"I went upstairs and called Jerry Wexler at Atlantic Records. This was before I ever met Jerry Wexler in person. I said, 'I got a song. You told me to call you if I ever found something that I thought was a hit. I heard a record just a minute ago, and I think it's an absolute smash.' I said, 'A Number 1 record. A Number 1—not Number 2 or Number 3. A Number 1!' He said, 'You really think so?' I said, 'Without any reservations whatsoever. I'd stake my life on it.' He said, 'Send it up to me.'"

The call paid off. Wexler signed Sledge to Atlantic, which released "When a Man Loves a Woman" in March 1966. Quin, Marlin, Rick, and Percy watched as the single flew to the top of the R&B and pop charts two months later, selling more than a million copies along the way.

After that resounding success, Muscle Shoals soon became Soul Mecca. Ivy and Greene would go on to have several more successful singles with Sledge, while Hall's Fame Studios racked up hit after hit via James & Bobby Purify's "I'm Your Puppet," Wilson Pickett's "Mustang Sally," Aretha Franklin's "I Never Loved a Man (the Way I Love You)," Etta James's "Tell Mama," and Arthur Conley's "Sweet Soul Music"—all before the Hour Glass came to town to lay down the tracks that would be rejected by Liberty Records.

Duane Allman had visited Muscle Shoals prior to the formation of the Hour Glass. Johnny Wyker remembers the days in 1967 when he and Duane stayed in Eddie Hinton's apartment: "Eddie had rented a small garage apartment behind a big Victorian house in Sheffield, over by the river bluff not far from Quin Ivy's studio. Eddie was writing with Marlin Greene and doing sessions, and Duane and I was just hangin' out, mostly. At that time, Duane's legend as a hot-shot studio guitar player had not taken off yet. The apartment was so dirty that anytime girls came over to visit, they would take newspapers and spread them all over the floor—the bathroom, everywhere. That little apartment was a real mess!"

Duane's stay with Wyker and Hinton would be brief. His next visit was briefer still, when the Hour Glass went to Fame Studios in April 1968. Later that year, after discovering Gregg had returned to Los Angeles, Duane made his third trip to Muscle Shoals—this time looking for work. In September 1968, he went to visit Rick Hall. "He came here wanting to break into the business as a studio musician," says Hall. "He was a huge fan of the things I was doing—Jimmy Hughes, Arthur Alexander, Clarence Carter, Joe Tex. He knew about all the records I was cutting and was heavy into black music."

There is an oft-told story of Rick Hall being so impressed with the Hour Glass tapes recorded at his studio that he sent a telegram to Duane asking him to come to Muscle Shoals. Hall says that was simply not the case. In light of the fact that the studio owner already had guitarists Albert "Junior" Lowe and Eddie Hinton available to him at a moment's notice, it seems highly unlikely that Hall—a man in constant motion—would actually take the time to try to track down Allman and invite yet another lead guitar player to join the roster.

"He came here and said, 'I want to be a session player,' Hall remembers. "I said, 'I really don't need a session player. I have people on draws. I have signed contracts with the staff players here. They come in every day and punch the clock and stay here six hours, and they get paid X amount of dollars.' I said, 'I've got guitar players running out of my ass here.' To which he said, 'Well, would you mind if I just kind of camped out around here, and if something comes up just, you know, when the opportunity arrives, pick for you and let you see what I can do?' I said, 'No, no. Be my guest. Come around. You're welcome. I just can't pay you any money, and I can't commit to you that I'm gonna make you a regular here because I've already got people that I'm using and committed to.' And he said, 'Fine.'

"I mean, this was Duane—he was hell-bent for stardom and nothing was going to stop him. You want it bad enough, you're gonna pay your dues. Nobody's gonna tell you that you can't, and the more people who tell you that you can't, the more determined you are to prove that you can. So I said, 'You're welcome to hang out here, but I don't know if I'm going to have anything for you.' At this time I hadn't even heard him play."

When Duane finally did get the chance to play for Rick Hall, he made a lasting first impression via his Coricidin bottle. "One day we were doing a demo and he had his bottleneck," says Hall. "To be honest with you, I hadn't saw many bottleneck players. I don't know if I had saw *any*. I mean, I knew about 'em. I knew about Muddy Waters and the Mississippi delta and the back porch blues and all that—but I hadn't really invested much time in it."

Duane and Rick Hall at Fame Studios, Muscle Shoals, Alabama

By the time Duane arrived at Fame in the latter part of 1968, the number of studios in the Shoals had begun to grow, but Rick Hall was still the godfather of the whole scene. His ability to recognize great artists, great songs, and great session players was uncanny.

Clarence Carter was a case in point. Rick took Carter into the studio in 1966 and began releasing a string of singles on his Fame Records label. The first couple of Clarence Carter singles reached the bottom of the Top 40 on the R&B charts, and one managed to skim the pop charts as well. Carter's third single, "The Road of Love," failed to make any noise at all.

Undaunted, Rick produced a track on Carter in early 1968 called "Funky Fever." It began to die after only three weeks of airplay. In the rush to release the single, "Slip Away," recorded at an earlier session, was picked for the B-side. By the second week of July, deejays all over the Southeast had begun to turn "Funky Fever" over and play the flipside instead. Soon "Slip Away" was scaling the charts. Purely by accident, Rick Hall had produced Clarence Carter's first Top 10, million-selling single.

When Carter's next single, "Too Weak to Fight," was released in November, it too became a million-seller. According to session sheets, Duane played on a number of Carter's recordings in October and November 1968. Although he's buried under horns and background vocalists on several of these sides, his unmistakable lead guitar work peaks out from time to time. And on Carter's 1968 re-recording of "The Road of Love," Duane is front and center.

Throughout the 1960s and 1970s, Rick Hall made a habit of recording many of the same songs from his Fame Publishing catalog time and again. Less than a year after his production of Clarence Carter's recording of "Tell Daddy," for example, Hall took Etta James into the studio to record the song as "Tell Mama." "Lollipops, Lace, and Lipstick"—the B-side of Jimmy Hughes's "Steal Away" in 1964—showed up again when Rick produced Donny Osmond's first solo album seven years later. The logic was simple: owning the publishing rights to a song was an additional—and lucrative—source of income beyond the royalties Hall would receive as the record's producer.

Making two versions of "The Road of Love" was more unusual, in that Rick produced the same song on the same *artist* twice. The first version had been recorded in July 1967, and in September of that year it was released as the follow-up to Carter's Top 40 R&B hit, "Thread the Needle." By October it was a casualty of the chart wars—just another 45 unable to garner any life-sustaining airplay. But Hall believed in the song. And when he heard Duane Allman's slide playing during that demo session, Rick Hall knew he had found the missing stripe down the center of "The Road of Love."

"When Duane played bottleneck guitar on a session, you had to have plugs in your ears because he would rattle the shingles," says Hall. "It was all full volume. He started playing the bottleneck on that thing, and guitar players were laying down their guitars and hiding because most of them had never heard anything like that. Of course, you can't capture that on a piece of plastic—the bigness and the funkiness and the whole thing of it. But I was knocked out, and Clarence was too."

"Clarence had just completed a recording session at Fame, and he called me," says Alan Walden. "I was Clarence's agent and manager at the time. He called me from the Muscle Shoals airport and said, 'Good God! Rick Hall has got this incredible guitar player.' That was the first that I ever heard of Duane Allman."

Duane had been playing slide on "Statesboro Blues" and other songs at live gigs during the latter part of the Hour Glass days, and he had also played slide on "Melissa" during the 31st of February sessions. But Clarence Carter's "The Road of Love" would become the first commercially released recording to feature Duane playing a slide guitar solo. (The 31st of February sessions, released on Bold Records under the misleading and misspelled title of *Duane & Greg Allman*, wouldn't come out until 1972.)

On November 12, 1968, Clarence Carter re-recorded his flop single of a year earlier. On this new version, several familiar elements from the original single remain: the hooky guitar riff that opens the song; the bass line that jumps in and lopes along; the Farfisa-like organ that enters on the second verse. The first real indication that something different is going on becomes evident at the beginning of the third verse, when a host of horns comes roaring in. And after that—the deluge.

At the end of the third verse—not quite a minute and a half into the record, just as Carter shout-sings, "Play that thing now!"—your ears catch what for just a moment sounds like four notes from an amplified blues harp. By the next measure, though, it's clearly a slide guitar. But this isn't some National Resophonic being picked by Roy Acuff's guy. This is electric. And it's not only loud. It's just plain *nasty*—so nasty that Carter cries out, "I like what I'm listening to right now!" In the middle of Carter's exclamation, the guitar leaps to the other speaker, and for the next half-minute it slides back and forth from one speaker to the other. Your ears have to race to follow what's happening. And then, just as quickly as it started, it's over. The song goes on for another verse, but the statement has already been made: Duane Allman has arrived in Muscle Shoals, and a thousand guitar solos on a thousand records will follow—but none with the intensity of what's happened here. Except one.

Even before *The Dynamic Clarence Carter* (the album with the new and vastly improved "The Road of Love") was released in early 1969, the session that would *finally* change everything for Duane Allman came to pass. But it was a session that would not have happened if Jerry Wexler hadn't had a falling out with Jim Stewart, the owner of Stax Records.

"I had Wilson Pickett under contract," Wexler explains, "and I was theoretically his producer. For a year we never got together on material. It was a time when I had sort of absconded from the studio. I had been making lousy records. I was bored. Like I said in my book [*Rhythm and the Blues: A Life in American Music*], I was out of inspiration; the musicians were out of licks; and the arrangers were out of ideas. But when I saw how Stax made records—*in*ductively—just building a rhythm track off a bunch of numbers instead of *de*ductively off a written chart—man, it inspired me and put me back in the studio. So I brought Pickett down to Stax, and we cut 'Midnight Hour' and all that good stuff."

The "good stuff" that the Wicked Pickett cut at Stax in 1965 included "In the Midnight Hour," "634-5789," and "Ninety-Nine and a Half (Won't Do)"—all produced by Wexler and backed by guitarist Steve Cropper and the rest of the crew at the Stax Records studio in Memphis. And then things fell apart.

"Jim Stewart didn't like the idea that his guys were fabricating hit records for my label," says Wexler. "He was jealous. So when Jim barred the door— 'Don't bring any more people down here'—it was a godsend. That's what sent me to Muscle Shoals."

"He came over here, and he liked what he saw," says Rick Hall. In fact, Jerry Wexler liked what he saw so much that he took Aretha Franklin, Don Covay, Wilson Pickett, and other Atlantic soul acts to Fame, producing hit after hit. With Pickett, the hits recorded there from 1966 to 1968 included "Land of 1,000 Dances," "Mustang Sally," "Soul Dance Number Three," "I Found a Love–Part 1," "Funky Broadway," and "A Man and a Half."

Then, one day in late 1968, Rick Hall was caught off guard when Pickett showed up at Fame, ready to record—but Jerry Wexler wasn't around to oversee the session. "I gave him the reins," says Wexler. "I said, 'Rick, can you produce this? I can't do this right now.'"

"Pickett came into the studio," says Hall, "and I said, 'We don't have any-thing to cut.' We didn't have a song. Duane was there, and he came up with an idea. By this time he'd kind of broken the ice and become my guy. So Duane said, 'Why don't we cut "Hey Jude"?' I said, 'That's the most preposterous thing I ever heard. It's insanity. We're gonna cover the Beatles? That's crazy!' And Pickett said, 'No, we're not gonna do it.' I said, 'Their single's gonna be Number 1. I mean, this is the biggest group in the world!' And Duane said, 'That's *exactly* why we should do it—because [the Beatles single] will be Num-ber 1 and because they're so big. The fact that we would cut the song with a black artist will get so much attention, it'll be an automatic smash.' That made all the sense in the world to me. So I said, 'Well, okay. Let's do it.'

"Nobody was here from Atlantic. I was on my own. Wexler had said, 'Whatever you want to do, just do it.' So Duane began to thump around on his guitar and caught the groove, and we're standing out in the studio listening. We started fooling around with it. His little groove was what we built the record around. Of course, after we cut the song, we decided that it would need horns. Horns was our thing. We just started coming up with horn lines with our guys."

Although he had worked with a lot of session musicians, by the latter part of 1968 Rick Hall favored a rhythm section that had been the backing band on quite a few successful singles. The four members were Jimmy Johnson, rhythm guitar (the same Jimmy Johnson who had engineered the Hour Glass sessions at Fame); David Hood, bass; Barry Beckett, keyboards; and Roger Hawkins, drums. Different lead guitarists worked with the group—sometimes it was Hinton, sometimes Junior Lowe. Occasionally, Rick would use Bobby Womack if he was in town. And, for Clarence Carter and this particular Wilson Pickett session, it was Duane Allman.

In his quest to be *the* lead guitarist in Muscle Shoals, Allman had to work hard to overcome one slight handicap: he couldn't read the number charts used by the other musicians. "He wasn't able to read charts," Jimmy Johnson recalls, "but you could play a song for him on a demo, or just somebody with an acoustic guitar, and it was unbelievable. We'd be looking at the sheet, following it along, and Duane would be standing there memorizing it. In one pass he could remember every chord and everything about it. It totally amazed us. You always hear about people like this, but you never meet 'em. Duane had that ability."

There was also the issue of how Duane looked and dressed. "It was almost scary to hang out with him because of his appearance," says Johnson. "Here was a man with hair down his back. At that day and time, you just didn't see anybody in Alabama wearing long hair. Even the Beatles didn't have hair like this."

Seeing Duane Allman at a session with the other Muscle Shoals players was like bumping into a member of Hell's Angels at a PTA meeting. Bassist David Hood recalls, "He was the first hippie I ever met. The rest of us had short hair and button-down collars. Even though we were in the music business, we looked pretty straight. All of a sudden this guy comes in with bellbottom pants and long hair and the mutton-chop sideburns and flowered shirts and everything. Duane was like a guy from another planet, almost. He was *so* different from the rest of us."

"He was wild," record producer Tom Dowd recalled. "I mean, most of the Muscle Shoals guys were kind of reserved—kind of shy. Duane wasn't afraid to talk to you man-on-man, one-on-one, and say, 'Did you like that? I think I can do it better.'"

On top of everything else, when it came time to record, Duane always played standing up. "I don't recall him ever sitting down for a session," says Hall. "He always had a long cord—that was part of his whole thing." While the rest of the musicians sat in chairs with their music stands in front of them, Duane stood off to one side, his headphones strapped over a shock of reddish-blond hair that was parted in the middle and hanging past his shoulders.

Duane's hair had already provided him with the first of his three nick-names. "He was called 'Dog' back then," says Hood. Apparently he considered it a badge of honor. In some of the photos taken during his Fame days, Duane is wearing a silk scarf around his neck, a wild-patterned shirt, black jeans, and Frye boots—a dog collar strapped like a spur around his right ankle. "He *always* had that dog collar around his boot," recalls Bobby Whitlock.

When Pickett arrived, Duane's second nickname arrived with him. "Wilson called him Sky Man," Hood recalls. "Duane already had the Dog nickname, and so somehow it eventually got changed around to Skydog."

"He was the most dynamic man that I'd ever had walk in the studio," says Hall. "He was very confident, but not cocky. He had an abundance of confidence that he could do anything and that we were going about the whole thing 'bass-ackwards.'" Looking back now, of course, it's abundantly clear that in the matter of "Hey Jude," Duane's confidence was justified, and his determination that Pickett should cut the song was nothing less than a stroke of genius.

It would seem that Duane's purpose for wanting to do this particular song—and to do it his way—was multifaceted. For starters, the record would, in fact, become a hit on both the R&B *and* pop charts, just as he had predicted. Secondly, by coercing Pickett, Hall, and his fellow musicians to record a song he already knew, Duane—unable to read the number charts—avoided the embarrassment of having to ask the other musicians to play an unfamiliar song through one time so he could learn it while Wilson Pickett sat around waiting for the hippie to figure out the damn changes. Thirdly, Duane obviously had developed a general idea of what he would play on "Hey Jude"—and what he would play on that song in that session on that day was so remarkable, it would change his life forever.

The Beatles' version of "Hey Jude" is over seven minutes long, mostly because of a four-bar coda that repeats some eighteen and a half times before the song finally fades out. The record surpasses the three-minute mark before the four-minute coda even begins. This is significant because the vast majority of Wilson Pickett's hits up to this point had hovered between two and a half and three minutes. In fact, until the Beatles released "Hey Jude," practically *everybody's* singles were two and a half to three minutes long. No matter what was going on in the rock world, there was simply no such thing as a song more than four minutes long on the R&B charts in the 1960s. In that era of AM radio, the whole idea was for the disc jockey to play as many records and run as many commercials as possible every hour. If a radio station wasn't squeezing in all the hits teenaged ears wanted to hear, the kids would simply switch to another station. The Beatles got away with it on the Top 40 stations not just because "Hey Jude" was a great song, but because they were the Beatles.

It's understandable, then, that Wilson Pickett did not want to cut a seven-minute song; nor a rock song; nor one that happened to be among the most popular songs in the world at that particular moment. But Duane gently refused to take no for an answer. Eventually, there was nothing else Pickett could do but accept the challenge. And once the singer had consented, Duane just might have taken a bit of pleasure in watching—and waiting—while the other musicians sat around figuring out the chords.

One of the contributing factors to the song's popularity is its unique structure: two verses, a bridge, third verse, another bridge, fourth verse, and then the long, mantra-like coda. The arrangement for Pickett's version, conceived and written out on the fly, is pretty basic, but beautiful in its simplicity—due, at least in part, to the fact that it had to be created so quickly.

On the Pickett recording, the song begins with a short intro featuring organ, guitar, drums, and whole-note roots on the bass—played on this session by Jerry Jemmott rather than David Hood. This instrumentation continues through the first verse, with Duane's guitar playing a musical response to every line Pickett sings. At the beginning of the second verse, the rhythm guitar kicks in while the bass begins to pump 16th-notes, giving the song substantially more punch. All the while, Duane's guitar continues responding to each line being sung. When the first bridge comes up, the horns finally appear, playing the equivalent of wordless background vocals. Everything continues in the same pattern as before through the third verse, the second bridge, and the fourth verse. When the coda hits at the 2:44 mark, Pickett lets out one of his trademark screams, and one would expect the song to quickly fade at this point, in an effort to keep from going too far beyond the sacred three-minute mark.

As it turns out, however, everything up to this moment has been a mere prelude to what comes next—the obvious reason Duane wanted to cut "Hey Jude" in the first place. Four measures into the coda, Allman unleashes an extended guitar solo that is light years away from anything anyone in the studio could have possibly expected. The coda rolls on with Pickett screaming his ass off, but the listener's attention is no longer focused on the singer. From the moment Duane plays his first lick ten seconds into the coda until the song fades out over a minute later, it is entirely his show. The background vocalists are singing those familiar "na-na-na-na's"—but it's all for naught. Rick Hall has pushed them so far down in the mix, they are merely ambiance. Absolutely nothing matters but Duane's guitar.

Wilson Pickett had taken a pop hit by the Beatles and turned it into a Southern soul ballad—only to have Duane Allman grab the song at the coda and turn it into a rock masterpiece. The result is a groundbreaking, trans-genre *tour de force*. Soon after the single was released, record producers in New York, Los Angeles, Memphis, Philadelphia, and elsewhere began incorporating rock guitars into soul settings. A lot of interesting recordings would be made, but none that would surpass the one captured on tape at Fame that November day.

Everyone in the studio was dying to hear the playback. Rick rewound the tape, and then—just as he had done when he heard "When a Man Loves a Woman" two years earlier—he grabbed the phone and called Jerry Wexler. Hall cranked up the volume, held the receiver near the speakers, and played the recording all the way through. The guitar player, naturally, blew Jerry Wexler away. "Who is he?" Wexler asked. Hall told Wexler that Pickett called him Sky Man. He said that Sky Man was a hippie from Florida who had talked Pickett into cutting the tune. Wexler persisted. "Who the hell *is* he?" "Name's Duane Allman," Rick replied.

Today, Wexler still marvels at Duane's ability to convince Pickett to record the song. "I named Wilson Pickett the Black Panther before there were Black Panthers," Wexler says. "He was made of whipcord and steel. Wilson sang 'Hey Jude' against his will, but look at the masterpiece that came out. It's just a fantastic record."

Pickett's single of "Hey Jude" was pressed and released so quickly that the Beatles' version was still receiving plenty of airplay when Pickett's 45 entered the charts. As the Beatles' record began to drop down the pop charts after a nine-week stay at Number 1, Pickett's "Hey Jude" was climbing both the R&B *and* pop charts—just as Duane had predicted. The Wicked One's single reached the Top 15 on the R&B lists and a very respectable Number 23 on the pop charts.

Allman played on several more songs during the Pickett sessions, including "Toe Hold," "My Own Style of Loving," and "Born to Be Wild." His guitar work is stellar throughout, but "Hey Jude" is the album's cornerstone.

This album's title track kicked off Duane Allman's career as a session guitarist—despite his being listed as "David" Allman on the LP's back cover.

Wilson Pickett and the guitarist he dubbed "Sky Man" at Fame Studios during the recording of the Hey Jude *album*

It would also become its title cut. Although there is no existing interview in which Duane mentions the credits on the back cover, it had to be painful for him when the album was released, listing the guitarist as "David" Allman. But he wasn't alone—the label got the bass player's name wrong, too. "I got used to my name being spelled wrong so many times," says Jerry Jemmott, "but as long as I could cash the check, I had no problem."

While Allman was still working on the Pickett record at Fame, blues keyboard player Barry Goldberg was at Quin Ivy's studio across town, recording an album with the help of his fellow Electric Flag alumnus Michael Bloomfield. The LP—its cover a photomontage of Goldberg and Jesus—would be released in early 1969 under the title *Two Jews Blues*. Between sessions at Fame, Duane hung out at Quin's place with his old friend Eddie Hinton, who had been recruited to play on Goldberg's recording of the Chuck Willis chestnut "You're Still My Baby."

"I became tight with Eddie Hinton," says Goldberg, "but there was also another guy hanging out in the studio—a hippie, with long blond hair. He was so friendly, and so wonderfully cool and soulful. I started talking to him, and he turned out to be a fan of Mike Bloomfield. I said, 'What's your name?'

He said, 'Duane Allman.' He told me he played slide, so he put some slide on one of my humble little songs ["Twice a Man"]. I'll never forget it. I was so impressed by him being such a down-home, wonderful kid—not at all pretentious or anything, like some of these guys now. Duane was just the opposite. He just hung out, playing on whatever he could, as much as he could, just for the sake of playing."

Pickett was still in town, so Duane offered to take Goldberg to the Black Panther's lair. "He invited me back to Wilson Pickett's motel room after he played on my session. He said, 'I want you to hear something.' I had been knocked out when Duane played on my record, but when I heard 'Hey Jude,' I almost passed out. I started shaking. And there was Duane and Pickett—they were jumping up and down on the bed like little kids, listening to the cut and just screaming! To be in on that before it came out, and to have Duane play on my record—those are two of my fondest memories."

After all of the flop singles and misdirected albums, Duane Allman—thanks to his incredible performance on "Hey Jude"—had *finally* played guitar on a hit record, and he instantly found himself in high demand as a session guitarist.

"Nobody's an overnight sensation," says Jemmott. "Years of playing in bars and clubs and dances—this is what you bring to the studio with you. All of that experience comes out in your music. And once the success is achieved, you just never know how long it's going to last."

CHAPTER ELEVEN

The Solo Album

"I was working in Muscle Shoals and Phil Walden liked my playing. He said, 'Listen, I've got this drummer over here in Macon who plays so weird, nobody knows if he's any good or not.'" — D.A.

After **"Hey Jude,"** Allman became Rick Hall's go-to guy at Fame. He even rented his own place in the Shoals. "Duane lived in Stokes Cottage on the Sheffield side of Wilson Lake," says Johnny Wyker. "It was a humble little cabin, but it had a lot of soul."

"He had a little girlfriend out there, and he was just fine," recalls Jimmy Johnson. "It was kind of secluded, and he liked it that way."

"I rented a cabin on this lake," Duane once said. "I just sat and played to myself and got used to living without a bunch of that jive Hollywood crap in my head. It's like I brought myself back to earth and came to life again."

Of course, living the simple life in a secluded cabin did have its drawbacks. "Duane didn't have a car back then," says Wyker, "so I had to drive out there and bring him into the sessions at Fame, and then give him a ride home afterwards."

By this time, Duane Allman had already achieved a string of solid accomplishments—although he had little money to show for it. (In fact, he still owed Hour Glass manager Bill McEuen $2,500). But in little more than two years, Duane had been the leader of two bands that had secured record deals, played on bills with many of the major rock acts of the day, and was in the early stages of becoming one of the most noted session guitarists of his generation. Without question, Duane could have made a good living if he had chosen to do no more than play guitar on albums by other artists for the rest of his life. But he was much too driven to settle for being a sideman. He wanted to make his own music his own way. He was a leader in search of followers.

Although he would continue to play on recordings by other acts long after the Allman Brothers Band was established—in fact, until the end of his life—in his heart he knew the life of a session player was too restrictive for him. To Duane, the solution was obvious. All he had to do was talk Rick Hall into letting him make a solo album.

"Duane was a 'buddy' kind of guy," says Hall. "He was lovable. He'd get under your skin and you couldn't say no to him. He would hug your neck and tell you how great you were. I'm the kind of soul who takes to that kind of stuff—the praise. He was a great salesman, a great guitar player, and had a tremendous personality. So he came to me and said, 'I want you to cut a record on me.' I said, 'Doing what? Can you sing?' He said, 'Yeah, I can sing!' But to tell you the truth, he couldn't sing.

"He talked me into cuttin' an album on him anyway. I didn't think I could cut a hit record on him, but he was such a great guitar player that I thought *maybe* he could overcome the singing with his guitar playing."

In December 1968, Duane entered into artist, production, and publishing agreements with Fame. There was, of course, the little matter of his still being under contract to Liberty Records. Perhaps the fact that Gregg was out in L.A. making solo records for Liberty was, in Duane's mind, fulfilling the contractual obligations of all the former Hour Glass members. This would turn out not to be the case.

For the time being, though, Duane would be too busy doing session work to start on his solo project. After hearing Allman's playing on "Hey Jude," Jerry Wexler had become very interested in him. In January 1969, he brought Duane and the entire Fame rhythm section up to Atlantic Recording Studios in New York to cut several songs that would appear on Aretha Franklin's album *This Girl's in Love with You*. Duane played on two tracks: "It Ain't Fair" and "The Weight," the latter featuring Duane's slide work throughout. "The Weight" was released as a single, eventually peaking at Number 3 on the R&B charts, as well as reaching the Top 20 on the pop charts. The other song, "It Ain't Fair," features a beautiful sax solo played by King Curtis. According to Atlantic's session notes, Duane also played on a King Curtis session that took place in New

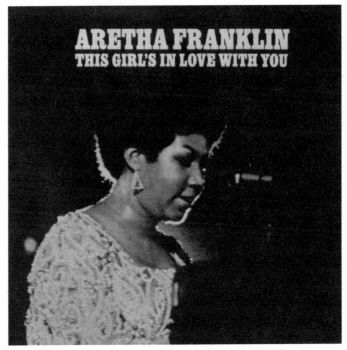

The entire Muscle Shoals rhythm section—including Eddie Hinton and Duane Allman—flew to New York to play on Aretha's This Girl's in Love with You *album*

York either right before or immediately after the Aretha sessions. Just where and when Allman and Curtis met is unclear. What *is* clear is that they instantly struck up a friendship that would last for the short remainder of Curtis's life.

Meanwhile, Phil Walden—an old friend of Jerry Wexler's—had a proposal for the Atlantic exec to consider. Phil, along with his brother Alan, managed a number of important R&B performers who recorded for Atlantic, as well as several artists on labels Atlantic was distributing, including Stax and its subsidiary, Volt. Sadly, the Waldens' hottest act, Stax/Volt recording artist Otis Redding, had died in a plane crash in December 1967.

By early 1969, Phil was making plans to set up a recording studio in his hometown of Macon, Georgia. According to Paul Hornsby, Walden was "trying to build this studio from the model of Stax and Fame. At that time, they had their own staff bands and that's what Phil Walden wanted to do. He wanted to build that studio and have everybody come there to record." And he wanted Atlantic to help finance the venture.

"We were on my boat in Florida," recalls Wexler, "and Phil said to me, 'I'd like to start a studio in Macon. Would you front me the money?' I said, 'Let's have you start a label instead.'" The two men decided that when the new record company was formed, it would be named after their mutual astrological sign. "We called it Capricorn because that was our sign," says Wexler, "but neither one of us believes in that horseshit."

The label was formed with a little seed money from Atlantic and, of course, with the understanding that Walden would use Atlantic as the label's distributor for the first three years.

At that time, Phil Walden Artists and Promotions was still *the* management and booking agency for many of Southern soul's most successful acts. But two major events had taken place in the late 1960s that prompted Walden to begin looking to represent artists outside of the R&B genre, the first being the death of Otis Redding.

"Otis was, without a doubt, the Number 1 R&B singer of our time," says Alan Walden. "He was the undisputed king in all of our minds. I started my career with Otis Redding, and it never got any better. To me, Otis *was* soul music. I don't know how to say it any other way. He was a joy to work with—not only talented, but just a wonderful person. The day he got killed, I was shattered. I was angry and bitter with the world. I just thought, 'Why would God take away this beautiful human being?' It truly bothered me a great deal. I know that it was hard for my brother as well."

The other event that had turned Phil Walden's head was the 13th annual convention of the National Association of Television and Radio Announcers (NATRA), an African American media organization. By the time of its meeting in August 1968 at the Sheraton Four Ambassadors Hotel in Miami, NATRA had begun to develop what some might consider radical overtones.

"Bill Cosby was the emcee," recalls Jerry Wexler. "It was the 'year of taking over,' where black disc jockeys were going to expropriate record labels and radio stations—and Bill Cosby was whipping them on. I was threatened and disparaged at that thing, and somebody came after me. King Curtis and Titus Turner both had guns, and they got me out of there."

"I can remember being at that convention in Miami," says Alan Walden, "and having to hide in a room for several days because the black mafia there was trying to run everyone white out of R&B music—and beating up several of my friends. Many people like my brother and myself all of a sudden said, 'Hey, we've had it with this shit.' It was like, when you'd go into a radio station, it was no longer, 'Hey, there's Alan' and 'Hey, there's Phil.' It was like, 'Hey, what's that white motherfucker doing in here?'

"Some of us got tired of it and started looking in other directions. And that's when Southern rock started to emerge. When Phil announced that he thought we should go from R&B into rock & roll, I wasn't quite ready for it, to be honest. I liked rock & roll, but I truly loved rhythm & blues music, and I wasn't quite ready for the transition. I believe that this was part of the reason that led to us going our separate ways."

"Phil Walden was and is my bosom buddy," says Rick Hall. "He's one of us Southern rock & roll boys who have a lot in common." Long before Otis Redding passed away, Walden and Hall had worked out a handshake deal that would serve them both well. "Phil said to me, 'Look, anything that you can find that don't have management that you produce, I'd appreciate you sending them to us. And in turn, anyone that I manage that needs a producer, I'll send them to you.' To give you an example, Phil sent me Arthur Conley."

"We brought Arthur Conley to Rick Hall and put him on Fame Records," says Alan Walden. "I believe he did four sides there—two singles. Rick decided that he didn't want to continue doing Arthur himself. But Otis believed in Arthur Conley, and he said, 'I'll take Arthur Conley and go to Fame Studios with my road band and produce him myself.' So Otis and Arthur Conley and I went to the studio with Otis's band. Jimmy Johnson was the engineer. We recorded 'Sweet Soul Music'—which, of course, became a million-seller."

"Otis and Phil were bosom buddies—and Alan, of course, was too," says Hall. "I might have been the fourth brother in that group because we were all very close in those days. We partied together. We drank together. We hung out."

But by February 1969 Otis had been gone for over a year, and Phil Walden—having gone through the negative experience of the NATRA convention in Miami—was trying to find rock acts to manage and possibly sign to his yet-to-exist record company. "Phil wouldn't have dared insert himself into anything I was doing because we were friends," says Hall. On the other hand, there was always the possibility of Walden becoming Duane Allman's manager—and if it just happened to turn out that Rick wasn't particularly happy with the album Duane was recording. . . .

Once Hall had agreed to let the guitarist work on a record of his own, Duane began recruiting musicians. "In early '69, I got a call from Duane saying he was getting ready to cut a record and wanted me to come up and play on it," says Paul Hornsby. Although Phil Walden was officially still merely an observer at the time, Hornsby recalls that it was Walden who suggested Duane use a particular drummer on the sessions: "Phil brought Jai Johanny Johanson—Jaimoe—up to play."

Jaimoe was born Johnny Lee Johnson in Ocean Springs, Mississippi, on July 8, 1944. Over the years, he has gone from his birth name to Jai Johanny Johanson to Jaimoe. As if three names weren't enough, he also managed—thanks to his most common facial expression—to acquire the nickname "Frown." He was a jazz lover from an early age, and his drumming skills led to gigs with a number of top R&B acts, including Otis Redding. But Jaimoe preferred variety, so he opted to play behind all the other acts in Redding's road show while drummer Woody Woodson backed Otis. After his tour of duty in Redding's road band was over, Jaimoe played drums for Percy Sledge, and later for Joe Tex.

When Phil Walden decided to put together a house rhythm section for the recording studio he wanted to build in Macon, Jaimoe got the call. When the drummer arrived in town, he discovered that he was a tad on the early side. The studio was nowhere near ready, and the remaining musicians had yet to be recruited. With no actual session work on the horizon, Jaimoe was about to give up and head to New York when he got another call—this time from his friend Jackie Avery.

In a *Hittin' the Note* magazine article entitled "Reflections: The World According to Jaimoe," the drummer told *HTN* editor John Lynskey about the call and what happened next: "I had just finished my last gig with Eddie Kirk at Club 15 in Macon. We played two nights—Saturday and Sunday. The first night I think we made six bucks each and two half-pints, and Sunday night it was three bucks. At the end of the gig, I get this call from Jackie Avery. Jackie is a great songwriter, piano player, and a great singer. Jackie called me and said, 'Hey Jai, Alan and Phil Walden have been trying to find you. They got this white boy down in Muscle Shoals—this hippie with long, reddish-blond hair. I'm not kidding, Jai—I never heard no white boy play like this. You gotta hear it—they call him "Sky Man." They want to know if you want to go down and play in a band with this guy.' I said, 'I don't know about that.' Jackie says, 'Jai—I think you'll like it.' I go, 'I'll tell you what, Avery. I was thinking about going to New York, because if I'm going to starve to death, then I might as well starve doing what I really love, and that's playing jazz. I think I should go to New York.' He said, 'Jai—Phil and Rick Hall are backing Duane.' And then what my mentor—Charles 'Honeyboy' Otis—had told me went off in my brain. Honeyboy told me this when I was in high school. He said, 'If you want to make some money, you go play with them white boys, because the Kingfish ain't gonna pay you a dime.' So when Avery was talking to me over the phone, I saw dollar signs in my head. Plain and simple, I went down to Muscle Shoals to make money. I just said, 'Forget this—I'm going to go make some money.' You see, every time that I ever left off of the road and went home, I had to borrow money from my mother to go back out and play with these stars—Otis Redding, Percy Sledge, Joe Tex."

While his solo project was still in its formative stage, Duane continued to play sessions at Fame whenever Rick called on him. Duane's new friend King Curtis had come down in early 1969. He recorded an instrumental version of the Joe South hit "Games People Play," as well as "The Weight"—one of the songs Duane and Curtis had played on together with Aretha just a few weeks before.

Allman's slide work on Curtis's version of "The Weight" was a reprise of what he had done on Aretha's record. But for "Games People Play," Duane reached back for a sound from his Hour Glass days. The song begins with Allman picking out the chorus's melody on his electric sitar before Curtis's sax takes over on the first verse. The electric sitar hangs in the background throughout the song, and Duane's electric slide guitar makes two brief but tasteful appearances during the course of the track.

A single of "Games People Play" was released in March. Although it touched neither the R&B nor pop charts, it made plenty of noise within the music industry, resulting in King Curtis receiving a Grammy for Best R&B Instrumental of 1969. (In those days, the Best R&B Instrumental category wasn't part of the annual Grammy ceremony, so Rick Hall got to do the honors at a NARAS event in Georgia. "At the time, Atlanta had a [NARAS] chapter, so I presented him with the Grammy award," says Hall. "It was the only one he ever received.")

Of the musicians Duane planned to use on his solo project, Jaimoe was the first to arrive, showing up during the King Curtis session. "Duane and I used to play after a session," says Jaimoe. "I would have my drums set up in Studio A or B down at Fame, whichever one they weren't recording in. I'd be over there with my headphones on, playing along with my records until Duane had finished, and then we'd play."

Members of the Fame rhythm section—no doubt curious about what Duane was up to—occasionally stopped by to watch Duane and Jaimoe jam. "These guys used to come in," says Jaimoe, "and they'd sit around the wall—and nobody would touch their instruments. You know how Duane was—'Hey man, c'mon and play something.'"

But Rick's session players were focused on the world of R&B. What Duane and Jaimoe were playing was something else entirely. And then Duane called on Berry Oakley of the Second Coming to come up and join the fun. "When Berry arrived, it was amazing," says Jaimoe. "It was like, 'Where did *this* dude

December 1968—Duane enters into recording, production, and publishing agreements with Rick Hall

come from?' It became a whole different ballgame, and at that point my perspective changed." For Jaimoe, it was suddenly no longer about seeing dollar signs. It was about playing a new and innovative kind of music.

"It had been so great playing with Duane," says Jaimoe, "but I thought we'd never find a bass player who could do the stuff that we were doing. You know, Dickey once asked me, 'What did it sound like when you, Berry, and Duane were in Muscle Shoals?' I told him, 'The closest I can relate it to is the first time I heard the Mahavishnu Orchestra.' That's what went off in my head. 'Damn! That's the stuff that Duane, Berry, and I were doing in Muscle Shoals!'"

In short order, however, it became apparent that things weren't going to work out on Duane's solo project quite the way the drummer had expected. "Jaimoe ended up not playing," says Hornsby. "Rick Hall produced the stuff, and he didn't feel like Jaimoe had the R&B backbeat that was needed for the project. You know Jaimoe's style of playing—he's a jazz drummer. Even in the Allman Brothers Band, Butch is the backbeat drummer and Jaimoe complements him—he plays *around* him.

"So," continues Hornsby, "Johnny Sandlin wound up doing the drums. The idea was to put a band together around Duane as the focal point, and Phil was talking to me and Sandlin and Pete Carr. Basically he wanted to put the Hour Glass back together. I didn't want to do it, or Sandlin, or Pete—none of us. We just didn't want to go through it again. I had things pretty much established back in Tuscaloosa. I was doing pretty well, playing in a band, playing weekends in clubs and stuff. So I wasn't hungry. I was making more money than I had made in the Hour Glass. I mean, at least I was *eatin'* regular. So I couldn't see going back and revisiting that."

Although Hornsby and Sandlin weren't interested in an Hour Glass reunion, they were both happy to support their former bandleader's solo project. So, in February 1969, Allman's solo sessions got under way. The songs were cut with Duane singing and playing guitar, Paul Hornsby on keyboards, Berry Oakley on bass, and Johnny Sandlin on drums. Rick Hall produced and engineered the sessions, with Jaimoe sometimes watching from the sidelines. They recorded eight songs: "Down Along the Cove," "Neighbor, Neighbor," "Bad News," "Steal Away," "No Money Down," "Goin' Down Slow," "Dimples," and an original composition of Duane's called "Happily Married Man."

As Hall notes, Duane wasn't a great singer. However, among the songs Duane recorded, there was one vocal standout: "Goin' Down Slow." Pianist Champion Jack Dupree had done the song on his 1958 album *Blues from the Gutter*, and it was this very album that had turned a young Brian Jones into a blues fanatic. Jones shared this obsession with his friends Mick Jagger and Keith Richards, and the band they formed—the Rolling Stones—would introduce a unique brand of blues-based rock & roll to the world. *Blues from the Gutter* had also made an impression on Duane Allman. His performance of "Goin' Down Slow" features not only two standout guitar solos but a bluesy vocal that sounds not entirely unlike his younger brother.

In fact, Gregg was on Duane's mind. "He'd talk about his brother all the time," says Rick Hall. "He loved his brother and was concerned about his well-being and what was happening to him. He said, 'If I had my brother here, we'd have the greatest band in the world.' But he wasn't giving up."

Duane might not have been giving up, but he certainly didn't seem to be in any hurry either. The recording sessions dragged on at a pace unfamiliar to Hall. "I think it took us two months 'cause he was really—I mean—a funny guy," Rick says. "He got his band together and brought all the pickers up and went into Studio B. And they'd sit back there and rap for 10 or 12 hours, and then pick up an instrument. I'd sit at the board waiting for them to play. Well, being the kind of man I am, that wasn't my thing."

And then there was the other issue—the reason Pickett called Duane "Sky Man." "He loved to indulge in drugs," says Hall. "I didn't go back and examine what he was taking, but he *loved* to indulge in drugs. Duane and his band would be in the studio, sometimes all day, with the doors closed. I'd go out and say, 'Why don't we cut some sides?' And Duane would say, 'Well, you know, the stars aren't right.' I'd say, 'That's horseshit! You guys get up and let's cut some sides.' But Phil always persuaded me to go along with it. I've always been a wet junkie [i.e., a drinker]. I've never known the other side of that world. Duane loved to smoke pot. I think there was a lot of speed, too, but I don't know. I never went back and said, 'What have you got in your pocket?' or 'What are you smoking?' I knew it was happening, but I just kind of turned my head and let it go.

"Phil Walden kept coming around and saying, 'Look, he's a superstar.' I said, 'Nah, I really don't think so. He can't sing. What can he do? I mean, you can't cut instrumentals on a guy and sell any records.' Phil kept saying, 'I'm telling you, he's gonna be a superstar. You've got him signed up. You just need to hang on to him and go in the studio and turn on the machine and let him hang out back there and screw around, and a year from now you'll make a million dollars with him.' I said, 'Phil, you're full of shit. I'm telling you, that's crazy! I'm not that way. I can't *do* that. I mean, I have to be involved. I want to be rewriting the song—I want to come up with the horn lines and stuff, you know?' But he said, 'Do it. Get a pack of cigarettes and go in the control room and just kick back and turn on the machine and let him go in there and screw around with his band.'"

Walden was persistent. He didn't really care about how long it was taking. If the stars weren't properly aligned, so be it. He could wait. Unlike Hall, Walden seemed to understand what Duane was all about. Allman wasn't just a guitar player who could pick well on other people's sessions. He was unique, one of a kind, a potential "superstar."

Walden believed that Duane represented his future. He wanted to be his manager, but Duane was still under contract to Bill McEuen. Phil would have liked to have Duane on Capricorn Records, but he was signed to Rick's label—

Tape box containing tracks
from Duane's unreleased
solo album

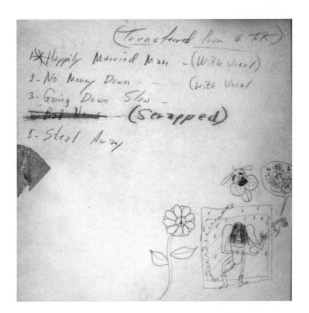

and Walden and Hall went too far back for Phil to make any improper overtures to Duane.

But Rick Hall was getting more and more uneasy. "Phil thought I was missing the boat," says Hall. "Of course, I was more mainstream. I want a hit record tomorrow. I don't have time to fart around. I was on a roll and I didn't want to be bothered. I didn't have time to play around and wait for Duane to write a song or any of that stuff." So, after weeks of Duane's "screwing around in the studio," Rick Hall decided to ease himself out of the project. "I was telling them, 'Let's go in and cut a record or go home.' I just wasn't patient, so I finally said, 'Hey, Duane, you guys can finish it up. I'm getting out of this thing.'"

In truth, Duane wasn't particularly happy with the way the project was going either. As Phil Walden told writer Dave Kyle, "It really wasn't working and Duane's enthusiasm waned by the day. He said, 'You know, I want to step back from this thing a little bit.' He would call me in Macon from time to time and tell me he was trying to visualize what he was trying to do. He knew he had something in mind, but he hadn't heard the players yet."

CHAPTER TWELVE

Two Days in March

"Me and Jai eased on down to Jacksonville, and Berry met us there. We all got together in a big house in Jacksonville, and Santa Claus came and brought us a band." — D.A.

Although Jaimoe hadn't played on any of Duane's solo recordings, the drummer and the guitarist had become good friends during their time together in Muscle Shoals. Jaimoe recognized Allman's talent, while Duane enjoyed the benefits of the musical education he was receiving from his new friend. "The jazz thing definitely came from Jaimoe," Gregg Allman told interviewer Alan Paul. "He had played with Percy Sledge and Otis Redding, but jazz was really his bag."

Jaimoe's "jazz thing" had begun to seriously affect Duane's approach to music. It had broadened the guitarist's musical landscape and shown him the value of extended improvisation. Duane would later tell disc jockey Ed Shane, "Miles Davis does the best job, to me, of portraying the innermost, subtlest, softest feelings in the human psyche. And John Coltrane was probably one of the finest, most accomplished tenor players. He took his music farther than anybody I believe I ever heard."

"Duane was always looking for a challenge—for something new," Jaimoe told John Lynskey. "He never grew tired of learning, of developing new ideas—exploring—and I always admired him for that."

Throughout the months he was living in Alabama, Allman had continued to return to Jacksonville whenever he could, hanging out with the Second Coming at the Green House on Riverside Avenue—and jamming with them and other musicians at the local park on weekends. When Duane's solo project ground to a halt, the guitarist decided to head back to Jacksonville for a while. But this time, he talked Jaimoe into making the trip with him.

The summer of 1967 had been called the Summer of Love. That year, while the members of the Hour Glass were just beginning to fight their futile battle against Dallas Smith, Jacksonville native Scott McKenzie was flying high on the charts with his single "San Francisco (Be Sure to Wear Flowers in Your Hair)." The Haight-Ashbury district of San Francisco was the epicenter of the new movement. It was also the home of the Grateful Dead—the place where the Dead and other bands would play in the park for free to a group of counterculture kids being called "hippies" by the mainstream press.

The following year, on the other side of the country—about as far away from San Francisco as one could get—this same movement began taking hold among many of the young people in the South. But the Southeastern United States wasn't like New York or Los Angeles or San Francisco. Alabama, Mississippi, Georgia, Tennessee, and Florida were strongholds of conservatism—a swath of America still referred to today as the Bible Belt. Compared to many other sections of the country, enforcement of the drug laws was stricter there and the sentences handed down were much more harsh.

As Jimmy Johnson points out, just going to a restaurant in Muscle Shoals with Duane Allman was a scary experience because no one else in town looked or dressed like him. It wasn't just that the locals had a preference for crewcuts and button-down collars. There was a near-violent reaction to those who chose to look so different—not simply because it was seen as improper or odd, but because it was considered to be nothing less than sinful.

On top of everything else, there was the issue of race. African Americans in the Southeastern United States were already a counterculture of their own. Only a few years before Duane Allman headed to Muscle Shoals to become a studio musician, Governor George C. Wallace had stood in the doorway of the University of Alabama, doing his utmost to refuse entrance to the school's first two black students. He failed, and the segregated South began the slow journey away from its tarnished past. (Not that the North was bigotry-free—even the school district of New Rochelle, New York, had to be sued by black parents before a federal judge finally enforced integration there in 1961. Many in the South merely chose to be less subtle about the matter.)

And so, in March 1969, a longhaired, strangely dressed, drug-using Duane Allman chose to head back to Jacksonville—this time with one of his "Negro" friends in tow. Allman was the living embodiment of everything the counter-culture of the late 1960s stood for, thumbing his nose at authority by virtue of his very existence.

Duane's first stop in Jacksonville was Butch Trucks's place. "One day there's a knock at my door, and it's Duane," Butch told interviewers Kevin Spangler and Ron Currens. "He's got this big black guy with him with this tank top on him, you know, and he looked like Schwarzenegger or something—really muscle-bound—and he's got these bear claws around his neck and everything. And Duane says, 'Hey Jaimoe, this is my old drummer, Butch. Butch, this is my new drummer, Jaimoe.'

"With my old Southern Baptist sensitivities, I figure I got this militant African guy here who's gonna rip my head off. He was *mean*-lookin'! He wound up staying for two weeks—he didn't leave! But once he opened up and started talking, I mean, we just hit it right off."

After dropping off Jaimoe at Butch's, Duane headed over to the Second Coming's latest residence. By early 1969, the band had left the Green House and moved a couple of blocks west to the Grey House. "The Second Coming played six nights a week at the Scene, and we also played on Sunday at the park," says Reese Wynans. "We'd just go down and set up at Willow Branch Park and do a free jam session. When Duane and Jaimoe came down, they'd play at the jam session every Sunday. That's when a lot of the local bands would come out—particularly people like the 31st of February. That's what Butch was doing at that time."

"Duane had been playing with Jaimoe, and Berry Oakley had been going up to Muscle Shoals with him," says Butch. "So they came to Jacksonville to find some more players to put together a whole band. Duane had told Jaimoe about Dickey, and they were looking for other people to fill out the band. We would get together on Sunday afternoons and get all the equipment in town and set up a mountain of gear, and everybody would play."

"Guys from the Second Coming and Duane and David Brown and Butch were all kind of gathering in the park," says Scott Boyer. "They had a stage set up, and they'd get up there and jam. Sometimes they'd play a song they knew, but often as not it'd just be some jam thing going on. Duane was checking people out—looking to put something together."

"The jam sessions were [made up of] musicians from different bands who had never played together before," says Wynans. "You never knew what was going to happen. The songs would always be lengthy, and it seemed like it was a real musical journey every song. I absolutely loved playing with Duane every time I was privileged to do that in those jam sessions—and it happened quite a few times. I still remember some of the tunes that we played—songs that don't have any names, you know—just progressions that he would start out and we would go from there. I was not any kind of a great player in those days. I thought of myself as being just past a beginner, and doing those jam sessions was a great education for me."

After a few weekends of playing in the park, Duane decided to call upon three members of the Second Coming—Berry, Dickey, and Reese—plus his "old" drummer, Butch, and his "new" drummer, Jaimoe, and get them all to join him for a private jam session. "Duane had been talking for a while about getting his band together," Wynans recalls. "He was excited about it, and he wanted us to play in it. He wanted *all* of us to play in it."

The date of this private jam session was March 23, 1969. Once the instruments were set up and everybody was ready to play, Duane kicked off the proceedings with a shuffle—a shuffle that lasted for hours. "We got into this jam, and it went here and here and here," says Butch. "Dickey and Duane were really having a good time with each other."

Duane later recalled the moment this way: "We set up the equipment and whipped into a little jam, and it lasted two and a half hours. When we finally quit, nobody said a word, man. Everybody was speechless. Nobody'd ever done anything like that before. It really frightened the shit out of everybody. Right then, I knew. I said, 'Man, here it is—here it *is*!'"

"That particular day, when Duane pulled that," says Butch, "I was sitting there crying one minute, had chills up and down my back the next minute—just shit flying *everywhere*. It was like my arms had been moving of their own volition. They just knew what to do. I'd look over at Jaimoe and he'd be grinning.

We finally finished and I looked over at him and said, 'Did you get off on that?' He just *smiled*!" As if the musicians in the room didn't already know that something incredibly special had just happened, to see a grin on Frown's face was the ultimate confirmation.

Duane Allman walked to the open doorway, stood in front of it, and said, "Anybody in this room not gonna play in my band, you're gonna have to fight your way outta here!" And then he added, "The only thing is, we need a singer—and my baby brother's the only one who can do it."

The time had come. Duane called up Gregg and managed to persuade him to get his ass back to Florida once and for all. During his stay in Los Angeles, Gregg had gone back in the studio to make two more 45s by "GREG ALLMAN & the Hour Glass." As had been the case with all of his other singles, radio and record buyers everywhere ignored them.

There are at least three different accounts of how Gregg got from Los Angeles to Jacksonville—each relatively plausible. The background for all of them is the same: By late March 1969, Liberty Records had undergone major changes. In 1968, an insurance company called Transamerica purchased the label. Already the owner of United Artists Records, Transamerica merged the two record companies, as well as their music publishing entities. Having signed to Liberty Records as part of the Hour Glass, Gregg was also under contract as a song-writer to Metric Music, the label's publishing division. When Transamerica merged Liberty and United Artists, Metric Music and United Artists' publishing company, Unart, ended up under the same roof.

Shortly thereafter, veteran music industry executive Eddie Reeves was put in charge of the publishing company's L.A. office. He tells the story of Gregg's departure this way: "One day I get a call from this guy, and he says, 'My name's Gregg Allman. I was in a group on Liberty Records called the Hour Glass. They've given our band a release from the contract, and all the other band members have gone back home. They gave us a release on the condition that I would remain here and cut four more sides. I'm waiting around for them to put the session together. They're gonna try to put another single out because they want to have a chance to recoup the investment they had made in us because we haven't sold any records. Meanwhile, while this is happening, I'm waiting around and I'm broke. I think the session's scheduled for next week sometime, but in the meantime I need to get back to Florida. I need $300 and I don't have any money.'"

According to Reeves, Gregg offered to let the company publish three or four more of his songs—including one called "Dreams"—in exchange for the $300 advance. Allman went to Reeves's office and played the songs for him. Eddie liked what he heard, but he had a hard time talking the home office in New York into coughing up an advance for a former member of a now-defunct band that still owed the company money. With a lot of persuasion, Reeves was able to get Gregg some of what he needed. "I called him back and told him I got him $200. I said, 'Look, I have a couple of songs by another writer that I've been looking for somebody to do the vocals on for the demos. I'll pay you 50 bucks a song to do the vocals, and then you'll have your $300." Gregg went into the studio, cut the two vocals, and Eddie gave Gregg the money he needed for the flight to Jacksonville.

And then there's John McEuen's version: "In the six months or so that Gregg was living in California, my brother Bill bought him a Chevy Corvair, because you can't get around L.A. without a car. One day Gregg comes over to my brother's house. Bill wasn't home, but I was there and Gregg was delivering the story of, 'Oh John, I got pulled over running a traffic light and the Man says that I, well, I gotta take the pink slip to show the judge that I didn't steal the car because, you know, they think I stole the car because I don't have the registration, but if I can bring in the pink slip. . . .' So I went and got the pink slip because I knew where it was in the file and said, 'Okay, Gregg, I'll tell Bill.' So he took the pink slip, signed it over to himself, and sold the car that day—because Duane was putting a band together [and he'd told him,] 'Gregg, you gotta come out to Florida because the players are all really good. Gregg, you gotta come out to Florida, the music's coming together finally. Gregg, come out to Florida, we need you.' So he finally heeded that brotherly call, or the call of the music. Who knows which it was? I think it was both. He sold the car and bought a plane ticket that day to fly to Jacksonville. If I hadn't given him that pink slip, he might have missed it, you know? That's about as close as I can come to saying I helped him get his big start."

And finally there's the story Gregg told Alan Paul about how the trip came to pass: "Duane said, 'I got this killer band together. We got two drummers.' I said, 'What for?' He said, 'We also got a great guitar player, too.' I said, 'Well, what do *you* do?' And he said, 'Wait'll you get here and I'll show you.' His deal there sounded good, so I was ready to go check it out. He sent me a ticket, but I knew he didn't have any money, so I put it in my back pocket and stuck out my thumb on the San Bernardino Freeway. I got a ride all the way to Jacksonville—the guy who gave me the lift was a bass player."

The bottom line is that Gregg Allman recalls (as do the other surviving members who were there that day) that he arrived in town on March 26. Almost 40 years later, however, some of the participants and observers of the March 26 jam session recall it being at the Green House while others say it was at the Grey House. According to Gregg, it was at neither. "We all got into the same room for the first time in Arlington—a suburb of Jacksonville," Gregg said recently. "It was actually Butchie's house, and I was the last one to get there. And there were all these guys I don't know *looking* at me. It was heavy." He stood and listened to the six musicians as they tore through Muddy Waters's "Trouble No More." As Dickey Betts later recalled, "Gregg put his hands against the wall and said, 'I can't play in this fucking band!'"

That was all it took to set Duane off. The elder Allman began using the same tactics he had always used to get his way with Gregg: "He starts in on me, 'Oh, you little punk! I told these people all about you, so you don't come in here letting me down.' He knew which buttons to push. He kinda pissed me off and embarrassed me."

Duane had written out the lyrics to "Trouble No More" and waved the paper in his brother's face. Gregg could either continue to endure his brother's wrath, or he could just sing the song. "I said, 'Count it off—let's do it,' and with that, they counted off and I did my damnedest," says Gregg. "I'd never heard or sung this song before, but by God I did it. I shut my eyes and sang, and at the end of that there was just a long silence. At that moment, we knew what we had."

What they had was the soon-to-be-named Allman Brothers Band—plus Reese Wynans. Duane had a decision to make. "I don't recall the exact words," says Reese. "I do recall him saying to me at one point that he didn't want to have two guitars and two keyboards. He thought that would be too much. And by the time Gregg arrived in town, I think he had pretty much settled on working with Dickey." Two guitar players meant one keyboard player, and that spot was definitely going to belong to Gregg. To use Butch Trucks's phrase, Reese Wynans was "odd-manned out."

Duane wasn't one who took pleasure in this kind of situation, and he eventually found a way to make up for having let Wynans go. "Duane did a real nice thing after the Allman Brothers were doing well," says Reese. "Boz Scaggs wanted to put a band together, and Duane recommended me. So David Brown and I got that gig—David Brown, the bass player for the 31st of February—and he and I relocated to San Francisco to work with Boz. I always appreciated that."

On March 26, there were seven musicians in the room, but only one of them knew anything about songwriting. "I had 22 songs with me when I came," Gregg told Alan Paul. "I sat down and started showing them to everybody in the band, and they kept saying, 'What else you got?'"

After going through a dozen or so, Gregg went to the Hammond organ and played "Dreams"—"which, to this day," he says, "is the only song I've ever written on a Hammond. We worked it up right away." After "Dreams," Gregg played them "It's Not My Cross to Bear." They worked that one up right away, too.

Just as the other members of the band had realized three days earlier, Gregg knew he was now in previously unexplored musical territory. Two things were certain: (1) he had to write more songs that would fit within the context of this new band; and (2) there would *definitely* be no dental school in his future.

"Within the next five days I wrote 'Whipping Post,' 'Black Hearted Woman,' and a couple of others," says Gregg. "I got on a real roll there."

CHAPTER THIRTEEN

The Calling of the Brotherhood

"Rock has never died, and it ain't never gonna die. As long as there's some place to go see rock and someone who wants to go there, I'll be there to play it for them." — D.A.

Less than a week after the younger Allman arrived in Jacksonville, the still unnamed band of Duane, Berry, Butch, Jaimoe, Dickey, and Gregg played its first gig. Not missing a beat, Reese Wynans and the remaining members of the Second Coming became the *New* Second Coming. "Larry Rheinhart, Monty Young, John Meeks, and I decided to stay together," says Wynans. "At that time, we were doing concerts at the Jacksonville Beach Coliseum. We had a series of concerts that summer—it seems like it was every Friday or Saturday night. We weren't playing at the Scene anymore. The New Second Coming was the feature act, and Duane's band was the opening act."

For a brief time, Duane called his new band Beelzebub. He soon decided to change the group's name to the more meaningful—and slightly less demonic—Allman Brothers Band. The new appellation was more than just a literal reference to the fact that Duane and Gregg were siblings. What Duane had brought together was truly a brotherhood. Although it might not be nearly so obvious decades after the fact, this interracial act, formed in the South of the late 1960s, was making a bold statement by referring to itself as a band of brothers. But it was noticed then—and members of the Southern Caucasian community weren't the only ones to raise an eyebrow. Not everyone in the African American community was happy either. "When I first started playing with the Allman

Brothers," Jaimoe told John Lynskey, "I had people come up to me and go, 'What are you doing playing with these white boys? Why are you in a rock & roll band?' All I said was, 'Hey man, these cats can play!'"

According to Butch Trucks, Phil Walden had originally conceived of the Duane Allman Band as a trio like Cream or the Jimi Hendrix Experience. But, Walden recalls, "Duane called me after the famous Jacksonville jam and said, 'I've got it!'" What Allman had was a band twice the size of the one Walden had envisioned.

There was still the issue of what to do about Duane's recording contract with Rick Hall. "To be candid," Walden told Dave Kyle, "I don't think Rick understood what Duane was attempting to do. In fairness to Rick, Duane had basically brought in a version of the Hour Glass, except that Gregg was not part of it. Duane was a one-of-a-kind guitarist, but you couldn't say the same about his singing. He was adequate, but it certainly didn't match his talent with the guitar."

Hall remembers, "Phil asked me, 'How many sides have you got cut?' I said, 'I've cut eight sides.' He said, 'What do you think?' I said, 'Nothing. Bullshit. Just a bunch of garbage. I mean, you can't get a deal on it.' He said, 'You don't want to work with him anymore?' I said, 'Not really.' So he said, 'Then I'm going to bring Jerry Wexler to hear it.'"

The opening Phil Walden had been waiting for had finally arrived. "So Jerry and Phil came in," Rick Hall says, "and Jerry says, 'Phil tells me that you got some sides cut on Duane. Would you consider selling him?' I said, 'Yeah, I'd consider it. What'll you give me for him?' He said, 'I'll give you $10,000.' I said, 'Write me a check.'"

Wexler recalls the event a little differently: "I bought Duane Allman's contract for $15,000. It's in the contract. There was no dialogue—no discussion. I just made the offer, Rick said, 'Fine,' and that was that. I didn't care about any masters in the can. It didn't interest me. Phil decided he wanted to start his label with these guys, but he'd said, 'I gotta get Duane loose from Rick,' so I just bought Duane's contract. It was not esoteric or complex. I just wanted to free up Duane so Phil could start his label with the Allman Brothers."

While Hall, Wexler, and Walden were doing their deal, the Allman Brothers were building up a following in Jacksonville. Walden's basic plan for Duane and the band was for Atlantic to acquire Duane's recording, production, and publishing agreements from Hall, followed by Walden's purchase of Duane's contracts from Atlantic, followed by Walden entering into recording, publishing, and management agreements with the entire Allman Brothers Band. He also wanted the group to move from Jacksonville to Macon, where his studio and record label were to be headquartered.

At first the band was hesitant to leave the state where the majority of the members had lived most of their lives. They had the steady Coliseum gig, the jam sessions in Willow Brook Park, and a growing fan base. On top of everything else, Jacksonville was a hip little city. Georgia—especially a small town in Georgia—just didn't seem that inviting. But when one of the band members was forced to toss his entire stash of pot out the window as the Jacksonville cops banged on his front door, the group decided that moving to Macon might not be such a bad idea after all. The very next day they packed their Ford Econoline and headed for the Peach State.

By early April the whole band was crammed into a two-room apartment in a house at 309 College Street. It was furnished with six mattresses on the floor and a soda machine to keep the beer cold, courtesy of Phil Walden. At the end of College Street was Rose Hill Cemetery—a graveyard that would become a special gathering place for the Allman Brothers. Gregg and Dickey found it to be a serene spot to write songs. Duane went there to play his acoustic guitar for a captive audience. It was also a place not frequented with any regularity by the Macon police department, making it possible to occasionally indulge in activities one might not be able to do in a more public setting.

"I was there when they arrived in Macon and was very much aware of the impact they had on our fair city, which has never been the same since," says Alan Walden. "They made it the hippest place in the world to live. Bear in mind, the Allman Brothers were the first longhairs in Macon, Georgia. We had one guy in town who had real long hair when the Allman Brothers arrived, and he wasn't even a hippie—we called him a beatnik. And when they arrived, the women went absolutely bananas. I mean, these guys could get laid sitting out in the front yard of their two-room apartment."

Back in Muscle Shoals, it had turned out that quite a bit of fancy footwork was necessary to untangle all of Duane's previous contractual obligations. The process had begun back in December 1968 when Duane signed his artist, production,

Entrance to Rose Hill Cemetery—Macon, Georgia

and publishing agreements with Fame—although he was still bound by the Hour Glass deal with Liberty Records that he had signed on June 15, 1967. Gregg's return to L.A. with the understanding that he would be fulfilling all of the other band members' obligations to the label was apparently based on a false assumption. Before Duane's contract with Fame could even become effective, Liberty would have to release him from his 1967 deal. There was also the matter of his management agreement with Bill McEuen. Walden had been making overtures to Duane about managing him ever since the guitarist had signed a recording contract with Rick Hall. But neither Hall nor Walden could move forward before Allman got out from under his still-effective West Coast deals.

In an effort to kill both birds with one stone, Duane had called McEuen back in December 1968. They had quickly worked out a settlement in which Allman agreed to pay $2,500 he owed McEuen, as well as $500 to one Lee D. Weisel to discharge a debt that had been guaranteed by McEuen. In addition, Duane assigned his former manager all of his rights in the Hour Glass name. In exchange, McEuen agreed to do more than just release Allman from his management contract. The final clause of Allman's settlement with his former manager stated: "McEuen agrees and guarantees that he will obtain for Allman a release from the recording contract with Liberty Records, Inc."

Bill McEuen worked his magic with Liberty, and on January 23, 1969, a deal was struck between Allman and his former label. The document read, in part: "It is our mutual desire to effect a termination of said agreement insofar as said agreement relates to your services individually or as a member of 'THE HOUR GLASS' and to execute mutual releases of all claims that any of us may have against the other in connection therewith." In other words, Duane was finally—if not paradoxically—set free from Liberty.

The release further stated: "Both you and we shall retain any and all rights and interests respectively obtained pursuant to the said agreement with regard to any record sides recorded pursuant thereto, embodying your services." With those lines, Liberty was confirming that Duane still had the right to be paid royalties (assuming the outstanding Hour Glass advance was ever recouped), and that Liberty still had the right to release future Hour Glass recordings if it so desired. For the duration of Duane's life, this clause would be meaningless. After his death, however, United Artists Records—successor-in-interest to Liberty—would take full advantage of its right to re-release "any record sides recorded pursuant thereto," as would EMI Records, successor-in-interest to United Artists.

Upon the date of Duane's release from Liberty Records in January 1969, his various agreements with Rick Hall officially went into effect. And so, on May 10, 1969, Atlantic Recording Corporation and Cotillion Music, Inc. (Atlantic's music publishing arm), entered into an agreement with Fame Productions, Inc., and Fame Publishing Co., Inc., acquiring the rights Duane had assigned to Rick. Schedules to this agreement list the eight masters Duane had recorded, the one song he had written ("Happily Married Man"), and the $8,877.20 in debts Allman had incurred in studio, musician, travel, and other expenses, including the $2,500 the guitarist owed to Bill McEuen and the $500 owed to Lee D. Weisel, as well as an advance to Duane of $925. Regarding all the monies owed by Allman, the agreement stated, "Insofar as you are concerned, we may charge same to Allman's account."

Paragraph 6 of the assignment called for Atlantic to pay Fame $15,000. Hall has claimed in numerous interviews that he sold Allman's contract to Atlantic for

Otis Rush's Mourning in the Morning, *featuring Duane Allman playing the blues on one of his final sessions at Fame*

$10,000. Writing off the nearly $3,500 in studio time Duane had managed to rack up, the remaining expenses incurred by Hall would have been a little more than $5,000, making Hall's final take from the sale very close to the $10,000 he remembers.

Ironically, since—on paper—Hall appears to have taken on the burden of Allman's outstanding debts, the agreement with Fame implied that Atlantic still intended to charge those debts back to the artist. Jerry Wexler says Atlantic didn't charge the outstanding debts to Duane "as far as I know," but if Atlantic actually did so, it would mean that the entire cost to Atlantic for acquiring Duane Allman's artist, production, and publishing contracts was only $6,122.80.

Regarding his sale of Duane's contract to Wexler, Hall now says, "I felt at the time it was probably the best deal I ever made. Of course, as history would have it, it was probably the all-time worst deal I ever made in my life."

Between the time Duane's solo sessions at Fame ran out of steam in early March and Wexler purchased his recording contract from Hall two months later, the guitarist's earlier session work had begun to yield impressive results. Aretha's single of "The Weight" had been released, as had King Curtis's version of "Games People Play" and Wilson Pickett's "Born to Be Wild," along with *The Dynamic Clarence Carter*. Just before Duane and Jaimoe split for Jacksonville, Otis Rush had come to Fame to cut his album *Mourning in the Morning*, where Duane got a chance to play straight blues on tracks like "Reap What You Sow." Only days after the Otis Rush sessions, however, there was a major shift in the Muscle Shoals recording scene. About the same time Duane and Jaimoe were leaving for Florida, the four members of Rick Hall's rhythm section departed *en masse* to open their own studio less than three miles away from Fame.

"The four of them kept appealing to me," recalls Jerry Wexler. "They said, 'We're leaving Rick. We can't take it anymore. We want to go with you.' I said, 'I can't do that because I met you guys through him. That would be a betrayal.' They all came up to my house on Long Island with an ultimatum. It was an ultimatum of affection. They said, 'We're coming here because we want to show you that we mean it. This is the last shot.' Meanwhile, I kept calling Rick, saying, 'Rick, your guys are getting very impatient. They can't take it anymore. You better shape up with them.' He said, 'Ah, I can always get me some new pickers, blah, blah, blah.' But they surprised him. They defected."

"It wasn't like we left him without any money or anything to do," says Jimmy Johnson. "We'd cut a bunch of hits. And so we came in and met with him and said, 'Hey look—we have gotten together and bought a studio.' He was shocked, but he said, 'Guys, I would have done the same thing.' He said, 'Now I think you've made a mistake, but, hey, I would have done it myself.' So that's how we split. We didn't know if we'd be a success or not. We left on decent terms, but there was a couple of strained years because there was a feelin' of competition for a while. Rick Hall's biggest success came after we left, so our leaving had no effect on his career at all. All we did was go for ours."

The rhythm section set up shop at 3614 Jackson Highway in Sheffield. The location had been a casket storage facility before a local businessman named Fred Bevis converted it into a recording studio. When the four players purchased the operation from Bevis, they christened it Muscle Shoals Sound Studios. Once the deal was done, Johnson put in a call to Jerry Wexler. "I said, 'Look, we got a four-track studio. We need to borrow some money.' And we borrowed $18,000 from Atlantic on a demand note. At any time they could recall it, right? I mean, you know, they had to do it in their favor. See, we were *musicians*. We couldn't borrow money from a bank."

"I loaned them the money with no collateral and no interest," says Wexler. "Would somebody not have asked something for that? Instead, I loaned them money and guaranteed them a year-and-a-half's worth of work. I could've asked for a percentage or something. Did you ever hear of a record guy doing that? 'Here's the money. Get started.' I gave them the money and guaranteed the work, and I was happy to do it. They talk about Muscle Shoals or Memphis—and you know damn well it's not about studios or towns. It's the players! And they were my players."

The four musicians took Atlantic's money and upgraded the studio to an eight-track facility before their first client arrived. In one of the strangest moments in a story filled with irony, the first act to arrive at Muscle Shoals Sound was Gregg Allman's future wife, Cher. Still one-half of Sonny & Cher at the time, by 1969 Cher had scored two huge solo hits with "Bang Bang (My Baby

Muscle Shoals Sound, 3614 Jackson Highway—The studio where Duane played on recording sessions by Boz Scaggs, John Hammond Jr., Ronnie Hawkins, and others

Shot Me Down)" and "You Better Sit Down Kids." Her album was engineered by Tom Dowd and produced by Dowd, Wexler, and another ace Atlantic producer, Arif Mardin. The rhythm section played on the whole album, with Eddie Hinton on lead guitar—but commercially the project was a bust. The singles all died and the album itself, aptly titled *3614 Jackson Highway*, lasted all of three weeks on the charts. It was "strike one" for Muscle Shoals Sound.

To keep a little money coming in while waiting for Wexler and Walden to work out their deals with Rick Hall and each other, Duane had no choice but to continue playing on sessions at every opportunity. In early May—the same week Atlantic finally purchased Duane's contract from Rick Hall—the guys at Muscle Shoals Sound were working with Atlantic's latest signing, Boz Scaggs. Scaggs had already made a trip to the Shoals, posing as a reporter for *Rolling Stone*. "He hung out for a little bit, then left," says David Hood. "Right after we bought the studio, Atlantic sent these acts down, and Boz was the second one. That was the first time we knew he was a recording artist." (The Muscle Shoals Sound rhythm section, ensconced in their own musical world, weren't aware that Scaggs had been a founding member of the Steve Miller Band, singing and playing guitar on Miller's first two albums before embarking on a solo career.)

"I had signed Boz [for management]," says Alan Walden. "Duane was leaving Macon to go to Muscle Shoals to play on Boz's first album for Atlantic. He dropped by my office, and he couldn't help but leave me with one thought. He says, 'Well, I'm going over there to Muscle Shoals to play on Boz's album.' I said, 'Oh, that's great. I'm real happy for you.' He says, 'Yeah, I want to show him he shouldn't pick up his damn guitar case with me around.' It was a little cut, but he went over there and made Boz's album what it was. 'Loan Me a Dime' was un*real*."

The album was produced by Scaggs, Marlin Greene, and *Rolling Stone* editor Jann Wenner, and Duane's guitar work was exactly what the doctor ordered. Allman's electric slide playing graces both "Now You're Gone" and "Finding Her"—the latter being the first recording to capture Duane's unique slide guitar "birdcalls." He also plays dobro on "Look What I Got" and "Waiting for a Train." But his finest moments are on the 6/8 blues dirge "Loan Me a Dime," written by Fenton Robinson although credited on the original album jacket to "W. R. Scaggs."

The song opens with a plaintive organ solo from Barry Beckett. Soon the rest of the rhythm section falls in for 12 bars of what might be one of the slowest blues progressions ever put down on tape. At the 1:20 mark, Duane's first solo begins. By the time Scaggs finally starts singing the first verse more than a minute later, the average single from 1969 would have already begun to fade out. Duane is back for another solo after verse two. He's in B.B. King mode for this 12-bar stretch, and then begins his familiar call-and-response playing between Boz's vocal lines throughout verses three and four. When Scaggs concludes the last verse, "Loan Me a Dime" has already surpassed the seven-and-a-half-minute mark. From that point on, it's all Duane's show. Horns blare as Allman and the rhythm section hit a double-time feel. For the next five minutes, Duane plays like a man possessed as the groove gets more and more intense. It is his most impressive work to date—and it will go virtually unheard during his lifetime.

Nobody seemed to care about Scaggs's first LP. Its initial release in 1969 sold even fewer copies than Cher's Muscle Shoals album. Although Boz would later have a string of hits for Columbia Records, prompting Atlantic to remix and reissue his debut album in 1978, Scaggs began his solo career with a commercial flop—"strike two" for Muscle Shoals Sound. Having played on a series of impressive sessions as a Muscle Shoals sideman, although receiving little personal

Boz Scaggs's debut (and only) album for Atlantic Records—one of the first recordings made at Muscle Shoals Sound

recognition, Allman (credited as Duane "Skydog" Allman) got top billing on the long list of musicians on the back of *Boz Scaggs*.

After the failures (at least as far as sales were concerned) of both the Cher and Boz Scaggs albums, Atlantic Records sent a completely unknown singer named R. B. Greaves down to Muscle Shoals. His very first single, "Take a Letter Maria," exploded onto the charts in 1969, selling over a million copies and securing Muscle Shoals Sound's status as a hit-making studio.

Duane hadn't played on "Take a Letter Maria." By the time Greaves arrived in Muscle Shoals, Duane and the rest of the Allman Brothers Band were already on the road. But the guitarist would continue to return to Muscle Shoals Sound between gigs with the ABB, despite having grown weary of the sideman scene. "Oh, man! Studios—that's a terrible thing!" he would later say. "You just lay around and you get your money, man." Specifically referring to the Muscle Shoals Sound rhythm section, he said, "All those studio cats that I know, like, one of them gets a color TV, see, and then the next day, man, they're all down to Sears or wherever: 'Hey man, I'd like to look at some color TVs,' you know. And this one place I know, man, all of these cats had Oldsmobile 442s. One of them traded for a Toronado, see, and so all of them traded for a Toronado. And now one of 'em's got a Toronado *and* a Corvette, and now they're *all* looking at new 'vettes! It's sickening."

"He couldn't quite understand the rest of us," says Jimmy Johnson. "We couldn't be too much of a free spirit at all, really. I mean, we had to stay home and make a living. But you could walk up to Duane—if he didn't have any work for a week or two—you could come up to him at eight o'clock one night and say, 'Hey, let's go to California,' and he'd say 'What time do you wanna leave?' He was that type of free spirit."

As soon as Duane signed off on the deal between Fame and Atlantic, he headed for Atlanta. Slowly but surely, the counterculture that had sprung up on the West Coast had finally made its way to the biggest city in the Southeast. By May 1969, rock bands had begun going to Atlanta's Piedmont Park to play free concerts there, and Duane wanted his band to be part of the scene. "Playing the park's such a good thing," Duane once said, "because people don't even expect you to be there. About the nicest way you can play is just for nothing, you know. And it's not really for nothing. It's for your own personal satisfaction—and other people's—rather than for any kind of financial thing." There was also one other reason. When an interviewer once asked Allman his favorite place the band had played, he responded, "Piedmont Park, Atlanta. You got up onstage and it'd be covered with dope. Piles of reefer on the stage and acid tabs—every color you could see."

The Peach State was now home for the Allman Brothers Band. They had a record deal, a place to live, and Piedmont Park to go to when they didn't have paying gigs. But playing live—whether for money or not—called for a crew to help set up, tear down, and get the band from one town to the next. For an act still making little money, the band had no problem recruiting a loyal gang of roadies. Twiggs Lyndon Jr.—an employee of the Waldens' management and booking firm—became the band's tour manager. Joseph "Red Dog" Campbell, a Vietnam War veteran who had first heard the band while attending Florida Junior College in Jacksonville, was soon on board as well. Kim Payne, a roadie Gregg had met during his solo months in L.A., also joined up, as did Berry Oakley's old friend from the Roemans, Mike Callahan.

Red Dog once said, "In the old days, when Duane was alive, if Phil Walden called a band meeting, he wouldn't just get Duane and five [other] musicians—he would also get the roadies. . . . Phil would ask, 'Do I have to meet with roadies?' Duane would answer, 'You called for a band meeting, and this is the band.'" In his book *The Legendary Red Dog: A Book of Tails*, Campbell referred to the formation of the band and its original road crew as "the calling of the Brotherhood." All the Brotherhood needed now was a record.

With the band established in Macon, Phil Walden was working on the next phase of his plan. As Walden and Wexler had planned, the Allman Brothers Band was now signed to Phil's Capricorn Records label, so it was time to get the rhythm section together for his Capricorn Studios. Since Duane had decided not to use any of the players from the Hour Glass for his new band, Walden saw a golden opportunity. Paul Hornsby recalls, "Phil says, 'I've got a studio I'm building in Macon. Would you consider moving to Macon and being in the staff band?' I said, 'Macon—where's that?' He said, 'Macon, Georgia.' I didn't even know what state it was in. I declined and Sandlin declined. But Phil kept calling us and went through about—it seems to me—a month of calls. And every time he called, the deal got a little more prosperous—sounded a little better every time—and finally he talked Sandlin into doing it, and Pete Carr, and then Sandlin called and convinced me. He said, 'We're going to do it,' and I thought, 'Well, if y'all are gonna do it, I'll do it.' We had always been kind of a bloc vote, so to speak, even in the Hour Glass. What one of us three did, the other two went along with. So that's how we ended up in Macon. We went to work as the rhythm section in the studio. Duane and his fellow band members arrived in Macon about a month before we did, so all of our careers sort of took off at about the same time at the same place."

CHAPTER FOURTEEN

The Allman Brothers Band

*"I like everything on the first album, man. We worked
some of it out when we first got together, and then as we
went along we became a little more proficient." — D.A.*

When it came time for the Allman Brothers Band to record their first
album, it was decided that the project would take place at Atlantic
Recording Studios in New York City rather than Capricorn Studios
in Macon. That way, the legendary Atlantic engineer and record producer Tom
Dowd could oversee the sessions. On the surface, it seemed an unlikely place
for the group to find themselves making music with such an obvious Southern
flavor. In the ensuing years, however—though no one in the original group
would actually take up residence there—New York City would become almost
like the band's second home. As loved as the Allman Brothers Band became
throughout the South, New Yorkers would take to the band in a manner that
surpassed every other major U.S. city. It is a testimony to the sophistication of
the Allman Brothers' music that the most cosmopolitan metropolis in America
would be so drawn to their sound.

But in August 1969, the Allman Brothers were still an unknown entity
when they arrived in Manhattan to lay down tracks for their first record. Ironically, Tom Dowd—who would go on to produce many of the band's most important recordings—was called away at the last minute, making him unavailable
to sit behind the board for the sessions. One of his colleagues, Adrian Barber,
took over the production chores.

Due, in part, to Dowd's work with a host of great musicians—John Coltrane, Ray Charles, Ornette Coleman, the Coasters, the Drifters, Otis Redding, Thelonious Monk, Aretha Franklin, Eric Clapton, Lynyrd Skynyrd, and many others—he would eventually be the subject of an award-winning documentary entitled *Tom Dowd & the Language of Music*. Sadly, Dowd would pass away on October 27, 2002, just as this tribute was being finished. Prior to the making of the film, in late 1993 and early 1994, Dowd had a series of marathon conversations with *Hittin' the Note* magazine's publisher, Bill Ector. Entitled "Tom Dowd—In His Own Words," the article drawn from those conversations is the Rosetta Stone of the producer's decades-long involvement with the Allman Brothers.

In one of those conversations, Dowd told the story of the group's debut LP: "I was supposed to have done the first album with the band up in New York, but some way or other I got detoured. Jerry Wexler made a deal to keep them in the studio for three or four days when they were supposed to be with me. But I had a panic call, and I couldn't tell you to this day whether it was Muscle Shoals or Memphis, but all of a sudden, 'Hey Dowd, get your ass down there. They need you.' So the chap who was working with me, Adrian Barber, and his crew did the first Allman Brothers album in three days in the New York studio."

In truth, the sessions took twice that long, but even six days was a ridiculously short amount of time for any band—let alone a brand-new one—to cut an entire album. The sessions began on August 3, with Barber serving as both recording engineer and producer.

Adrian Barber had been a member of the Big Three, a late-1950s/early-1960s Liverpool band managed by Brian Epstein. He was a guitarist with a knack for electronics who built enormous amplifiers and speaker cabinets that dwarfed the usual gear of the era. After leaving the Big Three, Barber eventually ended up stateside, where he used his electronics skills to become an engineer for Atlantic. By the time he was handed the Allman Brothers, he had manned the board on records by David "Fathead" Newman, Herbie Mann, Buffalo Springfield, and several others. When the Allman Brothers Band went into Atlantic Studios, it was not only their first album—it was also Barber's first time sitting in the producer's chair.

On the first day, the group recorded an instrumental version of the Spencer Davis-Edward Hardin composition "Don't Want You No More" that segued into Gregg's "It's Not My Cross to Bear." That same day, the band took a shot at

"Dreams," one of the songs Gregg had signed over to United Artists' publishing division just prior to his trip to Jacksonville, which they had already recorded as a demo at the new Capricorn Studios back in April. The band wasn't happy with the version they cut on August 3, so they decided to set it aside for the moment.

Two days later the band was back at work, putting down another of Gregg's compositions, "Black Hearted Woman," along with "Trouble No More." After one more day off, it was time to tackle "Whipping Post." "I wrote it on an ironing board cover," Gregg once said. "It came so fast, I didn't even have a chance to get the paper out. That's the way the good songs come—they just hit you like a ton of bricks.

"I didn't know the intro was in 11/4 time," Gregg would later tell John Lynskey. "I just saw it as three sets of three, and then two to jump on the next three sets with: it was like 1, 2, 3—1, 2, 3—1, 2, 3—1, 2. I didn't count it as 1, 2, 3, 4, 5, 6, 7, 8, 9, 10, 11. It was one beat short, but it didn't feel one short, because to get back to the triad, you had two steps to go up. You'd really hit those two hard, to accent them, so that would separate the threes. That's how naïve I was about the whole thing. My brother told me—I guess the day I wrote it—he said, 'That's good, man. I didn't know that you understood 11/4.' Of course I said something intelligent like, 'What's 11/4?' Duane just said, 'Okay, dumbass, I'll try to draw it up on paper for you.'"

In the end, it would take the entire August 7th session for the band to record "Whipping Post" to their liking. On the following day, they took a shot at the number that had inspired Duane to take up slide playing. "'Statesboro Blues' was a song that me and my brother had known for a long time," says Gregg. "The song just kind of stuck with us over the years, so when the ABB got together, 'Statesboro Blues' resurfaced." Although the band gave it their best shot, they simply weren't able to capture "Statesboro Blues" in the studio with the same kind of power they could achieve when performing it live. The same could safely be said about everything they were recording in New York, but the difference in the energy level between live performances and the studio version of "Statesboro Blues" was so obvious that they decided to scrap the song—and the session—for the day.

Three days later, the band recorded Gregg's composition "Every Hungry Woman." They returned to the studio one last time on August 12, to try once more to capture "Dreams." This time, it all came together.

"They were out of their element in New York, hustled by a chap with an English accent," Tom Dowd told Bill Ector. Dowd said the process of recording under Barber's direction was "perhaps intimidating, or push-push, shove-shove. 'Do what the guy says and let's get out of here.' I think better could have been had on all points, but that's no reflection on them or Adrian. Whatever they went through then probably made it better for the second time."

But work on the second LP was still half a year away. For the moment, the Allman Brothers Band had managed to record an entire album in six days—and on the seventh day, they did not rest. There were gigs to be played in Florida and Georgia.

As hard as the band was working, Duane was working harder still. In September and October he played on sessions by Lulu, Judy Mayhan, and Ronnie Hawkins at Muscle Shoals Sound. One of the highpoints of the Hawkins date was Duane's slide solo on "Down in the Alley."

Ronnie Hawkins was an Arkansas native who moved to Canada in 1958 with the idea of trying to make a name for himself in a music scene not nearly as competitive as the one in the U.S. By the following year, thanks to a gig in New Jersey, he had secured a deal with Roulette Records. He cut a series of singles, including "Forty Days" and "Mary Lou," both of which hit the charts. Hawkins chose to remain based in Toronto, though, and his popularity subsided in the lower 48.

The Hawks, his backing band, rose to heights Hawkins could only dream of after they left him in 1964, soon to join forces with Bob Dylan and then become The Band. Hawkins made an album on the Yorkville label in 1968 and was signed to Atlantic's Cotillion subsidiary the following year. He went to Muscle Shoals Sound to record with the rhythm section there, augmented by Eddie Hinton, harmonica player Richard "King Biscuit Boy" Newell, and pianist Scott Cushnie. Allman played on Hawkins's remake of "Forty Days," as well as "Matchbox," "One More Night," "Who Do You Love," and the aforementioned "Down in the Alley."

When "Down in the Alley" was released as a single in January 1970, Atlantic/Cotillion put its muscle behind the 45 in a big way, with no less than John Lennon making a radio ad for the record. But it was all for naught. Both the single and the album, *Ronnie Hawkins*, died with hardly a whimper.

In his liner notes for the Rhino Records collection *The Best of Ronnie Hawkins & His Band*, Colin Escott wrote of Hawkins's attempt to later thank Allman for putting his signature slide licks on "Down in the Alley." "He was so ripped he couldn't even remember doing the session," said Hawkins. "When I told him what a good job he'd done, he said, 'Down in the *what?*'" Duane's inability to remember every session he'd worked on—even when he wasn't high—was perhaps understandable. As soon as he had finished the Mayhan, Lulu, and Hawkins sessions, he was on his way to Criteria Studios in Miami to record "Pullin'" for Aretha's next album.

Only a few weeks later, Allman was heading back to Muscle Shoals. John Hammond Jr.—son of the famed Columbia Records A&R man who had discovered Aretha Franklin and Bob Dylan, and who would later sign Bruce Springsteen and Stevie Ray Vaughan, among others—had been sent by Atlantic to Muscle Shoals Sound. Hammond's forte was performing songs by artists such as Robert Johnson, John Lee Hooker, Elmore James, and other classic blues artists. When he showed up at 3614 Jackson Highway in Sheffield, Alabama, expecting to find a group of seasoned R&B session players, everyone in the studio was in for a shock.

"When I arrived, they thought I was going to be black and I thought they were going to be black!" Hammond said in an article for *Guitar Player* magazine. "So they got pretty cold to me, and I didn't know what to make of this. It was Roger Hawkins, Barry Beckett, Jimmy Johnson, David Hood, Eddie Hinton—and for three days I tried to get them into what I was playing, and they just seemed to play a little bit awkwardly.

"Then on the scene arrives this guy with long red hair down his back, eyebrows that crossed, and a moustache that went all the way into his sideburns, wearing a T-shirt that said 'City Slicker' on it. He pulled up in this milk truck, and everybody said, 'Hey, Duane, how you doin' man?' Everybody just fell all over themselves for Duane, you know. He was their idol. He said, 'Where's this John Hammond guy? I want to meet this guy—I really dig him.' They said, 'You *do?*' And they all looked at me with new respect.

"I was introduced to Duane, and he said, 'I sure dig your stuff, boy, and I sure would love to play on your record, if it's okay.' I said, 'Sure, I guess so.' I had never heard him play before, but these guys worshipped him. As soon as Duane gave me the okay, the session went fantastic."

On the album that would be titled *Southern Fried*, Allman played on "Cryin' for My Baby," "I'm Leavin' You," and "You'll Be Mine," but reserved his best performance for Willie Dixon's "Shake for Me." His guitar slides in after the first line of the second verse and hangs on for the duration, weaving and winding its way in and out of each line of Hammond's vocals. Duane takes a slide solo after the third verse, and then, once again, his guitar responds to every line when the singer comes back for the final verse. When the lyrics are done, Allman takes over, attacking again with a second slide solo that is clearly just beginning to warm up as the track fades. "I was floored," says Hammond. "There was a lot more that was edited out in order to fit the album. I mean, he played on and on and on! He was just incredible."

On November 21, when Duane arrived in Muscle Shoals to introduce himself to John Hammond Jr., he might well have been feeling some apprehension. It was just a day shy of two weeks since the Allman Brothers' debut album had hit the stores, and there was yet to be any indication whether the LP might sell well or not.

After the band had finished recording, photo sessions for the album cover were set up. Stephen Paley was the photographer, and the shots for the front and back were no problem—taken at various locales in Macon. But this was to be a gatefold LP, meaning there were nearly 25 inches of space to be filled in the album's foldout center. "The [inner sleeve] photo was taken in Round Oak, Georgia, down behind my log cabin there, which is also the back of [Otis Redding's] Big O Ranch," says Alan Walden. "It was Phil's idea that they all be bathing in the creek. There was supposed to be bubbles all in the water, but the creek water was moving, so the bubbles kept blowing away—going on down the creek. They only brought one bottle of bubble bath, so it didn't last very long. It was a little bit risqué for that time period. We had some good reviews and some bad reviews on that."

In the infamous inner-sleeve photograph, the entire band is naked, except for Butch's hat. The creek is shallow, but just deep enough to keep the shot from looking like a *Playgirl* spread. Butch is the only one standing up, but Berry is sitting in front of him, keeping Butch's private parts private.

The advertising campaign was interesting, to say the least. Instead of emphasizing the rather ordinary-looking front-cover shot, the print ads featured one of the photos taken at the creek, along with a quote about the band being a "bad bunch of electric Southern longhairs"—a line from Ed Ochs's *Billboard* review of the single, "Black Hearted Woman."

"I remember sending out a postcard with that picture on it," says Alan Walden. "It said, 'The Allman Brothers will tear your head off with their new album, *The Allman Brothers Band*.'" Duane sent out some postcards, too, including one to Jerry Wexler that read, "Thanks for your help, guidance, confidence, but most of all your friendship. Love to you and yours always, Duane Allman."

Whatever fate held in store for *The Allman Brothers Band*, Duane and his fellow musicians had done the best they could, working with a record producer they didn't know; using a studio only Duane had previously worked in (thanks to the Aretha Franklin and King Curtis sessions earlier that year); and cutting seven usable tracks over the course of six days. Plus, there was the matter of the album being released under the auspices of a record label owned by a manager of R&B acts making his initial foray into the rock world. In fact, the album was released on one of Atlantic's subsidiary labels, Atco. Walden hadn't even created a logo for Capricorn Records yet, so the LP had an Atco label with a barely noticeable line that read "Capricorn Records Series."

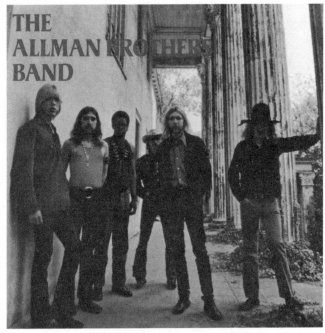

The ABB's (and Capricorn Records') first album, recorded in New York under the tutelage of Adrian Barber

At first glance, it doesn't seem that a lot of thought was put into the album's sequencing. Excluding the scrapped initial take of "Dreams," the first four songs appear on the LP in the order in which they were recorded. The first two, of course, had to go back-to-back as one leads directly into the other. The opener is the Allmans' instrumental arrangement of "Don't Want You No More," with the two guitarists playing the melody line an octave apart. Only 27 seconds into the piece, though, the tune suddenly turns into something else entirely. The guitars and bass take the band through an eight-note passage that dives into an organ solo by Gregg, complemented by Jaimoe on congas. This is followed by solos from each of the guitarists before the whole band locks in together, racing through an ascending unison lick followed by a series of quarter-note triplets that slow down significantly, signaling a shift in tempo. It's clear that *something* is about to happen, but no one—back in November 1969—could have been prepared for whiskey-voiced Gregg Allman to make his formal singing debut on an Allman Brothers record. Gregg would later comment, "If you got somebody from, say, Tibet, and played them the Hour Glass records, and then played an Allman Brothers record right after it, and then told them it was the same guy singing, and the same guitarist, they wouldn't believe it. I can't believe it sometimes!"

As the band sustains the final note of "Don't Want You No More," a line from Duane's guitar rides over the top, bridging into Gregg's ballad "It's Not My Cross to Bear." As Duane's phrase ends, Gregg's singing begins—a blues-laden shout of "Yeah, yeah, yeah" that's at least two planets removed from the same catch-phrase as sung by the Beatles some five years earlier. This isn't an upbeat, mop-topped cry of joy; this is a serious warning that a sorrowful story is about to be told. But the listener has to wait until the singer is good and ready because, in a musical move unfamiliar to rock record buyers of the time, Duane plays a wailing guitar solo that goes on for 45 seconds—the duration of an entire verse—before the singer finally returns to tell his story.

Up next is "Black Hearted Woman," another Gregg Allman original, which opens with a two-guitar riff that clearly indicates both guitarists have played a few Hendrix covers in their day. The girl Allman sings about might have a black heart, but she also sounds like a foxy lady caught in crosstown traffic. Despite this and other influences that can be heard here and there in the music, the Allman

Brothers' sound is uniquely their own: twin lead guitars, melodic bass, the gritty voice of Gregg Allman, and a pair of drummers who fear no time signature.

The last track on Side One is the song that became Gregg's audition piece when he arrived at the March 26 jam session. On much of the album, producer Adrian Barber chose not to emphasize the band's double-drum attack—often moving Jaimoe to congas, or Butch to timbales or maracas. On "Trouble No More," though, the two drum kits kick off the song. Through Duane's slide solos, Dickey's solo, and all five verses sung by Gregg, the Butch-and-Jaimoe rhythm assault never stops.

Side Two opens with Gregg's "Every Hungry Woman." Jaimoe's back on congas, and the guitarists show off their proficiency in the twin lead department once more. But the organ sound is distorted, and the overdubs aren't just obvious—they're practically announced. If the band's debut has a "filler" track, this is it. It hardly matters, though, because of what follows.

"Dreams" is the musical equivalent of its title. It is a strangely muted work—haunting and ethereal. If this were a Grateful Dead song, the twirlers would be out in full force. It is clearly still the Allman Brothers, but it's a gentler side of the band. "'Dreams' is the effect that good jazz has on us," Duane once explained. "If you can get the music flowing out there where you don't have to listen to it, it just takes you away." On this waltz-time track, the band achieves Duane's intent to perfection. "Dreams" inevitably takes the listener away, no matter how many times it's been heard. Perhaps the song's most mystical aspect is its deceptive length. It is an aural illusion. Although the track seems to begin and end within a couple of minutes, it's actually more than seven minutes long—in fact, it's the longest track on the album, by more than two minutes.

In the classic tradition of leaving the listener wanting more, the album ends with "Whipping Post." The song begins with two measures of Oakley's pounding bass, laying down that unmistakable 11/4 riff. In the second measure, a high-hat subtly joins in, followed by two measures of Duane's guitar. Dickey's guitar soon arrives, playing against Duane and Berry's line. Rather than distracting from the proceedings, the contrapuntal effect of Dickey's playing actually pushes the rhythm forward. Gregg's organ sneaks in just before the first verse begins. Duane—in the fashion that will become familiar, but never commonplace, to Allman Brothers fans—plays bluesy fills between the lines of Gregg's vocals. As the singer reaches the chorus, the harmony lead guitars go to work. After the second verse and chorus, Duane takes the first solo. Gregg sings the concluding verse, and then Dickey's solo picks up right where Duane's had left off. It is a moment of musical brilliance that works to perfection. At the end of Dickey's solo, the whole band joins in, starting at the tonic note and then, playing each note four times, climbs up the scale and into the stratosphere. The effect of the whole ensemble arriving at the final note together is almost earth shattering—but the song's not over. Gregg returns to sing the chorus one last time while Duane's guitar wails behind him. After the excitement of all that has come before, the band brings the album to a gentle close, concluding "Whipping Post" with a few final improvisational flourishes as the song slowly disappears.

The Fillmores, Part 1

*"Anyone who doesn't respect Bill Graham has
got their head messed around."* — D.A.

Duane Allman and Bill Graham had first crossed paths during the Hour Glass days, when the band opened for Buffalo Springfield on December 21–23, 1967, at the original Fillmore Auditorium on the corner of Fillmore Street and Geary Boulevard in San Francisco. Graham had been producing rock shows there for two years, booking acts like the Jefferson Airplane, Quicksilver Messenger Service, the Byrds, and, of course, the Grateful Dead.

In July 1968, Graham moved his S.F. operation to the Carousel Ballroom at Market Street and Van Ness Avenue, renaming the venue Fillmore West. Earlier that year, he had taken over the Village Theater at Second Avenue and Sixth Street in New York City, changing its name to the Fillmore East. Both Fillmores became *the* hallowed spots to play for the best-known acts of the era. Being asked to play at the Fillmore—East or West—was the ultimate sign of success for rock bands of the time, until Graham closed both venues in 1971.

The Allman Brothers Band played its first gig at the Fillmore East in December 1969. Their debut album had been released the previous month, and a giant blow-up of the inside cover photo—with the boys naked in the creek—was already adorning a wall in the Fillmore East lobby. None of the Fillmore's employees had heard the record yet. So, as Fillmore staff member Alan Arkush told author Robert Greenfield, the assumption was that these guys from Georgia must be "a bunch of redneck yo-yos."

To unintentionally further the "redneck yo-yos" image, the band showed up late to its first gig. But once they set up and began their sound check, the Fillmore staff came pouring out to watch the Allman Brothers rehearse—the ultimate compliment from a jaded bunch who had heard many of the world's greatest rock bands over the previous couple of years.

"The Fillmore in itself was a temple of rock & roll," Dickey Betts told interviewer Kirsten West. "It was *the* temple of rock & roll." And then he added, "It was the lowest paying gig out there.

"But everybody wanted to play the Fillmore, because it was the artistic presentation of rock & roll music. And it was because Bill Graham made it a point to present rock & roll in an artistic form instead of on some old stark stage with a bunch of metal fold-up chairs and a white spotlight. You know, he had created this whole atmosphere."

Those first three nights at the Fillmore East—December 26–28, 1969—the Allman Brothers were third on the bill behind Appaloosa and Blood, Sweat & Tears. It was a strange musical mix, to say the least. And, being the opening act, the Brothers were allowed to play only 45-minute sets—hardly enough time to get warmed up. (For the Allman Brothers, there were nights at other venues when one song could last almost that long.)

As was usually the case early in their career, the Allman Brothers were dead broke the first time they played the Fillmore East. "I remember the stories of Twiggs Lyndon standing at the toll bridge panhandling so they could get money to go through the toll to play at the Fillmore," says Alan Walden. "By then they were a happening band, but financially they were not stable yet." In fact, Alan Arkush had to personally loan Duane money just so the band could eat while they were in New York.

Better days were looming, though. The whole staff at the Fillmore had loved what they'd heard, and they immediately decided to bring the ABB back as soon as possible—and to have them open for a band more musically aligned with what the Allman Brothers were all about.

But before returning to the Fillmore East, the band headed to San Francisco in January 1970 for a four-night stay at the Fillmore West, opening for Buddy Guy and B.B. King. This engagement had to be a major thrill for Duane.

"It was Phil's idea that they all be bathing in the creek." (L–R) Butch, Berry, Jaimoe, Gregg, Duane, and Dickey in the photo that adorned the lobby wall of the Fillmore East

B.B. King had left a lasting impression on him ever since he and Gregg had first seen King perform when the boys were teenagers. Duane once said of the bluesman, "He could sing 'Happy Birthday' and bring tears to your eyes, man." And now, thanks to Bill Graham, Duane got to share the stage with the idol of his youth.

The following month—on February 11, 13, and 14—the Allman Brothers returned to the Fillmore East on a bill with Love and the Grateful Dead. It was the beginning of a beautiful friendship for the Allmans and the Dead. (Later that year, Duane would tell disc jockey Dave Herman, "I love the Dead. As for Jerry Garcia, Jerry Garcia could walk on water. He could do anything any man could ever do. He's a prince.") Before the first night was over, most of the Allman Brothers Band were onstage with the Dead, jamming on "Dark Star" and "Turn on Your Love Light."

Luckily, Grateful Dead sound mixer Owsley Stanley—who frequently recorded the Dead's shows—had the presence of mind to capture the Allman Brothers on tape during those February gigs. In 1996, selections from the Allman Brothers' set would be released on Grateful Dead Records under the title *Fillmore East, February 1970*. The seven tracks on the CD show what a strong live act the band had already become in the 11 months they had been together. And, as was the case in the old Hour Glass days, the Allman Brothers didn't confine themselves to performing songs they had already recorded.

Emphasizing this fact, the set opens with "In Memory of Elizabeth Reed," a Dickey Betts instrumental that wouldn't appear on record until *Idlewild South* some seven months later. It's followed by "Hoochie Coochie Man," with a lead vocal by Berry Oakley (whom Duane introduces as "our bad sex symbol").

Duane's blossoming slide work can be heard on "Statesboro Blues" and "Trouble No More," before the band tackles another blues chestnut, "I'm Gonna Move to the Outskirts of Town." *Fillmore East, February 1970* concludes with "Whipping Post" and "Mountain Jam," the former being a rather straight reading while the latter stretches beyond the half-hour mark, as usual.

By early 1970, the Allman Brothers' improvisational process had been developed to near perfection. As off-the-cuff as the band's live playing might have seemed to their audiences, there was always a conscious, formal structure holding everything together. Years later, Gregg explained the underpinnings of the band's onstage work to John Lynskey: "All the arrangements are pre-rehearsed down to the letter," he said. "But with the solos—you can take it as long as you want. When it comes to the solos, each soloist goes around twice—it's never just once. It takes twice to get out what you really want to say."

CHAPTER SIXTEEN

Idlewild South

*"I like the second album better myself because
it's farther on up the road." — D.A.*

Sales of the Allman Brothers' debut album started off slowly—very slowly. In December, the band played gigs up and down the East Coast, including the initial shows at the Fillmore East, trying to kick-start the record. But by the beginning of 1970, *The Allman Brothers Band* was still hovering somewhere underneath *Billboard*'s Top 200 Pop Albums chart.

In January, the band played the Electric Factory in Philadelphia and the Fillmore West in San Francisco before heading to Los Angeles for Duane and Gregg's first engagement at the Whisky a Go Go since their Hour Glass days. After the dismal failure of both Hour Glass albums, they must have felt somewhat vindicated when *The Allman Brothers Band* finally hit the charts on day three of the band's four-night stay at the Whisky. Granted, the album was barely clinging to the bottom of the Top 200, but it was enough to prove that the ABB was more than a regional outfit. They were on the national album charts at last.

Their first single was another story. Capricorn put out a 45 of "Black Hearted Woman" b/w "Every Hungry Woman," stamping "Black Hearted Woman" as the "plug side." Releasing a 45 with the word "woman" in the title of both songs wasn't the most brilliant marketing move the label could have made. Along with that, "Black Hearted Woman" had been whittled down from 5:08 to just over three minutes in an effort to appeal to Top 40 radio. It didn't help: pop radio stations ignored the single despite Ed Ochs's rave review in *Billboard*.

After L.A., the Allman Brothers played a couple of gigs at Pappaliski's in Dayton, Ohio, and three more nights at the Fillmore East—the aforementioned shows with the Grateful Dead—before returning to Macon in mid-February to start work on their second album.

By this time, the cramped space at 309 College Street had been a part of the band's past for several months. Dickey had moved down the street, while Duane had begun domestic life with Donna Roosman in an apartment a block-and-a-half away from the band's original crash pad. Their daughter, Galadrielle (named after a character in J. R. R. Tolkien's *Lord of the Rings* trilogy), had been born in August 1969. Meanwhile, Berry and his wife, Linda, had moved into a nearby apartment upstairs from Butch's place.

Late in 1969, Linda Oakley, Berry's sister Candace, and Donna found a potential new residence advertised in the paper. The house was located at 2321 Vineville, and it was *huge*. In December, Linda made the rental deposit for the place that was soon to be known by the band members, their families, the roadies, friends, and associates as the Big House—not the most creative name in the world, but certainly appropriate. It was a three-story affair with French doors, more than a dozen rooms, lots of fireplaces, and plenty of stained glass, built on a massive lot covered with water fountains, fish ponds, and trees everywhere—and the rent was all of $235 a month.

The Big House was initially home to three "family units": Duane, Donna, and Galadrielle; Berry, Linda, and their daughter, Brittany; and Berry's sister, Candace, and Gregg—Candace and Gregg being romantically involved at the time. The band members and their children got the bedrooms, but there were often guests at the Big House, including the occasional roadie crashing on the living room sofa.

Berry was determined to make the Big House a real home for everyone living there. He put himself in charge of organizing the meals, starting with the purchase of a dining room table large enough for the crowd that gathered at the house on those few occasions when the band wasn't touring.

Duane settled on the first-floor sunroom as the proper spot for the band to work, putting baffles on the walls himself to help keep the sound from bounc-

The Big House—2321 Vineville Avenue, Macon, Georgia

ing all over the house (and the neighborhood). This would become the band's rehearsal room, the place where they would practice, jam, and work out arrangements for new songs—songs that were often being written in other parts of the house (primarily the kitchen) by Gregg and Dickey.

Although the first album had been out for three months by the time the Allman Brothers came off the road in February, Tom Dowd had not yet heard the band play live. Luckily, he happened to be in Macon shortly after they got back to town. "I have no idea what the hell I was doing there," Dowd later recalled to Bill Ector, "but for some reason I had to be there. I came walking out of the hotel one day . . . and I heard this band in the rehearsal room at the studio. I walked on down the street to Phil Walden's office and asked him, 'Who the hell is that I just heard in the rehearsal room?' He says, 'It's the Allman Brothers.' I said, 'Do me a favor. Tell them to stop playing. Put them in the goddamn bus and ship them to me in Florida. They are ready to record. They are wasting their time in there. They'll lose it.' So he shipped them down to Miami, and we commenced recording somewhere in early 1970. And that's the way we started *Idlewild South*."

In truth, although several of the album's tracks would be cut at Criteria in Miami, the first tracks Dowd produced were recorded in Macon. Johnny Sandlin remembers the first *Idlewild South* session well because he was under the impression he was to be co-producer of the project. "[Dowd and I] would do it together," Sandlin told Michael Buffalo Smith in a *Gritz* magazine interview. "That's how it was put to me [by Phil Walden]." Unfortunately for Sandlin, nobody had put it that way to Dowd.

"So when Tom came in to produce the album, in my head I was there to co-produce it with him," Sandlin continued. "I didn't know until the end of the first day, when I was trying to discuss things with him—which you would do if you were a co-producer, but you wouldn't do as a bystander. He didn't seem interested in what I had to say. I felt like it was strange. Then, at the end of the session, I think it was Gregg who said that Phil had decided that Tom should do the record. I felt like the biggest ass in the whole world."

Johnny Sandlin would go on to play a vital role in Allman Brothers' recording sessions in years to come. In fact, he would eventually produce the biggest hit single of the band's career. But for now, with the exception of one song, Tom Dowd would be producing *Idlewild South*.

The band cut the album between February and July 1970, working in recording dates around a touring schedule that was becoming more and more hectic as the group's popularity increased. The first album had hung onto the charts for just over a month, peaking at a less-than-impressive 188 on the Top 200, but word was beginning to spread that you didn't want to miss the chance to hear this Southern band with the incredible slide guitarist.

In April, the ABB played two nights at what could safely be described as the hippest venue in Cincinnati. Ludlow Garage was just that—a former garage turned rock venue on Ludlow Avenue in the city's gaslight district. It had opened as a concert hall in 1969, run by a collective determined to give the locals an opportunity to hear and see the latest rock groups. Santana, Dr. John, Neil Young, Alice Cooper, and a host of other hot acts of the day played there during the venue's two-year lifespan.

But, as would later be the case with the Fillmore East, the group the Garage's organizers favored above all others was the Allman Brothers. Even with a pack of roadies who looked too hardened to be allowed to join the Manson family, the band always brought with them a certain atmosphere of Southern charm that endeared them to club owners around the country. "Ludlow Garage was was one of our favorite gigs back then," Dickey once said. "That was a real dungeon, but it was a great place to play—just a great crowd. We always had a good gig there."

During the Allman Brothers' visit to Ludlow Garage in early April, the show was recorded through the soundboard on a Teac A-6010 reel-to-reel machine. The eight songs taped that night would, with one exception, remain in the can for the next 20 years. When PolyGram Records finally released *Live at Ludlow Garage: 1970* on a two-CD set in 1990, Allman Brothers fans got a taste of what the live band was truly like at the time.

The set list is a familiar collection of songs from this era, including "Dreams," "Statesboro Blues," "Trouble No More," "Every Hungry Woman," "I'm Gonna Move to the Outskirts of Town," and "Hoochie Coochie Man." "In Memory of Elizabeth Reed" failed to make the album due to technical problems with the recording, but there is a rare opportunity to hear Duane sing on "Dimples," an old blues tune written by John Lee Hooker. It's the only ABB recording with a vocal by Duane (and can also be heard on the Duane Allman collection *An Anthology, Volume II*).

The showpiece of the record is a monumental "Mountain Jam" captured in its 44-minute entirety—a version that some critics feel eclipses the one on the band's 1972 album, *Eat a Peach*. "Mountain Jam" fills the entire second CD of *Ludlow Garage*. Based on the melody of the Donovan song "There Is a Mountain," it's a wide-open jam that gives everyone in the band a chance to shine. Duane and Dickey weave in and out of each other's solos, frequently unleashing harmony leads. Gregg stretches out on the B-3 before Duane and Dickey come back for more, with Dickey at one point playing a lick that sounds very close to what would become the lead line of "Ramblin' Man" some three years later. One-fourth of the way through the track, Butch and Jaimoe solo together for nearly six minutes before Berry comes in with his own lengthy solo, showing his truly exceptional melodic skill on bass.

At no point does this sound like a band playing just for the sake of filling time. Every note seems to make sense. No matter how far any one solo is extended, the piece never becomes tedious. And just at the moment when it sounds as if someone is about to head too far off the trail, suddenly the whole group reunites on the theme. And before they're done, they somehow turn "There Is a Mountain" into Ray Charles's "What'd I Say"—a musician's joke straight out of the jazz world. Finally, after more than 40 minutes of carrying the audience along on an incredible musical journey, the band returns to the theme one last time and "Mountain Jam" is over. It is the most apt title imaginable.

The same month the band played at Ludlow Garage, Duane went to Criteria Studios in Miami to work with Delaney & Bonnie & Friends. D&B had just lost their entire backing band to Joe Cocker, with the exception of keyboard man Bobby Whitlock. But it was time for a new album, so Delaney pulled together the best musicians he could find under the circumstances, including Jerry Scheff and Ronnie Tutt, the bass player and drummer from Elvis Presley's TCB band.

"I was excited about recording Delaney & Bonnie," says Jerry Wexler, "but they came down without [drummer] Jim Keltner and [bassist] Carl Radle. They came with Tutt and Scheff—very routine rhythm players. They were downbeat players. They didn't understand syncopation. So then Delaney said to me, 'Why don't you get Ry Cooder?' Ry was a good friend of mine. I called Ry, and Ry couldn't do it. I said to Delaney, 'I got somebody that you won't regret.' So I brought Duane in."

"Jerry brought Duane down," recalls Whitlock, "and wow, what a great player he was—a big happy smile and you fell in love with him right away. He was all serious about playing; sat down and played some serious slide guitar. It was just totally awesome. What he had found out through records that he had listened to, studying Robert Johnson and Elmore James, all of that was pouring through him. It wasn't coming from him; it was coming through him—that pure essence.

"There was instant camaraderie. He was one of those people who you felt you had always known from the instant you met him. [After that session] anytime Duane was available he was always with us, because he just loved Delaney & Bonnie. He was pretty much a constant, popping in and out of our lives."

On the album that would be titled *To Bonnie from Delaney*, Duane played acoustic slide on a medley of "Come On in My Kitchen," "Mama, He Treats Your Daughter Mean," and "Going Down the Road Feeling Bad," as well as electric slide on "Soul Shake"—the song that would become Delaney & Bonnie's first hit.

After such high points as the Ludlow Garage gigs and playing on the De-laney & Bonnie sessions, the month of April ended with one of the low points in Duane's professional life. On the 28th, the band had played a show on the campus of the State University of New York at Stony Brook. Their next show was more than 450 miles away in Buffalo at a place called Aliotta's Lounge. The band rode all night to get there. They played two shows on the 29th, leav-ing their gear at the club for the roadies to pick up the next day. When Kim Payne and Mike Callahan arrived at Aliotta's to load out and get the check for the previous night's performance, the club owner, Angelo Aliotta, refused to pay them. He claimed the band had shown up late for the show and told Payne and Callahan he would pay only if the Allman Brothers played again that night. Not only was Aliotta's demand preposterous, it was impossible—the band had to be in Cleveland on the following day.

Payne called tour manager Twiggs Lyndon and told him about the prob-lem. Twiggs went to the club and demanded the money from Aliotta. When the club owner still refused, a scuffle broke out. Lyndon pulled his knife and stabbed Aliotta three times. A short time later, Angelo Aliotta was dead and Twiggs Lyndon had been arrested on a charge of first-degree murder. It was a very dark day for the band. They had no choice but to travel on, leaving Lyndon in a Buffalo jail. Incredibly, he would later get off on a plea of temporary insan-ity due, in part, to his lawyer arguing that touring with the Allman Brothers Band was enough to drive anyone insane. A few moments of a virtually incoher-ent Berry Oakley on the witness stand helped to prove the lawyer's argument.

During short breaks from the constant touring, the band would get together with Dowd to continue work on their second album. "They didn't record an album in one sitting," recalled Dowd. "They would record maybe five songs. Then they might say, 'I don't think that song was good enough,' or, 'I don't think that song was ready to record.' Then among them, Duane being the leader, he would say, 'Okay, we'll work on it.' They wouldn't waste any more time doing it. They would work harder on the songs that were ready to go.

"They would have to go back out and then rehearse, and then . . . Phil would call me and say, 'Hey, the band is ready. Do you want to hear them?' I might zip into Macon or catch them on a gig someplace for a night, and then we'd go in the studio . . . because they *played* the songs into shape. It made the studio time shorter. That was generally the way it worked."

By 1970, most bands were taking advantage of the multi-track technology available to them. A rhythm track might be recorded first, followed by the vocals, with instrumental solos and other overdubs added after everything else was done. The order in which the tracks were laid down varied depending on the musicians and their producers, but seldom did a rock band go into a studio and record with the entire band playing together.

As usual, the Allman Brothers weren't interested in doing things the way everyone else did them. "Everything was cut live," said Dowd. "The only overdubbing would be to repair a guitar part where maybe somebody botched a note or something. There were at least five or six people playing simultaneously whenever we were recording, in a full setup like a live show. The idea is that part of the thing of the Allman Brothers is the spontaneity—the elasticity. The parts and the tempos vary in a way that only they are sensitive to."

Although they managed to get several tracks cut in early 1970, finishing the second album wasn't an easy task. "They had to get on the road to support themselves," Dowd recalled. "They were working 300 days a year. So they would just blow in and do some songs and blow out. That was it—in and out—just like that."

On top of the rigors of road life with the Allman Brothers, Duane was still being called upon to contribute to other artists' recording sessions. In those rare instances when the other members of the ABB could return to Macon for a short break, Duane was frequently heading to Muscle Shoals, Miami, or New York, earning session money wherever possible to help support the band. "Any sessions I do now," he said at the time, "I just go in there and do it and leave." Ironically, on one of his own sessions—recording overdubs for *Idlewild South*—he almost didn't leave soon enough.

On July 3, 1970, the Allman Brothers were booked to play at a three-day event billed as the Second Annual Atlanta International Pop Festival. The first AIPF had been held at the Atlanta International Raceway in Hampton, Georgia, but the locals decided one pop festival in the neighborhood was more than enough, leaving promoter Alex Cooley to find another home for this weekend of music. The venue he settled on was the Middle Georgia Raceway in the town of Byron, about 20 miles south of Macon. Governor Lester

Maddox didn't like that location either. He wrote the owner of the racetrack, emphatically (if redundantly) stating, "The best interests of the fellow citizens of Georgia would be served best by the immediate cancellation of the festival." Racetrack owner Lamar Brown declined the governor's request, paving the way for Cooley to put a fence around the track—a couple of dozen acres in all. The promoter also brought in hundreds of Port-A-Potties, as well as securing several hundred nearby acres as a campsite.

"The people had more of a tribal concept about themselves at that time," Dickey Betts once said. "People gathered a week before the music started—to camp and just make ready for the festival." Attending the festival wasn't just about hearing the music, said Betts. "It was more like a celebration of life."

By the time of the second AIPF, the Allman Brothers were practically superstars in the state of Georgia. Prior to the ABB, successful rock bands had emanated from San Francisco, New York, Los Angeles, and other parts of the country. The South had produced a host of notable R&B and soul artists, but a Southern band that played rock and had a record deal and a growing following—that was unheard of. The band's fellow Southerners were proud of their home-state heroes, so Cooley—a promoter who knew his audience—booked the Allman Brothers to open the festival on July 3rd and then take the stage again to close it two days later.

For everybody but Duane, getting to Byron required only a short drive from the Big House in the band's new Winnebago. Duane, on the other hand, had a slightly longer haul—almost 600 miles. After the Allman Brothers had finished a gig at the North Georgia Fairgrounds in Marietta on June 26, Duane had driven to Miami to do overdubs on *Idlewild South* at Criteria. He left South Florida early enough to give him plenty of time to get to Byron—but he hadn't counted on the Woodstock-like traffic jam he encountered as he drew closer to the venue. As the minutes ticked away, it became clear that his Ford Galaxie wasn't going to make it through the backup that stretched for miles along the highway. A motorcycle on the other hand. . . .

Duane pulled into a truck stop, hailed a ride on the back of a bike, and arrived at the Second Annual Atlanta International Pop Festival only moments before the band was due to hit the stage.

The Allman Brothers, along with Thom Doucette (the harmonica player Dickey "kept running into" in Florida back in the pre-Second Coming days), pulled out all the stops for their first set: "Statesboro Blues," "Trouble No More," "Don't Keep Me Wonderin'," "Dreams," "Every Hungry Woman," "Hoochie Coochie Man," "In Memory of Elizabeth Reed," and "Whipping Post" kept the crowd of more than 100,000 people on their feet. But when it came time for the Brothers to close their part of the show with "Mountain Jam," the festival took on another Woodstock-like overtone when—ten minutes into the song—the skies opened up and the rain came down hard. With no awning over the stage, the band had no choice but to stop and wait. With no music, the crowd got restless. There were still plenty of people stuck on the other side of the entrance gates, and in short order—as had been the case at Woodstock—Alex Cooley decided the best solution was to simply let everybody in for free and turn the weekend into a much less profitable event than he had originally hoped it would be. When the rain subsided, the Allman Brothers returned to the stage and played another six-and-a-half minutes of "Mountain Jam" before calling it a day.

Throughout the weekend, Duane had a ball hanging out and jamming with some of the other acts. Many of the Woodstock headliners were there, including Jimi Hendrix, Country Joe & the Fish, Sly & the Family Stone, Richie Havens, John Sebastian, and Johnny Winter, as well as Jethro Tull, Procol Harum, the Chambers Brothers, B.B. King, It's A Beautiful Day, and more.

When the Allman Brothers returned to the main stage to wrap up the weekend, the crowd had swelled to nearly half a million. The set list was quite a bit shorter than it had been for the opening show, most likely due to the fact that it was nearly four in the morning when the band started playing. Once again they closed with "Mountain Jam," this time with Johnny Winter sitting in.

Less than two weeks later, the Allman Brothers were headlining the Love Valley Rock Festival in North Carolina. This time, depending on who's telling the story, the crowd numbered anywhere from 20,000 to 75,000 people. The festival was the brainchild of Love Valley's founder and mayor, Andy Barker. In 1954, he had built an entire Western-themed town in the foothills of the Blue Ridge Mountains, prompted by his childhood dream of being a cowboy. At the time the festival was held, Love Valley consisted of a saloon, a church, and a general store. The sidewalks were made of wood, with hitching posts for horses. It was Barker's utopian experiment—a "Christian community" in a rural area of the state.

When Barker's daughter had heard about the upcoming festival in Byron, she asked her dad if she could go. "No, honey," he replied, "we'll hold our own music festival here instead." It was a bold and daring move for the deeply religious Barker, but he pulled it off by bringing in primarily Southern acts, many of which were Capricorn artists. The festival was held July 17–19 and featured the Allman Brothers, Wet Willie, Johnny Jenkins, and Tony Joe White. Barker even flew in the post-Janis Joplin version of Big Brother & the Holding Company from San Francisco.

The Allman Brothers played sets at Love Valley on both the 17th and 19th, then headed to New York for a gig in Central Park. While there, they continued working on *Idlewild South*.

"Now, *Idlewild South* was done in Miami and Macon, except 'Please Call Home' was done in New York with Joel Dorn producing," recalled Tom Dowd. "Joel was doing predominantly jazz recordings for Atlantic."

"I started making records in the mid-'60s when I was still a disc jockey in Philly," says Dorn. "Then I started to do some things for Nesuhi [Ertegun, brother of Atlantic Records founder Ahmet Ertegun]. Then, in June 1967, I came to Atlantic full time. All of a sudden some of my jazz albums started to sell, and they crossed over into R&B, and I started to catch a groove. The reason I mention that is because I was in a strange area of jazz-ish R&B, R&B-ish jazz, or something. I started using non-jazz sidemen, so I'd use [guitarists] Eric Gale, Cornell Dupree—guys like that—and I started hearing about Duane. Everybody who worked with him was talking about him, so I thought, 'I'd like to meet this guy.'

"I'm doing a session one day, and this guy walks in and says [Dorn puts on a Southern drawl], 'Are you Joel Dorn?' and I said, 'Yeah.' He said, 'I'm Duane Allman.' I said, 'Oh man, nice to meet ya. I've been hearing so many great things about you.' Now, I don't know if I'd heard him play or not. I'd just heard *about* him. I think he had just played on an Aretha session. We started talking. The odd thing was that I'd figured, 'Well, if I ever get a chance to meet this guy, I'd love to have him play on a record, say, with Fathead Newman or Hank Crawford—something where a great Southern blues guitarist would really fit.'

"The first thing he said to me was, 'Man, I would really like to make a record with Rahsaan.' That was Rahsaan Roland Kirk. And that's the last person in the world I'd think someone like Duane Allman would ask to make a record with, so it struck me as odd. And then he said, 'Yeah, I like the stuff you made with him, and I like that stuff you made with Yusef Lateef.' So I figured, 'Wow!

This guy is not your typical Southern R&B player.' This was a whole different thing. So we started hanging out a little bit when he would come to New York. We had a lot of common interests in music."

Only months after his initial meeting with Duane, Dorn found himself in the producer's chair for the Allman Brothers. "As I remember it," says Dorn, "Tommy Dowd was stuck down south and the band was in New York. Tommy said to Duane, 'Look, I can't get up there,' and Duane said, 'Well, this is the only time we can record.' So Tommy called me and said, 'Listen, I asked Duane who he wanted to work with and he said you, so would you do a session with the Allman Brothers?' I said, 'Of course I would.' It would turn out to be the only chance I ever really had to work with Duane.

"We did the sessions at Regent Sound, where I did most of my recording. I know we cut two things; we might have done a third. But the only one that made the album was 'Please Call Home.' I did the session and then Tommy, of course, did the mixing because it was his album.

"As the producer of that track, I had little to do with forming it. I was following Duane's lead. The reality of it is that I was coming in basically doing somebody a favor—being available just to guide 'em through some New York waters. It wasn't like I said, 'Hey guys, here's what we're gonna do.' I just said to Duane, 'You know what you wanna do?' He said, 'Yeah.' I said, 'Let me nail it for ya.' I just tried to capture what it was that they did. I did the track, and on my résumé I can say I worked with the Allman Brothers. It was just that one cut, but it turned out pretty well."

While in New York during the Dorn-produced sessions, the Allman Brothers played the Schaefer Music Festival in Central Park. The New York trip also gave Duane the chance to help Delaney & Bonnie finish the album they had begun working on in April at Criteria. Allman's work on the Miami recordings had been impressive, but his finest slide playing with D&B would come during a session at Decca Studios in Manhattan. The only holdover from the backing musicians in Miami (by this time even Bobby Whitlock was gone), Allman unleashed a slashing slide solo on the Delaney-penned rave-up "Living on the Open Road." It could have been Duane's theme song.

The Schaefer Music Festival had started in June and would continue through most of August. Acts of virtually every musical genre were on the bill. Along with the Allman Brothers, the performers included Ray Charles, Peggy Lee, Dave Brubeck, Miles Davis, Jethro Tull, Iron Butterfly (with Larry Rheinhart, formerly of the Second Coming, on guitar), Ike & Tina Turner, the Four Seasons, the Supremes, Buddy Rich, Little Richard, and many more—including Delaney & Bonnie & Friends on a bill with Seals & Crofts.

Delaney & Bonnie's show took place on August 5, and Duane was there. That night, sitting in his apartment overlooking Central Park, jazz flutist Herbie Mann was so taken by what he was hearing that he made his way to the stage—flute in hand—and joined in. Mann and Allman immediately took to each other musically, improvising solos that stirred the crowd into demanding a number of encores.

After the show, Herbie cornered Duane. "I told him I'd love to have him play on my next album. He said, 'Sure!' Now some people will call him a rock & roll guitarist, but basically he was a Southern blues improviser," Mann recalled years later. "He was a wonderful player, and he had the kind of feeling that I wanted on my records." (Mann was always open to using innovative guitarists, including Sonny Sharrock—inventor of the "machine gun" guitar solo—who appeared on a number of Mann's recordings.)

It would be almost a year before Duane would be able to make good on his promise to play on an album with Herbie Mann. The road was calling, and there were other sessions to do. But after years of listening to Miles and Trane, Duane looked forward to the opportunity to make a record with a genuine jazz musician.

One day during the making of *Idlewild South*, Tom Dowd got a phone call from Eric Clapton's manager. "Normally when there is a recording session," Dowd recalled, "I don't take phone calls. I just shun that kind of nonsense. But if Ahmet Ertegun or Jerry Wexler called, then they put the call through. When they interrupted and said there was a call, I thought, 'All right, who is it?' They said it was Robert Stigwood. I thought, 'Holy cow . . . I haven't spoken to this man in two or three years. What the hell does he want now?'

"So, in the middle of the session, while the Allman Brothers are recording, I just turned the monitor down and took the call and listened to Robert. The band finished playing and they were looking in the control room. Here I am with my head down, with the phone in my ear. They thought I was crazy. I was

getting this input on what . . . Robert wanted me to entertain doing. When I finished speaking, I put the phone down and half the guys were wandering into the control room.

"I said to Duane, 'I apologize. I do not normally take phone calls, but that was Robert Stigwood and he was asking me if I had time to record Eric Clapton in a couple of weeks.' Duane lit up like a Christmas tree, and he says, 'You mean the guy from Cream? If we're in town can I come by? I want to see him.' I said, 'Of course. He seems to be a nice guy, and the two of you would get along fine.'"

It had taken almost half a year and three recording studios in three different cities, but by the end of July the Allman Brothers' second album was finally done. Side One of the original vinyl version of *Idlewild South* opens with a song that perfectly encapsulates the message that Duane and the band were trying to get across. Entitled "Revival," it's Dickey Betts's first composition to appear on an Allman Brothers record. Surprisingly, the opening bars are played on an acoustic six-string, but it's soon joined by the familiar sound of Duane and Dickey's dual lead electric guitars. The melodic theme is similar to "Jesus Is Just Alright," a song that had appeared on the Byrds' album *The Ballad of Easy Rider* the previous year. The introduction is so long that first-time listeners might have thought the opening track was an instrumental, as had been the case on the Allman Brothers' debut album. But a little more than a minute-and-a-half into "Revival," Gregg begins singing the first verse with its uplifting message that "love is everywhere." When everyone joins in on the chorus, the song takes on a gospel feel that becomes even more pronounced when old-fashioned church-like hand clapping begins. There are rapid-fire solos on the bass, electric guitar, organ, and acoustic guitar before everyone but the drummers falls out. The chorus line is sung a cappella by the group as Gregg's gospel-shout vocals wail over the top, and then all of the instruments come back to repeat the theme one last time.

Lest anyone mistakenly assume that the first song was a signal that the Allman Brothers have become too happy to play the blues, "Don't Keep Me Wonderin'" is a strong reminder of the band's roots. The introduction is a brilliant meshing of Duane's slide guitar and Thom Doucette's harmonica: the harp and guitar slide up to the first note in unison before the whole band joins in. Gregg sings two verses about the strange way his woman has been acting lately before Duane comes back with one of his most succinct slide solos on record. Gregg returns with one more verse before Duane takes a second solo that rides out the rest of the song. At one point he slides up to the G above high C, hammering away on that single note for two-and-a-half measures before a flurry of 16th-notes leads back into the rest of his solo. Other bands might have allowed the song to simply fade out, but the Allman Brothers slam to a close. As Dowd pointed out, this was a band that played live in the studio, and "Don't Keep Me Wonderin'" is an excellent example of how well the process worked.

The next track, "Midnight Rider," is among the very best of Gregg's compositions. Co-written by roadie Kim Payne, it's the tale of a desperate man on the run. According to Gregg, the lyrics weren't based on anyone in particular. "It wasn't like a 'who' or 'what.' It seemed like the type of thing you'd listen to when you're traveling—I've always kind of dug that. The track was laid, and the lyrics just kind of found their way into the groove." The song is primarily acoustic. It's an unexpectedly mellow piece for a rock band—especially *this* rock band. It would later be a hit for Joe Cocker, Willie Nelson, and even for Gregg

Elizabeth Reed Napier's tombstone—inspiration for Dickey's song "In Memory of Elizabeth Reed"

himself when it was released as a single from his first solo album. It would go on to be covered by Bob Seger, Alison Krauss, Stephen Stills, Waylon Jennings, Hank Williams Jr., and many others. It *should* have been the Allman Brothers Band's first smash-hit single, but when the 45 came out, it inexplicably failed to touch the charts at all.

The A-side closes with Dickey's second contribution to *Idlewild South*, "In Memory of Elizabeth Reed." It's the first studio recording of a piece that had already become an important staple of the band's live act. The instrumental opens with Gregg's organ, Berry's bass, Butch on drums, and Jaimoe on congas. Duane and Dickey enter, playing the melody line together. "Elizabeth Reed" goes through a couple of tempo changes and some tricky melodic work before Dickey takes the first solo. This is, by far, the most complex composition the band had attempted to tackle up to that time. Dickey's playing is followed by a tranquil organ solo from Gregg—and then Duane takes the song to a higher plane before Butch and Jaimoe are featured via a brief drum/conga duet. The whole band returns to reiterate the theme before concluding the song.

Years later, Dickey would comment, "From the beginning, we were influenced by the jazz players. Just go back and listen to 'Elizabeth Reed,' and I think that will be clear." Another influence on the song was Rose Hill Cemetery, the final resting place of one Elizabeth Reed Napier. Betts originally wrote the piece as a tribute to a woman he was secretly seeing at the time, but he chose not to put her name in the title, he says, "because I didn't want to get shot."

The second side opens with Berry Oakley's Johnny Winter-inspired vocal showcase, "Hoochie Coochie Man." Cut less than two decades after Muddy Waters made his landmark recording of the Willie Dixon composition, the Allman Brothers' version is almost twice as fast, and everyone sounds hell-bent on plowing through the song with as much intensity as possible. There's no room for congas here. Both drummers pound their kits from beginning to end. Oakley sings lyrics that are only an approximation of what Dixon originally wrote, but no one seems to care. This track is all about feel, and by the time it's over the Allman Brothers have proven they can play blues-rock better than any band around.

The Joel Dorn-produced "Please Call Home" is such a stark contrast to the song that preceded it, it's almost a shock to the senses. A beautiful ballad with gut-wrenching vocals by Gregg, "Please Call Home" ranks among the younger Allman's finest songs. If "Midnight Rider" hadn't been on the same album, *this* is the song that might have gotten all the cover versions. Duane's mournful guitar work behind Gregg's singing exemplifies why he was in such demand as a session player. No matter what style of song was being performed, he always seemed to be able to create the perfect accompaniment.

The album ends on an uptempo note with "Leave My Blues at Home." After opening with Gregg playing a gospel-like acoustic piano intro, the drums and guitars come in, quickly turning "Leave My Blues at Home" into an almost straight funk piece. Gregg sings two verses and a bridge—with lyrics so esoteric, only he seems to know what he's talking about—before the two guitarists break into a twin lead melody that recalls the guitar riff of "Revival," beautifully tying the entire album together. Butch and Jaimoe share a short drum feature that takes Gregg into the final verse, and then Duane and Dickey trade lightning licks as the song slowly fades out.

The second album's title refers to a house near Macon that the band had rented at one time. Scott Boyer and Chuck Leavell would later take up residence there. "It was like a hunting cabin," says Boyer. "The back of the house had a porch that was built out over a manmade lake that was maybe five or six acres. It was a cabin made out of old pinewood, and it had been there a long time. The floor had sort of a 'manta ray' thing going on. It sloped down from the fireplace—which was in the middle of the house—and came up at the edges. It had one bedroom, and there was a kitchen that you'd have to walk through to get to the bedroom. Then there was one big room that had a bathroom in the near corner. I don't know exactly how old the place was, but it looked like it had been around for a while.

"The Allman Brothers used it as a rehearsal facility—that and a place to go maybe to consume a little something that wasn't quite legal. There were parties out there. It was in the middle of 130 acres of land—there weren't any houses next door for anybody to hear what you were doing. Hell, they had target practice out there. Butch almost shot his foot off one night practicing a quick-draw. When I moved in, there was a hole in the floor next to the fireplace where he'd been practicing. He accidentally pulled the trigger while the gun was in the holster, and the bullet went in the floor about a half-inch outside of his foot. It didn't hurt him, but if his foot had been over a couple of inches, it would've been bad."

The house got its name from the constant flow of people coming and going. Prior to being renamed JFK, New York's international airport had been called Idlewild. Thus, with so many folks constantly passing through the Allman Brothers' rehearsal and party house, the band had christened it "Idlewild South."

After all of the work on the second album was done, Duane shrugged his shoulders and said, "You know, a great record is easy to make. I ain't impressed by great records—but a great *performance* isn't so easy." Despite everything he had accomplished, there was still new ground to break. The Allman Brothers Band had made two very good records. Now Duane's dream was to find a way to capture the band's ferocious power in a live setting and put *that* on vinyl—the perfect marriage of a great record and a great performance. It was only a matter of time.

CHAPTER SEVENTEEN

Duane, Eric & *Layla*

"I'm as satisfied with my work on Layla *as I could possibly be. I was glad to have the opportunity to work with people of that magnitude—with that much brilliance and talent."* — D.A.

By August 1970, Eric Clapton was being hailed as one of the greatest guitarists of all time. Clapton's résumé was, in many ways, the history of British blues-rock. After gaining star status as a member of the Yardbirds, he left the band in 1965 to become one of John Mayall's Bluesbreakers. After that came Cream, the power trio with Jack Bruce on bass and Ginger Baker on drums. (The very concept that Phil Walden had originally envisioned for Duane's band, although the guitarist wisely chose not to move in that direction.) Tom Dowd first hooked up with Clapton in 1967 when he engineered Cream's second album, *Disraeli Gears*—the classic LP that included "Tales of Brave Ulysses," "Strange Brew," and "Sunshine of Your Love." Dowd worked with the trio again on their next release, the half-studio/half-live double album *Wheels of Fire*, which featured "White Room," "Crossroads," and a nearly 17-minute take on "Spoonful"—the latter two songs having coincidentally been recorded by the Allman Joys some two years earlier.

Cream disbanded in late 1968 and was followed shortly thereafter by Clapton's next group, Blind Faith. Frequently referred to as the first rock "supergroup," Blind Faith consisted of Clapton and Baker from Cream, Steve Winwood from Traffic, and the lesser-known Rick Grech from the equally lesser-known band Family. Blind Faith released one album in 1969 and went on tour that same year. Clapton was growing restless, though. Although his fame was based on his blazing electric guitar work—thus the intentionally ironic nickname "Slowhand"—his ears had begun to catch the beauty of the subtle ensemble work of The Band.

In the summer of 1969, Delaney & Bonnie & Friends were touring with Blind Faith. Although George Harrison has frequently been credited for bringing Delaney & Bonnie to Clapton's attention, Bobby Whitlock disagrees. "Opening up for Blind Faith—that's where we met Eric the first time. I don't care what anybody says, but George never came into the picture until we were actually on tour."

Perhaps the "anybody" Whitlock is referring to is his old bandmate, Delaney Bramlett. "When George came to see us with Alan Pariser, I got to say hi to him," Bramlett told interviewer Dave Kyle. (Whitlock strongly disagrees: "It was Gram Parsons who came with Alan Pariser. If it had been George Harrison, I would've jumped over my keyboards to meet him.") "Pariser came up to me," continued Bramlett, "and said, 'Can I manage your group? I think I have a way to get you started.' That was when Jerry Wexler had said he wanted the act. I told Pariser we were getting ready to do some stuff with Atlantic Records, and he said, 'Well, I know Jerry. Let me see if I can work something out.' Then he asked if I knew of a group called Blind Faith, which of course I did. He said, 'What do you think about me arranging for you to be the opening act for them?' That looked like a pretty good opportunity."

"We opened for Blind Faith and blew 'em away everywhere we played," says Whitlock. "It was all about Delaney & Bonnie. You gotta understand, the band was Jim Keltner, Jim Gordon, Jim Price, Bobby Keys, Rita Coolidge, Leon Russell, me, Delaney & Bonnie, and J. J. Cale. It was a pretty stout band. We were a tough act to follow—and Eric loved us. We were hanging out in hotel rooms, playing and doing 'that thing' before the gig, after the gig, on airlines, on the bus. Wherever we were, we were playing and singing, no matter what. Eric liked the whole camaraderie of it."

"About four or five shows into that tour," Bramlett recalled, "Eric asked me, 'Would you mind if I come out and just jam with you guys while you're playing tonight?' I said, 'No, I don't mind at all. That's how I put the group together. It's called "Friends," so come on and play.' Pretty soon, every show he was out there picking with us, you know, riding on the bus with us—jamming and having *fun*! Finally, he said, 'Can I join your band? Would you take me as your guitar player?'"

"We were in Toronto," Whitlock says. "We were opening for Blind Faith, and Delaney pointed at Eric and said, 'What do you think about him playing guitar with us?' I went, '*What?*' He said, 'Yeah, what do you think about him playing in our band?' I said, 'Well, he's going to have to do something about those pink pants, that's for sure.' He had on pink silk pants and high-heel boots and his hair all frizzed out."

After Blind Faith broke up in October 1969, Clapton got rid of the pink pants and became one of Delaney & Bonnie's "Friends," formally joining the band for some dates in Europe. His decision resulted in the awkwardly titled album *Delaney & Bonnie & Friends on Tour with Eric Clapton*—and, ultimately, in the formation of Derek & the Dominos.

In January 1970, Clapton went in the studio with all of Delaney & Bonnie's then-current band members—including Leon Russell, Carl Radle, Bobby Whitlock, and Jim Gordon—to make his first solo album, *Eric Clapton*. It was cut at Village Recorders in L.A., with Delaney producing and Bonnie singing background vocals, and there to mix the finished product was none other than Tom Dowd.

Clapton then headed back to England to be a guest artist on other people's records while waiting for his own album to come out. Meanwhile, most of Delaney & Bonnie's Friends had apparently ceased feeling very friendly toward the Bramletts. The split primarily had to do with money (what else?), and the entire gang left D&B to become much of the band on Joe Cocker's Mad Dogs & Englishmen tour. That is, the entire gang except Bobby Whitlock.

Bobby had been with Delaney & Bonnie from the beginning, playing on their first album, *Home*, recorded at Stax Studios in 1968. The other musicians on those Memphis sessions had included the usual Stax crew: Booker T. Jones, Donald "Duck" Dunn, Al Jackson Jr., and Steve Cropper. Two years later, Whitlock was starting to regret having stuck with D&B while everyone else was off partying with Joe Cocker. The proverbial straw that broke the camel's back, according to Whitlock, took place on US 101. "They got in a fight [in the car], and she grabbed the keys and threw them out on the Ventura Freeway at like 3:30 in the afternoon—traffic just blocked everywhere. She grabs the keys and throws them out. I'm in the middle of the two of them fighting, and I said, 'Oh man, I can't take any more of this.'

"So I called Cropper and said, 'I gotta get out of here. They're making me nuts.' He said, 'Why don't you go see Eric?' I said, 'I don't have any money.' Delaney paid me $96.50 a week and $12 per diem when we were on the road. I wasn't in there to make money. I was in there for the music. Money was not my complaint, but it seemed to be everybody else's complaint. I was in there for all this great music. So I said, 'I don't have any money.' He said, 'Well, call Eric and see what he's doing. Ask him about you coming over to visit. Go over and hang out with him a little bit.' So I said, 'Okay.'

"I called up Eric and said, 'What are you doing?' He said, 'I'm getting my hair cut.' I said, 'I need to get out of here. These people are making me nuts. Can I come visit?' He said, 'Sure, come on over.' He didn't think I was serious. So I called Steve Cropper back and said, 'He said, "Come on over."' Cropper said, 'Well, I'll have you a ticket there tomorrow.' The next morning there was a ticket at the airlines waiting for me. That afternoon I went and caught a plane. I didn't have but about $150, and I planned on just going over for a few days and hanging with Eric. That was it.

"When I showed up, he couldn't believe I was there. I said, 'Well, you *said*, "Come on over!"' So I was hanging with Eric and we were just playing and singing and having a good time. It was like two days later when he said, 'Let's put a band together.' And I said, 'Great!' Everybody was still out with Mad Dogs & Englishmen. So we went in and talked with his manager at the time, Robert Stigwood, and Eric said, 'Bobby and I are going to put a band together, but we need some cash.' So we got us a cash flow going. He had one already, but I didn't. I wasn't hip to all that. But we got a few pounds in our pockets, and we sat around and played and sang."

While formulating their plan, Whitlock and Clapton stayed busy with session work. "We did P. P. Arnold sessions, Doris Troy sessions, all sorts of different things, Eric and I," says Bobby. "I lived with him for six months out at [his country house] Hurtwood Edge. We talked about having Jim Gordon and Carl Radle in our band. Actually, Jim Keltner was going to be our drummer—I made the phone call to him, but he was doing a Gabor Szabo album. Jim Gordon and

Carl had just come off the road from Mad Dogs & Englishmen. Eric and I, we were just chomping at the bit, ready to play."

And then came a call from George Harrison. "When it came time to do *All Things Must Pass*, George said something to Eric about, 'What's the possibility of getting Jim and Carl and Bobby?' And Eric said, 'I imagine it'll work.' We were the core band for *All Things Must Pass*. Had it not been for Steve Cropper, odds are none of that would've ever happened."

The quartet of Clapton, Whitlock, Radle, and Gordon were soon to be known as Derek & the Dominos. In fact, the band cut a single—"Tell the Truth" b/w "Roll It Over"—using Harrison's producer, Phil Spector, while the *All Things Must Pass* sessions were in progress. "It was just entirely too fast," Whitlock says of that recording. "We did it with Phil Spector's Wall of Sound, and it just was not us at all. We withdrew the single and upset everybody, but we could because, hey, that wasn't us. It sounded terrible and wasn't a good representation of the band. We didn't even mean for that to come out. We recorded it and then the label put it out. So we said, 'Pull that thing now!'"

"Tell the Truth," which would appear in its better-known version on Derek & the Dominos' *Layla and Other Assorted Love Songs*, was an early Whitlock/Clapton composition. "We were always jamming," says Bobby, "and I had written 'Tell the Truth'—all but one part of the last verse. See, Duane had showed me all these open tunings. I was breaking strings left and right trying to get open *C*, open *D*, open *A*. When Duane was playing, his thing was open *E*, and that's a pretty standard open tuning. I was messing around with it out at Eric's place one afternoon, different inversions, trying to make something. So with 'Tell the Truth,' all of those chords, everything is backwards. I was up all night writing this thing."

Between hearing strings snap and listening to Whitlock laboring over the song until dawn, Clapton had gotten very little sleep. "The next morning I told Eric, 'Man, I've got this great song!' and he says, 'I know! I know! I already have my part,'" says Whitlock. "Then he hit me with the last part of the last verse, and that was it. That's how that particular song came together."

With Harrison's album in the can, Derek & the Dominos began the first leg of a U.K. tour. Meanwhile, even though Cream was gone, there were still recordings to be exploited, resulting in the release of *Live Cream* in April 1970.

Right on its heels, Clapton's solo album came out. What better time than now to have Robert Stigwood call Tom Dowd and set up a recording session at Criteria Studios? (This was the phone call Dowd had taken in the middle of one of the *Idlewild South* recording sessions.)

Clapton, Whitlock, Radle, and Gordon arrived at Criteria in August and went to work. They had been there only a few days when Tom Dowd's phone rang again. As Dowd recalled in his interview with Bill Ector, "It's Duane, and he says, 'Hey man, are they there?' I said, 'Yeah, they're here.' He said, 'We're going to be playing tonight. Can I come by?' I said, 'It's not a problem. We'll have a ball.'

"I put the phone down and thought, 'I'd better pump Clapton.' So when he went by, I said, 'Hey, Eric, there's a guitar player chap from a band called the Allman Brothers that I record for Atlantic, and they were here a couple of weeks ago and they heard you were coming, and that was Duane on the phone.' Eric says, 'You mean the guy that plays on the back of "Hey Jude?"' I said, 'Yeah. There're doing a concert, and he would like to come by after the concert and see you play.' And Eric looked at me and said, 'I want to see *him* play! When are they playing?' I said, 'In about an hour.' He says, 'Let's go.'

"So we go down to the concert. They had this barricade set up with sand-bags and four-foot-high railings for the photographers and so forth. We crawled in on our hands and knees and sat with our backs propped up against the barricade, so we were three feet from the stage looking almost straight up. When we walked in and sat down like that, Duane was playing a solo and the band was grinding along pretty good. Duane turned around, opened his eyes, and stopped dead in the middle of the solo. Dickey is chugging away on rhythm, and he doesn't know why Duane stopped."

Betts looked at Duane, saw him staring down at someone, followed his eyes to Clapton, and then turned to face his amp—knowing he'd be unable to play, too, if he had to watch Clapton watching him. "Duane and Dickey like to fell down," Whitlock says, laughing. "They looked out and there was Eric and me and Jim and Carl and Tom." As it turned out, Duane Allman had no reason to be nervous. "Eric was completely blown away," Whitlock says. "It was nothing for me, because I'd been knowing and playing with Duane for a couple of years."

"They go through the rest of the show," Dowd recalled. "The show is over, then we all meet backstage and we're talking, and I said, 'Well, we're going back to the studio because we have to listen to a couple of more things we were working on today.' Duane says, 'Can I come by?' By the time we got to the studio, it was probably 12:30. Along with Duane came the whole goddamn band! All of a sudden there's Eric and Duane and they're strapping on guitars and trading licks and showing each other, 'No, no—put it on this string—do it this way—this is how . . .' And they're swapping stories with each other while they're playing. I said, 'Hey, keep tape on the machine. Just keep it rolling.' Into the morning and on into the early afternoon, they were still chopping along with each other. They had a good time, and they were talking and swapping instruments and doing all kinds of things. Two kindred spirits met."

"They came and jammed and it was that brotherly love thing right away," recalls Whitlock. "They recorded a bunch of it. I remember Gregg did some piano. I played piano. I played organ. And it was just a bunch of all-nighter stuff you know, just jamming, jamming, jamming."

Sometime over the course of the night and day while the two bands were hanging together at Criteria, Dowd played some of the *Idlewild South* tapes for the assembled musicians. When Clapton heard Allman's slide playing on "Don't Keep Me Wonderin'," he knew he'd found the missing element his new band needed. "It was just immediate," says Whitlock. "Like, 'Hey man, this guy is great!'"

On August 28, the Allman Brothers were scheduled to play the first of a string of shows in Pensacola, so Duane had to move on. But before he could get out the door, Eric asked him to come back and play on the remaining sessions. Duane said he'd be back as soon as the stretch in Pensacola was over.

In his absence, the quartet cut "I Looked Away," Bell Bottom Blues," and "Keep on Growing." Upon Duane's return, the five musicians recorded the rest of the album. The Allman Brothers had more shows coming up—as usual—but Clapton's record wasn't finished yet. For the first and only time, Duane Allman voluntarily missed a couple of ABB concerts, opting to stay and play with Derek & the Dominos.

In a late-1970 interview with Ed Shane, Duane talked excitedly about his work on the album. "I was just going to play on one or two songs, and then as we kept on going, it kept developing. Incidentally, Sides One, Two, Three, and Four—all the songs are right in the order they were cut from the first day through to 'Layla,' and then 'Thorn Tree' was last on the album."

More than 35 years later, Bobby Whitlock remembers the sequencing just as Duane did: "If you listen to that album from the start to the end, everything is where it was and how it came about. It is exactly how it went down." The dates on the session sheets tell a different story, but it appears that whoever wrote down those dates wasn't always precise. On the "Layla" sheet, for example, the overdubs are boldly dated "10/1/70," which would have been impossible since the band (minus Duane) was back on the road for the second leg of their British tour at that time.

If the Allman and Whitlock accounts are accurate, the first piece Duane played on with Derek & the Dominos was "Nobody Knows You When You're Down and Out"—the song from the Scrapper Blackwell album that Bill McEuen had played for Duane back in the Hour Glass days. It was one of five covers on the album, the others being "Have You Ever Loved a Woman," "It's Too Late," "Little Wing," and "Key to the Highway"—the last beginning with a fade-up on Eric's guitar solo caused by an extremely rare faux pas on Tom Dowd's part.

Dowd was accustomed to producing the acts that arrived at Criteria, and he had expected that to be the case with Clapton and crew. But the band envisioned things otherwise from the beginning. "We had been in there hammering away and hammering away," explains Whitlock. "We were a band that had been on the road and we had all our stuff worked out. We produced the *Layla* album—the band did; Tom was executive producer.

"We were sitting out there playing away, and he walked out with all these charts one day. I looked at Eric and said, 'What the fuck is this?' He said, 'They're charts—we don't need these things!' I said, 'No, I can't even read 'em.' He said, 'Me neither.' We called Tom back in and I said, 'Hey Tom, what's up with this?' He said, 'I thought you guys needed some charts.' We said, 'Man, we just got through touring the whole of Great Britain. We know these songs inside out. We don't need any charts.' I told Eric, 'We gotta have a little powwow.' So we excused ourselves. We agreed that he needed to stay behind the glass. I said to Eric, 'Why don't we just talk to him—tell him to stay back there. We'll produce the record. He'll be executive producer, and all he needs to do is just make sure everything's turned on. And if anybody comes in here, whether it's you by yourself, me, Carl—whoever comes in—he'll turn on the tape. It's just tape. Then we'll have everything.'

"It was my suggestion to Eric to have Tom turn everything on and leave it on. The only time that he didn't was on 'Key to the Highway,' and that's why it fades into the song. That's the *only* time that he didn't have it on. Had we not recorded all of that, we wouldn't have had all those outtakes." (Several of the outtakes Whitlock refers to were released as two additional CDs of material on *The Layla Sessions: 20th Anniversary Edition* in 1990.)

As the *Layla* sessions progressed, so did the drug use. "There was a whole lot of nonsense that went down in the hotel," says Whitlock. "A lot of drugs went down, man. We were always experimenting—doing probably a whole lot more of everything than we should've. We were invincible, you know, according to us. That whole 'sex, drugs, and rock & roll' thing was more like 'drugs and rock & roll,' truth be known. I haven't known too many people who do a lot of drugs and drink a lot who have much sex. They didn't give us six months to live, and that included Eric, because during those sessions is when he started his heroin thing."

According to Clapton, the record label had booked the band into a hotel that turned out to have "a little nest of dealers in there who supplied us." After Ahmet Ertegun got word of how intense the drug use was becoming, he flew down to Miami and begged the band members to straighten out. But it was to no avail.

Tom Dowd later said: "I would be a blind, blind fool if I said that they didn't use drugs and that there weren't drugs there. I'd also stand up and say this about that collection of people: If we're breaking off tonight and I say, 'All right, two o'clock tomorrow, let's start,' I'm going to tell you, everybody was there between 1:30 and 1:45 waiting for two o'clock to make the first sound. They were ready to play. It didn't matter if it was Duane, Eric, or whoever—and I don't care if they went out the night before on a stretcher or in a police car. The next day they were there.

"These people accepted the responsibility of being entertainers and the responsibility of 'we've got this studio; we've got this chance; let's take advantage of it.' They weren't saying, 'You get here first because you take longer to tune up.' They weren't copping out on each other."

Eric Clapton and Duane during the recording of Layla and Other Assorted Love Songs

Among the ironies surrounding the *Layla* sessions was the band's decision to record Jimi Hendrix's "Little Wing." In the decades since the album's release, many pop music historians have presumed that this song was selected as a tribute to the late guitarist. In truth, though, Hendrix was still alive on the day they recorded the tune. His drug-related death didn't occur until Derek & the Dominos were back in England, just over a week after having recorded the song. "Eric and I were supposed to have been with Jimi Hendrix the night that he died," says Whitlock. "We both had a few too many of whatever it was that we were doing, and we didn't make it to be with Jimi that night."

In the years since his very public cleanup, Clapton has been outspoken about the dangers and pitfalls of drug abuse. He has even founded the Crossroads Centre, a drug rehab clinic in Antigua. But in September 1970, he and his bandmates were deep in the abyss. And Duane might have been the worst of the lot.

After his glue-sniffing when he was barely a teenager, Duane had quickly moved up the ladder through pot, speed, mushrooms, cocaine, and seemingly anything else he could get his hands on. According to Whitlock, he even recommended coke as the drug of choice when learning to play slide guitar. "I asked Duane, 'Man, how do you play slide so effortlessly?' And he says, 'Little brother, you can do this. It's just like seeing, man.' He tells me, 'There's a certain way to put your thumb up against the back of the neck, and it gives you a place to always come right back to.' He said, 'You can play every song that there is right here between these three frets.' And for sure, you can. Every symphony ever written was written between *C* and *C*, no matter what. But Duane's thing was like, 'I tell you what you do. You get you a fishing pole, a sack of cocaine, and some beers, and take your dobro and your slide and you go down by the creek and you sit there and you keep on. And one day you'll get it.' Well, I tried it and I gotta say that did *not* work!"

Despite Duane's substance abuse, Whitlock backs up Dowd's position on the guitarist's professionalism in the studio: "It was all business. When it came to playing, man, it was *all* business. There wasn't no bullshit coming down with Duane Allman. He was serious as all get-out. When it came to laying it down, he was your man. He was for real. It wasn't just a bunch of talk. He could back it up all day long—and all night."

Clapton would later refer to the *Layla* sessions as the starting point for what he called "the black-out years." His drug use at the time was exacerbated, at least in part, by falling in love with the wife of a close friend. Unfortunately, the friend in question was George Harrison. Clapton and Harrison had been pals for years by the time the *Layla* sessions began. Harrison had gotten Clapton to play lead guitar on the Beatles' recording of "While My Guitar Gently Weeps," and Clapton had returned the favor by asking Harrison to play rhythm guitar on Cream's "Badge." And then there were the *All Things Must Pass* sessions. Over the course of spending time with Harrison and his wife, Patti Boyd, Clapton had fallen head over heels for the beautiful young model. The immediate result was a collection of great songs and an attempt to ease the pain via heroin in a Miami hotel room.

If record sales and radio success are any indication of a great song, the greatest of all the compositions derived from Clapton's pent-up feelings for George's wife was "Layla." The song's title was taken from the female lead in the Persian poet Nizami's "The Story of Leyla and Mejnun." The poem tells the tale of Mejnun's love for the beautiful yet unattainable Leyla. Her unavailability—brought about by Leyla's parents' refusal to allow Mejnun to see her, no less marry her—drives the young man mad (*mejnun* being Arabic for "crazy").

Throughout the sessions at Criteria, Clapton was recording songs that expressed his silent love for Patti. "I Am Yours," "Why Does Love Got to be So Sad," even the old Freddie King hit "Have You Ever Loved a Woman"—they all told Clapton's story of frustration and sorrow over his inability to openly express his love for his friend's wife.

"Layla" was, without question, the most lyrical song on the album. But melodically it was pretty simple—three great verses in search of a hook. Clapton was desperately in need of a guitar line that would bring more life to the song. He had created some of the greatest guitar riffs in rock, but he was stuck when it came to "Layla." When Clapton told Allman of his dilemma, Duane went to work, soon coming up with the seven-note phrase that is now one of the best-known guitar licks in the history of rock: 16th-notes ascending from *A* to *C* to *D* to *F*, and then descending back down to *D* and *C* before returning to a long, vibrating *D*. It was exactly what "Layla" needed.

It would be some time before Clapton would find out that Allman's brilliant line wasn't entirely original. Duane had simply taken the first phrase of the melody from a blues ballad called "As the Years Go Passing By" and sped it up. "That's Albert King's lick," says Whitlock today. In point of fact, although the song appears on King's album *Born Under a Bad Sign* (where Duane probably heard it), the true composer of "As the Years Go Passing By" is open to debate. The song is credited to one Deadric Malone—a pseudonym frequently used by Don Robey (owner of the Houston-based Duke and Peacock record labels) upon having purchased a composition from a writer for a flat fee. "As the Years Go Passing By" was first cut in 1959 by blues singer-guitarist Fenton Robinson (the composer of "Loan Me a Dime" from Boz Scaggs's debut album). According to blues expert Jim O'Neal, Robinson always claimed that the true author of "As the Years Go Passing By" was another blues singer-guitarist named Peppermint Harris.

In truth, the actual number of composers who contributed to "Layla" (although officially credited to Eric Clapton and Jim Gordon) might be closer to half a dozen—not only because of the interpolation of "As the Years Go Passing By" but also due to the question of how many people were involved in the crea-

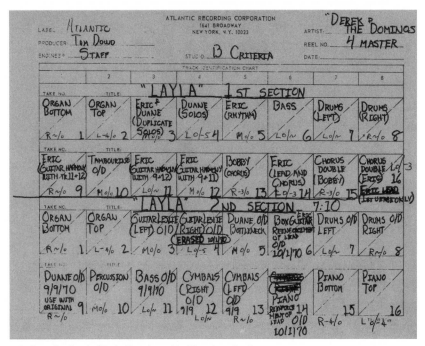

*Track sheet for "Layla," including the added "2nd section"
and an incorrect overdub date of "10/1/70"*

tion of the piano piece that makes up the second half of the song. Along with Gordon, two other writers are said to have contributed. "Rita Coolidge wrote that, when we were still with Delaney & Bonnie, up in John Garfield Jr.'s guest house," says Whitlock. "It was a song called 'Time.' The melody was actually a song, but Jim Gordon ripped it off." And according to another source, saxophonist Jim Horn deserves at least partial credit for the piece as well.

Eric Clapton told *Guitar Player* magazine, "Jim Gordon . . . had been secretly going back into the studio and recording his own album without any of us knowing it. . . . We caught him playing this one day and said, 'Come on, man. Can we have that?' So he was happy to give us that part. And we made the two pieces into one song."

"It was overdub time," says Whitlock. "Duane was there. Everybody was there, and they decided to put that part on. They stuck it together and that was that."

Duane had already played some remarkable slide solos on the album—particularly on the blues covers "Have You Ever Loved a Woman" and "Key to the Highway"—but his top-of-the-fretboard slide playing over the piano coda of "Layla" is now one of the most familiar solos in rock history. Eric and Duane both play slide guitars at the end of "Layla," with Duane's slide staying primarily on his high E string, seldom dropping below the upper frets of the B string. And, of course, those trademark birdcalls at the song's conclusion were created somewhere high above the E string's top fret.

A short time after the album's release, when an interviewer remarked that it was difficult at times to tell who was playing which solo, Duane responded, "Here's the way to really tell: He played the Fender and I played the Gibson. The Fender is a little bit thinner and brighter—a sparkling sound—while the Gibson is just a full-tilt screech."

"After the overdub session happened," says Whitlock, "that's when we did 'Thorn Tree in the Garden.' That was the very, very last thing that was done for that whole album, period."

"The thing about *Layla*, studio-wise—I don't think we spent as much as three weeks in the studio," said Dowd. "Then Duane and the Dominos had to go on their merry ways. We put a schedule together where I mixed the whole album down in their absence, and then they came back and listened. When the overdubs were done, we remixed them . . . and boom, it was done, and, 'That's it, goodbye, and put it out!'"

During and immediately after the recording of *Layla and Other Assorted Love Songs*, Clapton and Whitlock did their best to get Allman to come on board permanently. "Derek & the Dominos was a great band," says Whitlock. "Duane's addition to it just pulled that band together and made the whole thing unique. We tried to get him to leave the Allman Brothers but he wouldn't do it. He said, 'The only way I'll do it is if I can bring my brother.' I said, 'No, we don't need two keyboard players, but boy, you'd be a great addition.'" How could Duane argue with that logic? It was exactly what he had told Reese Wynans when Gregg had arrived in Jacksonville back in March 1969.

Duane had already missed a couple of Allman Brothers' gigs just to have the opportunity to record with Clapton, and the temptation to run off with a band fronted by one of his guitar heroes must have been strong. But in the end, as Clapton later said, "He had to be loyal to his family." As things turned out, it proved to be a wise decision.

The second leg of Derek & the Dominos' U.K. tour began on September 20 and ran through October 11. Four days later the band was in America, opening their U.S. tour in Trenton, New Jersey. The Fillmore East shows of October 23–24 were recorded for an eventual live album, and then the band headed west.

The following month, *Layla and Other Assorted Love Songs* was released on Atco. Whitlock says, "We did not record the *Layla* album to have a hit record and to make a lot of money"—which was a good thing, because it didn't exactly fly up the charts. Clapton's decision to hide behind the name "Derek" plus the fact that it was a double album hindered the record's potential sales.

"As I walked out of that studio," Dowd recalled, "I said, 'This is the best goddamn album I've been part of since *The Genius of Ray Charles.*' And then . . . nothing happened. It just sat there, and I thought, 'This is absurd.'"

The two-record set got good reviews, but it took a while for the general public to realize that Derek & the Dominos was actually Clapton, Allman, and the rest. Plus, when the single of "Layla" was released, it came out in an edited, under-three-minutes version—fading out more than 20 seconds before the piano coda even began. Despite its brevity, it was, perhaps, a bit too heavy for Top 40 radio—a world where the Carpenters and the Osmonds (whose bubblegum records were being produced by Rick Hall, of all people) were currently ruling the airwaves.

"The album wasn't promoted very well," says Whitlock. "That record was *never* promoted in the sense that record companies would usually get behind an album and do their thing."

After a gig on November 22 in San Diego, Clapton's group turned around and headed for the East Coast again, playing in Chicago, Cincinnati, St. Louis, Cleveland, and Owings Mill, Maryland. Finally having a short break from the Allman Brothers' constant road schedule, Duane caught up with the band at Curtis Hixon Hall in Tampa, Florida, on December 1, and then played with them again the next night in Syracuse, New York. Those two shows would turn out to be the only times Allman would have a chance to perform live with Derek & the Dominos. On December 6, the tour ended. Unbeknownst to anyone in the group, it would be their final concert.

In April 1971, Clapton, Whitlock, Radle, and Gordon went to Olympic Studios in London to begin work on a second studio album. They recorded "Got to Get Better in a Little While," "Evil," One More Chance," "Mean Old Frisco," and "Snake Lake Blues," but the atmosphere was all wrong. So wrong, in fact, that Clapton's reaction was to simply stop going to the studio. The drugs had finally won out over the music.

The truncated version of "Layla" had struggled about halfway up the Top 100 Singles chart before sliding back down and fading away. The album would eventually fare better, slowly but surely climbing into the Top 20. Sadly, Duane would already be gone for over half a year before mainstream radio finally caught on to the beauty and power of the full-length version of "Layla."

"It became a hit on its own," Whitlock says. "There was a guy at a college station who started playing the album cut over and over—like Dewey Phillips did [with Elvis's] 'That's Alright, Mama'—and it just took off. And the next thing you know, boom! But, you know, before this thing became a hit, the band had broken up and Duane was dead."

CHAPTER EIGHTEEN

The Fillmores, Part 2

*"We want people to listen with their eyes closed—
to just let the music come inside them so they
can forget their worldly cares."* — D.A.

As the Allman Brothers' popularity grew, Bill Graham continued to show-case the band at both Fillmores. Only days after Duane finished work on the *Layla* sessions, PBS affiliate WNET shot footage at the Fillmore East for a planned documentary. The lineup included the Allman Brothers, the Byrds, Albert King, Van Morrison, Elvin Bishop, and others. Duane and the band performed "Don't Keep Me Wonderin'," "Dreams," "In Memory of Elizabeth Reed," and "Whipping Post." It was one of the few times a performance by the Allman Brothers with Duane would be captured on film.

In the Fillmore footage, the front line from left to right is—as always—Gregg, Duane, Dickey, and Berry. Behind them, Jaimoe sits between Duane and Dickey, with Butch positioned between Betts and Oakley. It's an unusual configuration and one that emphasizes the band as a brotherhood. No other rock group prior to this had placed its primary lead vocalist off to the side of the stage, hidden behind a massive Hammond B-3. And despite the fact that Duane is obviously the leader—snapping his fingers to set the tempo and count off each song; using his guitar neck like a conductor's baton to bring each song to an end—he, too, chooses not to stand center stage.

The film is a fascinating glimpse into the band nearing its apex. There is so much interaction among the players, the various cameras never seem to know what to focus on. When one camera finally settles on showing the two drummers playing simultaneously—but playing completely different parts—it's difficult to take in. It looks as if it should sound cacophonous, but it all meshes perfectly. Another camera zeros in on the two guitarists standing next to each other and playing lead licks together, but the cameraman is soon stumped. He focuses on Dickey for a while until he figures out that it is the *other* guitar player who has suddenly taken off into the stratosphere.

Duane Allman, onstage, is a charismatic figure. He doesn't jump around like Mick Jagger or flail his arms like Pete Townshend. All of the movement is in his hands and not a motion is wasted. As the Coricidin bottle slides up and down the neck of his Les Paul, his pick-free right-hand fingers fly across the strings. But this is 1970—a time of flamboyant rock stars—so the camera pans up from his fingers and zooms in on his face. If the camera is hoping to find the requisite looks of pain and anguish, it won't find them here. There is expression in Duane's face, but it is a combination of concentration and serenity. As he plays a passage near the top of the neck, his brow furrows for a moment. Other times his mouth opens slightly, as if he's coaxing each note into its proper place.

"A cat comes to my band to pick, not to show off his fancy clothes," he will tell a reporter a few months later. "We want to share our music with the audience, but there's no stage show. This ain't no ballet." It might not be a ballet, but there is a gracefulness to what is going on among the musicians onstage that no other rock band of the day could match.

After Duane had finished his two-concert interlude with Derek & the Dominos, he met up with the rest of the Allman Brothers Band in Columbia, South Carolina, on December 4. The band opened for Johnny Winter And (the albino virtuoso's oddly named group with fellow guitarist Rick Derringer) at the Carolina Coliseum, and then moved on to the Music Factory in Greenville, North Carolina. Dates at the Fillmore East were coming up on December 11–12, so Duane headed to New York for a radio interview to promote the shows.

On December 9, Allman arrived at WABC-FM to chat with disc jockey Dave Herman. The general idea for the evening was to preview the Fillmore shows, talk a bit about the Allman Brothers and Derek & the Dominos, spin a few records, and take phone calls from listeners. But the interviewer's best-laid plans instantly flew out the window when Duane showed up late and out of it.

"I'm drunk, man," he told the DJ. When Allman attributed his condition to a bottle of Jack Daniel's, Herman calmly asked, "Black label or green?" "*Black* label, of course," Duane responded indignantly. "I'm from Tennessee, man. My grandfather washed his *feet* in Jack Daniel's."

For the next hour, Dave Herman had his hands full. Allman, who usually spoke slowly and articulately, was in overdrive. One has to suspect that much more than Jack Daniel's was at play. Duane did manage to subtly plug the upcoming dates by bragging about Betts ("If you've never heard him play, come down to the Fillmore this weekend, man, and hear him. I'm the famous one, man. *He's* the good player."). But there were other, more personal things on his mind.

In the most brutally honest statement he would ever make during any interview, Allman talked openly—perhaps much too openly—about his recently failed relationship with Donna, and about his daughter, Galadrielle. "I got rid of my old lady and my kid. I said, 'No old ladies, no kids, man. Just guitars.'

"She's a teenage queen," Duane continued. Herman, confused and perhaps sensing he was losing control of an interview that was turning into a monologue, asked, "Who's a teenage queen—your kid or your . . . ?"

"My old *lady*," Duane responded before Herman could even finish his question. "My kid is a *kid*. She's mine. She's part of me. You can see me in her. I look at her and say, 'Hey, me. How you doin'?'

"Children are good, man, if you love 'em—if you've got time to do it. It's not good if the old lady ain't nowhere, man. And my old lady . . . she's just, 'Do you love me, son?' No I don't love you. I just seen you. You come by the gig and asked me if I'd ball you, and I said, 'Okay, yeah.' And then ten months later, 'I'm pregnant. What'll I do? What'll I do?' I said, '*I* don't know what to do.' So she comes down and she gets a crib, see, she gets an apartment and she says, 'Duane, here's your home! Here's your home!' And I said, 'Well, I've been looking for home. This must be it.' So I run on in the door, man, and right away I start getting pulled at and shoved at. I don't want none of that, man. I don't want *none* of that. So I says, 'Okay, here's your bucks. Here's your car. Here's your trip. Hit the road.' So, it's just me and my old guitar."

Listening to the interview decades later, it is still a spine-chilling speech. Had Allman been a superstar at the time, his cruel confessional most likely would have been career-wrecking front-page news in the tabloids. But in December 1970, as far as the mainstream media was concerned, Duane Allman was just another guitar player in a rock & roll band.

Despite everything, the conversation wasn't short on levity. Duane was talking a mile a minute, explaining in an almost incoherent fashion about the formation of the Allman Brothers Band when Herman jumped in. "You do a two-and-a-half-hour interview in ten minutes," he told Allman. When the disc jockey added that he thought "people from the South are supposed to talk slow and mellow," Duane responded, "Oh, I am—but you get up here, you have to talk fast or somebody'll talk in front of you."

When phone calls started pouring into the station, one listener spoke of seeing the Allman Brothers open for Blood, Sweat & Tears at the Fillmore East the previous year, and then asked Duane what he thought of the group. After a lengthy silence, Allman finally responded, "My mother told me when I was a child, 'If you can't—don't.'" Moments later, the interview was finally, mercifully, over. Through a haze of alcohol and whatever else was in his system, Duane Allman had once again found a way to—in the words of Paul Hornsby—"show his ass." This time, however, it wasn't in the privacy of an Hour Glass recording session. It was on a radio show with thousands of listeners.

Perhaps Duane just got drunk and high that night for the hell of it. It certainly wouldn't have been the first time. Maybe all the Christmas decorations in Manhattan were a reminder that the anniversary of his father's murder was approaching. On the other hand, the upcoming Fillmore dates could have played some small part in his desire to get shit-faced before going on the air. On the 11th and 12th, the Allman Brothers would be second on the bill behind Canned Heat. Remarkably, Duane's old nemesis, Dallas Smith, had finally figured out how to make a blues-rock record. His production of *Boogie with Canned Heat* with its hit single, "On the Road Again," had turned Smith into a bona fide rock producer of no small renown. The irony wouldn't have been lost on Duane that the musically superior Allman Brothers Band had to open for a Dallas Smith-produced act.

After the Fillmore East shows, the band rounded out December with concerts in Washington, Boston, Macon, Los Angeles, and New Orleans. In January 1971 they played a gig in Statesboro, Georgia. Bill Ector recalls Duane opening the show with the line, "I think this song seems apropos . . ." just before the launching into "Statesboro Blues." That same month there were concerts in Boone, North Carolina; Atlanta; Pittsburgh; and Port Chester, New York. Then the band traveled across the country for a series of nights at the Fillmore West, beginning on January 28.

The headlining act was the Jefferson Airplane offshoot Hot Tuna. To call the show eclectic would be an understatement: this time, the Allman Brothers found themselves wedged between one of San Francisco's favorite acts and something called the 24-Piece Trinidad Tripoli Steel Band. But the ABB's perseverance in playing at Bill Graham's showcase venues—even on sometimes bizarre bills—was about to pay off. In March, the band returned to the Fillmore East to make what *Rolling Stone* would one day hail as rock's greatest live recording.

With two studio albums under their belt, the Allman Brothers were about to fulfill one more of Duane's dreams. In 1970 he had told disc jockey Ed Shane, "You know, we get kind of frustrated doing the [studio] records, and I think, consequently, our next album will be . . . a live recording, to get some of that natural fire on it." The live recording that Duane had hoped for would eventually consist of performances from Friday, March 12, and Saturday, March 13. The band actually played three straight nights at the Fillmore, beginning on Thursday. Ads for the show read: "Bill Graham Presents in New York—Johnny Winter And, Elvin Bishop Group, Extra Added Attraction: Allman Brothers." Extra added attraction indeed. No matter that Johnny Winter was billed as the headliner—by the final night, the Allman Brothers were closing the show.

Tom Dowd was back to produce the album, but this time he was flying by the seat of his pants. He hadn't even planned to be in New York when the live album was being cut. "I was supposed to be in Europe," he told Bill Ector. Dowd had been in Africa, working on the film *Soul to Soul*. From there he planned to vacation in Rome, but when his plane touched down, he discovered it was snowing. "I looked and I thought, 'I don't need Rome in the snow.'" So Dowd caught the next plane to Paris, eventually arriving in New York at the crack of dawn on March 10.

After checking into a hotel near the Atlantic Records office, he slept all day. The following afternoon he called Jerry Wexler to let him know he was in town. "That's great," said Wexler, "because the Allman Brothers are recording tonight at the Fillmore." With such short notice, Dowd had no time to speak to Duane or any of the other band members. He took a taxi down to the Fillmore East and hopped into the truck that housed Location Recorders' mobile studio.

"The band didn't even know I was back," said Dowd. "I'm sitting in the truck and prompting the engineers. So the band comes onstage and all of a sudden I hear horns, and I like to nearly wet my pants! I went out of that truck, I mean, I came tear-assing down. And when they came off, I grabbed them and said, 'Get the fucking horns out of my life. They are out of tune, they don't know the songs—whose stroke of genius was this?'"

When the band finally calmed him down, they asked Dowd if they could keep one horn player and Thom Doucette on harmonica. He agreed, but the initial show was a lost cause. "The first show, half the tracks that I could have used were wasted because I had horns on guitar parts, and they were terrible. It was pretty grim," said Dowd. "So that night, in order to make a point, we went up to my studio with the tapes under my arms, and I played the whole concert back to them. They were sitting there and said, 'Yeah, you're right.' When they did the next night, I didn't have to worry about the horns."

Although the eventual album would include tracks from both the 12th and 13th, Dowd felt the contributions by saxophonist Rudolph "Juicy" Carter— who had been featured on some of the second night's performances—weren't quite gelling with the band. By Saturday's gig, Carter was sitting out. In fact, for a while on Saturday—thanks to someone phoning in a bomb threat—it looked as if everybody might be sitting out. But after the Fillmore had been searched, the show resumed. Much of what was recorded during the post-bomb-scare set on the night of the 13th became the material on *At Fillmore East*.

Technically, the Allman Brothers' late show actually took place on the morning of March 14. By all accounts, the band didn't hit the stage until sometime after 2:00 a.m. Recollections of the duration of that final set vary greatly, depending on who's telling the story—but it's safe to say that it went on for well over three hours. The final encore (which didn't make it onto the original album) was "Drunken Hearted Boy," featuring Elvin Bishop on guitar and vocals, Steve Miller on piano, and Bobby Caldwell on percussion. At the end of the song, Duane said, "That's all for tonight." But nobody wanted to go home. As the crowd continued to cheer for more, Duane—in semi-disbelief—told them, "Hey, listen. It's six o'clock, y'all." When the cheers continued, he tried a different tactic: "Look here, we recorded all this. This is gonna be our third album, and thank you for your support. You're all on it. We ain't gonna send you no check, but thanks for your help." And with that, the Allman Brothers' three-night stand at the Fillmore East was finally over.

"Each night after the shows," Dowd said, "the band and I would boogie on up to Atlantic Studios, listen to the tapes, and make some instant decisions. When we listened to them, we knew what we had nailed and what we might have to work on. And we started editing: 'We don't need to do this song tomorrow. Let's change the set.' [On the second night] we mixed two or three songs down. The third night, we go back up to the studio after the show, listen to it, and say, 'Yeah, that's it.' They were gone and the album was done. What wasn't mixed was talked about being mixed . . . like, 'If you can scissor this one to that one, or make this one fit that one, go ahead.'"

Dowd mixed the album quickly. He did, in fact, "scissor this one to that one" in a few cases. But by 1992, when Dowd was asked to remix the tapes for a CD reissue called *The Fillmore Concerts*, he had forgotten, in some cases, exactly which edits were performed where for the original LP release. "Nobody ever got mad at me for the one or two I switched, and they knew I was doing it," he would later say.

Songs from the March 12 and 13 Fillmore shows that didn't make the cut for *At Fillmore East* would later surface on *Eat a Peach*, the two Duane Allman anthologies, and the Allman Brothers' *Dreams* boxed set. Recordings from both nights eventually appeared together in one form or another on the aforementioned 1992 two-CD set and on the 2003 release of a two-CD "deluxe edition" of the Fillmore shows. But the reissues—even with their constantly improving aural qualities, longer durations, and nifty packaging—don't seem to have the same weight and power as the original seven-song double album.

Tom Dowd had 20 reels of tape from which to create the live album. According to Phil Walden, Jerry Wexler wanted Capricorn to edit the material down to a single LP, "and he was adamant about that." Wexler confirms the assertion. "It's true," he says. "As an executive—a person in the company concerned about finances—I didn't want a two-record set, and I didn't want it to go for $6.95."

But Walden was equally adamant about making it a double album, and about selling it for the price of a single disc. After negotiating a reduced rate with all of the publishers, he convinced Wexler to give in. "In a subtle way," Walden explained, "we were trying to suggest that the Allman Brothers Band was the people's band, and we wanted the album to carry a price tag they could afford."

With Tom Dowd producing, the final selections—and even the sequencing of the album—helped to make the two-record set one of the most critically acclaimed and best-selling live recordings of all time.

The disembodied voice of low-key announcer Michael Ahern opens *At Fillmore East* with the simple introduction, "O-*kay*, the Allman Brothers Band." It is the only low-key moment over the course of the ensuing one hour, 18 minutes, and 19 seconds.

As soon as they are announced, the band kicks into "Statesboro Blues," the song written and first recorded by Blind Willie McTell in 1928. At the outset, the Allman Brothers' version appears to be a close copy of Taj Mahal's 1968 rendition, which inspired Duane to learn how to play slide guitar. But there's an electricity to the ABB's take on the song that makes all previous interpretations pale in comparison. For the first time, the full, raw power of the band has been captured on record. The fact that there are *two* drummers has never been more apparent—one comes out of each stereo speaker, playing different parts that flawlessly interlock.

Duane's 40-second slide intro leads into the vocal, and then his guitar returns to respond to every line Gregg sings. After the second verse, Duane takes his first solo on *At Fillmore East*. From this moment on, there's no turning back. If there was ever a question of who was in charge of this band over the course of the first two studio albums, the answer is right here.

Gregg comes back in with the third verse, and then Betts takes his turn in the spotlight. On the fourth verse, Duane is back on slide—once again complementing Gregg's every phrase. The song ends and the applause clearly indicates that this was recorded before an appreciative audience.

Up second is "Done Somebody Wrong"—a number Duane introduces as "an old Elmore James song we'd like to play you. This is an old true story. . . ." Whether it's really true or not, the implication is enough to make one pay close attention to the lyrics. Best known for his recording of "Dust My Broom," with its soaring slide guitar introduction, Elmore James had a unique talent for essentially rewriting the same song multiple times. But the Allman Brothers were savvy enough not to settle for covering James's biggest hit. Nor did Duane settle for copying the slide work made famous by the old blues master.

As with "Statesboro Blues," Duane kicks off the song with a slide intro. Gregg sings the first two verses, and then Thom Doucette—the sole survivor among the originally planned collection of additional musicians—takes a solo on blues harp. His contributions to this and other songs prove that the combination of Duane's instincts and the compromise the band struck with Dowd on the first night resulted in a setting that made perfect musical sense. Decades after the fact, it is no more possible to imagine *At Fillmore East* without Doucette than it is to imagine what the album would have sounded like with the addition of a three-piece horn section.

Doucette's solo is followed by 24 bars of pure Betts before the song hits the third verse. Duane's slide intertwines with Gregg's vocals throughout the lyrics, and then—unexpectedly—the band breaks out of the shuffle and builds up to a dual-lead guitar, triplet-based crescendo, culminating in Duane's slide coming out over the top for his first solo of the number. Gregg repeats the first verse, Duane takes one last, short slide solo, and the song is over.

After the two uptempo tunes, the band slows things down. "While we're doing that blues thing, we're going to play this old Bobby Bland song for you," Duane tells the audience. Then he adds, "Actually, it's a T-Bone Walker song." He's right on both counts. Texas bluesman T-Bone Walker had first recorded "Stormy Monday" on the Black & White label in 1948; Bobby "Blue" Bland's cover of Walker's composition came out in 1962. Both versions were major hits on black radio, with Bland's interpretation managing to make a little bit of noise on the pop charts as well.

Bland remains one of the unsung heroes of blues-based rock. His 1961 hit "Turn on Your Love Light" was covered by virtually every bar band in the country and was a highlight of most Grateful Dead shows throughout Pigpen McKernan's tenure. And, as Paul Hornsby pointed out, both the 5 Men-Its and the Allman Joys had "Stormy Monday" in their repertoires. But just as Bland's "Turn on Your Love Light" might be thought of today as a "Grateful Dead song" in some circles, the Allman Brothers' performance of "Stormy Monday" on *At Fillmore East* simply took the song away from Bobby "Blue" Bland and made it theirs—and theirs alone.

Duane (sans slide) starts the song alone on guitar for four measures before Dickey and the rest of the band join in for an intro that extends the length of a full verse prior to Gregg's vocal entrance. For a few fleeting seconds, Doucette's harp can be heard during the intro as well. While Gregg sings the first three verses of the song, Duane and Dickey trade blues licks. At the end of the third verse, Duane takes off on a solo filled with glissandos and bent strings.

When Duane is done, Gregg takes his first organ solo of the album as the rhythm shifts effortlessly into an uptempo 6/8-time jazz feel. It's as if Jimmy Smith has suddenly jumped onstage. But as soon as the organist's brief moment in the spotlight is over, everything downshifts back to a slow blues for Dickey's solo, followed by Gregg's singing of the last verse. The song draws to a close on a sustained note, while Duane's guitar and Doucette's harmonica continue to whittle and wail until they both finally meet up with the rest of the band on the last chord.

Thom Doucette's contributions to "Stormy Monday" are so tastefully subtle as to seem almost nonexistent. It would take the release of *The Fillmore Concerts* in 1992 for one of Dowd's amazing "scissor" jobs on *At Fillmore East* to become apparent. As the 1992 set reveals, Doucette had actually taken a minute-and-a-half harmonica solo between Dickey's guitar solo and the final verse of the song, but even the keenest ear would have a difficult time detecting Dowd's edit on the original album.

"You Don't Love Me" encompasses the entire second side of *At Fillmore East*. Written by journeyman blues singer and harmonica player Willie Cobbs, the song had been covered by a host of artists by the time the Allman Brothers began performing it. Three years prior to *At Fillmore East*, "You Don't Love Me" had appeared on the Al Kooper/Michael Bloomfield/Stephen Stills LP, *Super Session*. (Interestingly, that same album included a long jam based on Donovan's "Season of the Witch"—a precursor to the Allman Brothers' monolithic take on Donovan's "There Is a Mountain.")

As the track opens, Duane encourages the audience to "put your hands together for this." He plays for eight bars before Dickey joins in and the riff begins to take shape. Eventually everyone is on board, including Doucette. Gregg sings the first two verses and then Duane takes his first solo of the piece. Up to this point, the album has been all blues—but on this solo, Duane rocks. The singer comes back with verse three and then it's Dickey's turn. Gregg's organ takes up where Dickey's guitar left off, followed by Doucette's solo and the fourth verse.

By this time, the song has been going full steam for six-and-a-half minutes. Duane begins what at first appears to be another long, rocking solo—but after less than 30 seconds, the whole band drops out, leaving Duane alone. Suddenly all jazz has broken loose. It's the first sign that from here on out, the audience won't be listening to just another blues-rock band from the South. Duane's solo slowly winds and stretches its way through what could be an entirely different number. This isn't about rhythm or melody. It's all about feel. Finally, Duane slides down to a low *A* and simply lets it vibrate, allowing Dickey to take over and simultaneously bring the song back up to its original tempo. Both drummers join in, and for the next three minutes the ABB becomes a trio. Oakley jumps in a couple of times to establish a bit of foundation, but he's soon gone again and it becomes Dickey's turn to go into free time.

When Betts hits his last long sustained note, the whole band, including Doucette, jumps back in. Soon the two lead guitarists are playing together in harmony, and it sounds for all the world as if the band is about to bring the song to its logical conclusion. But once again Duane is suddenly alone in the spotlight. He drops the tempo as he plays a series of slow, bluesy licks. And then *it* happens: exactly 16 minutes and 16 seconds into "You Don't Love Me"—in the middle of a natural pause between two notes during Duane's freeform solo—a voice from the audience cries out, "Play all night!"

It is one of the defining moments in rock: a single jubilant fan caught up in the excitement of the greatest live rock concert ever captured on tape, expressing the feelings of an entire audience—an audience that would grow from fewer than 2,000 in attendance that night to millions of listeners around the world in the decades to follow.

Duane continues to play. He picks up the tempo for a moment and the audience claps along, and then he's back out in space and the audience pauses in mid-clap, waiting to hear what's going to happen next. The drummers and Oakley work their way into the mix. Gregg's organ fades in, holding long chords—seemingly waiting to see where it's all going. Now the whole band is back while Duane plays over the top, eventually letting his guitar ring out with the melody of "Joy to the World"—the cue that he's finally ready to wrap it up. As the song concludes with an old-fashioned three-note ascending blues ending, the audience goes wild. Seconds later, Berry Oakley's rumbling bass begins the introduction to "Whipping Post," but it rapidly fades and Side Two comes to an end.

Surprisingly, Side Three doesn't pick up where the previous one left off. "Whipping Post" is coming, but not until Side Four. (In fact, the "Whipping Post" on *At Fillmore East* is from another set.) Instead, Side Three opens with "Hot 'Lanta," a short instrumental credited to the entire band. The piece begins with Gregg's organ intro, followed by both guitars playing the melody in unison, then repeating the pattern in harmony with each other. Gregg takes a solo on the B-3, followed by Duane and then Dickey. Not quite three-and-a-half minutes into the song, Butch and Jaimoe tear into a 16-bar drum solo (or, more accurately, drum duet). When the drums are done, the theme is repeated one more time before the piece goes into free time. Everything seems to simply float momentarily as one note vibrates through Gregg's spinning Leslie speaker. Jaimoe's snare drum raps out a few quick rolls while the suspension continues. Then, as if anything else unexpected could possibly happen after all that's come earlier, the sound of tympani can be heard—very quietly at first, and then building to a huge crescendo. And just like that, the instrumental is over.

Duane introduces the next track as "a song Dickey Betts wrote from our second album—'In Memory of Elizabeth Reed.'" The first section of the song features Dickey playing volume swells, making his guitar work sound almost violin-like. The instrumental goes through a couple of tempo changes before Dickey takes off on a solo. Gregg's organ is up next, and then it's time for Duane. Once again, he leaps well beyond the bounds of rock. The performance is taking place at a point in time when many jazz artists have begun playing what will soon be labeled "fusion"—the playing of rock in a jazz context. With his solo on "Elizabeth Reed," Allman does the opposite: he's playing jazz in a rock context.

"You know," Duane would later tell writer Robert Palmer, "that kind of playing comes from Miles and Coltrane, and particularly [the Miles Davis album] *Kind of Blue*. I've listened to that album so many times that for the past couple of years, I haven't hardly listened to anything else." What Duane found so captivating was the modal improvisation pioneered by Miles in the late 1950s—extended soloing based on a single scale, or a sequence of scales, rather than a chord progression. This concept gave great freedom to soloists to take the music in new directions—a freedom that the Allman Brothers Band embraced.

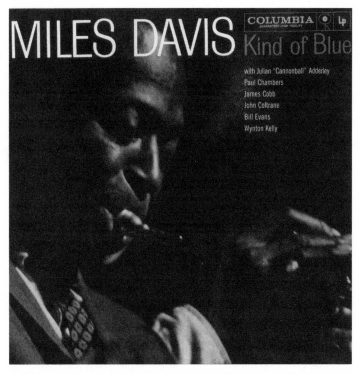

Kind of Blue—
the Miles Davis
album was a
major influence
on Duane's
approach to
improvisation

When Duane's solo in "Elizabeth Reed" ends, the drummers extend the improvisational concept, taking center stage with a solo straight from the repertoire of *Kind of Blue*'s drummer, Jimmy Cobb. The whole band comes back in, plays the theme one more time, and then ends the song so abruptly that there's a moment of silence before the audience erupts.

At Fillmore East ends with "Whipping Post." No longer the five-minute song it had been on the band's debut album, by 1971 "Whipping Post" had become one of the main set pieces the band would use to extend the boundaries of popular music. Taking up all of Side Four, this performance of Gregg's composition clocks in at 23 minutes. (When print publisher Hal Leonard put out a three-volume set of Allman Brothers Band songbooks in 1995, it would take 42 pages to transcribe the guitar solos in this version of "Whipping Post.")

"We got a little number from our first album we're gonna do for ya," Duane tells the crowd. "Berry starts 'er off." But before the bass player can begin, someone in the audience shouts "'Whipping Post!'" Just as Duane responds,

"You guessed it," Oakley begins to play what is now one of the most familiar bass patterns in the history of rock.

One by one, Duane, Dickey, and Gregg add their instruments to the mix before Gregg sings the first verse. At this point, Duane takes his most electrifying solo of the album thus far while Dickey's rhythm guitar pushes the song forward. Then, after Gregg finishes the second verse, Dickey plays lead while Duane takes the rhythm guitar part. Ten minutes into the song, the band once again slips into free time, leaping into the unknown. It feels as though everything could simply fall apart at any second, but Dickey continually pulls things back together at what—as usual—seems to be the last possible moment. At one point the music almost grinds to a halt as Betts slows the tempo to a dirge. Oakley plays a series of melodic bass lines behind Dickey. The drums and organ follow along, waiting for the inevitable instant when the tempo will once again return to its original speed. When that moment arrives, the whole band kicks into gear, building to an ascending crescendo that comes to a dead stop before Gregg begins to sing the chorus.

The chorus ends—and had this been any other band in the universe, so would the song. Instead, everything is left hanging in mid-air momentarily as Dickey plays a few more notes, eventually leading into the melody of "Frère Jacques." Duane and Berry join Dickey in reprising the melody as everything seems to be wrapping up once more. But the band *still* isn't done, and Duane begins playing a line that sounds straight out of the soundtrack of a Middle Eastern movie. Finally, Gregg is back to sing the chorus one last time, Butch's kettle drums return, and "Whipping Post" comes to an end.

As the applause breaks out, Butch has already begun playing the tympani intro to the next song. The other instruments join in, but the sound quickly fades. With almost eerie foreshadowing of what lies ahead, the final side of *At Fillmore East* concludes with the opening notes of "Mountain Jam"—a track the Allman Brothers' record-buying audience won't hear in its entirety until four months after Duane's death.

"Recording the Fillmore East album was probably the easiest way to record that there is," Gregg once said. "It's probably the cheapest way to record—and it's *definitely* the most fun way to record because it was live, and you had the excitement of the crowd, and you had two trucks outside with all the gear in

At Fillmore East *album front cover (in which Duane hides his stash in his hands while the rest of the band cracks up) and back cover (with a photo of the incarcerated Twiggs Lyndon superimposed on the wall)*

it, you know? We just took the best from each night and put it together."

"That was our pinnacle," Dickey told Kirsten West. "The Fillmore days are definitely the most cherished memories that I have. If you asked everybody in the band, they would probably say that."

For the album cover, photographs were taken of the band in front of the Fillmore East—their name on the marquee above them. When nobody was happy with the way the pictures came out, photographer Jim Marshall was flown down to Macon to take new shots. With the Fillmore East more than 900 miles away, Marshall had to make do with what he had—and what he had was a brick wall in an alley near Capricorn Studios. The photographer stenciled "THE ALL-MAN BROTHERS BAND AT FILLMORE EAST" on one of the road cases, and then had the roadies stack all of the cases in front of the wall before bringing out the band to gather in front of them.

Despite Jim Shepley's comment about a teenaged Duane Allman dreaming of being a rock & roll star someday, once that day finally arrived the guitarist chose to downplay the star image as much as possible: "Nobody [in the band] is going to get dressed up real fine to satisfy someone's vicarious need to be a rock star," he once said. And so the entire band scowled as they sprawled in front of the road cases. Just when things were beginning to look hopeless for the photographer, Duane spotted a local dealer hovering nearby. As Jim Marshall looked through the lens, Duane disappeared. When Allman returned and sat down—baggy in hand—the whole band cracked up, Marshall snapped away, and the now-classic cover of *At Fillmore East* was captured on film.

Always loyal to the road crew that had been so loyal to the band, Duane insisted that the back cover be a group shot of the roadies. "He wanted to do that because they were the unsung heroes," Gregg told Alan Paul. "He really had a lot of respect for the people that make the shows possible and set up the equipment just perfect every night."

The back-cover photo included Joseph "Red Dog" Campbell, Kim Payne, Mike Callahan, Joe Dan Petty, and Willie Perkins. Joe Dan and Willie were the two latest additions to the road crew; Petty had been the bass player in the Jokers, one of Dickey's pre-Second Coming bands, and Perkins—a college-educated former bank auditor—had been brought in to replace Twiggs Lyndon. (The photographer's decision to have Red Dog, Kim, and Joe Dan holding cans of Pabst Blue Ribbon while he took their picture probably did more for PBR sales than any ad campaign the beer maker could have devised.) Marshall didn't even try to get the roadies to stop scowling while he was shooting them. It was more than obvious that they were still pissed about having to stack all the cases in the first place.

Since Twiggs was unavailable for the photo shoot (he was still awaiting trial in Buffalo), Red Dog went to Duane with an idea. "You know," he said, "we can put a picture of Twiggs up on that brick wall. Just 'cause he's in jail, it doesn't mean that he's still not here with us." Allman liked the sentiment and decided to have Lyndon's photo superimposed on the wall above the rest of the crew, right next to the album's track listing.

At Fillmore East was recorded in March and released in July. "The reason for that long a period of time between recording and releasing the album was actually pretty simple," recalled Dowd. "Looking at it from the record company's side, the Allman Brothers never . . . concentrated on single records. So the album came out when they started their tour in July. It was a concerted effort. Touring and concerts and all were so different in those days. But you didn't want somebody going out there and after they come off the road you put their album out—you're a goddamn fool. Put it out when they were going out and get some attention."

At Fillmore East got some serious attention—quickly. The ABB's two previous albums had taken a month or more after their release to hit the charts. This time, the record started going up the album charts within a matter of days. Throughout the summer of 1971 it continued to climb, eventually reaching Number 13 on *Billboard*'s Top Pop Albums chart. By October, *At Fillmore East* had gone gold. Ironically, before the album even entered the charts, Bill Graham had closed the doors of the Fillmore East for good.

The concert scene had changed dramatically since the first Fillmore had opened in the mid-1960s, and Graham didn't like what he was seeing. In the early days, he had dealt with the bands themselves. But as rock music went from an underground community to an industry controlled by managers, agents, and record company executives, the cost of producing rock concerts on both coasts became, if not prohibitive, then certainly a lot less enjoyable for Bill Graham.

In May 1971, he wrote a letter to the *Village Voice* explaining his decision. In the early days, Graham wrote, he and his staff had chosen every act that would be performing at the venues. Eventually he found himself being forced to package shows according to the dictates of agents and managers. In the letter, he complained of everything from the lower quality of some of the current rock acts to the lower level of the audiences' musical appreciation. But in the end, he concluded his explanation by saying he was simply "tired." The final show at the Fillmore East, he announced, would be on June 27, 1971.

The acts for that final series of concerts at the Fillmore were Albert King, the J. Geils Band, and the Allman Brothers Band. The first two nights were open to the general public; the final night was for friends and family only.

For Duane Allman, the weekend held special significance beyond the closing of New York's hallowed rock venue. Kurt Linhof—a vintage guitar dealer from Texas—was flying in with the Les Paul of his dreams. "I met Duane in March 1971 in San Antonio," Linhof recalls. "ZZ Top opened for them. Billy Gibbons introduced me to Duane, and he introduced me as this great guitar finder." When Allman told Linhof what he was looking for, the guitar dealer responded, "Sure, I can find that tobacco Les Paul"—even though he had never actually seen one. "I thought, 'Why not? I can find anything else.'"

By late June, Linhof had located the guitar Duane had described, along with "a load of tweed Fender Bassman amps for each of them, and a '60 Fender Jazz Bass for Berry." On the day of the first show of the Fillmore's closing weekend, Linhof arrived in New York with the gear. "I shipped all the amps up and flew with the guitars—brought it all to the gig. Jay Geils was hanging around with Duane because he wanted to see this guitar. As soon as he saw it, he offered to sell me *his* guitar. He had a cherry sunburst Les Paul. He said he couldn't play it anymore after seeing Duane's."

While hanging with Allman at the Fillmore, Linhof had the opportunity to take in the whole early-1970s rock & roll experience. "Backstage there were about 20 dealers, about 20 chicks giving blowjobs, and about 30 musicians in all those little dressing rooms. It was a zoo. Behind every door there was some serious nonsense going on."

"The Fillmore East was the best gig there was," says Butch Trucks. "I think probably the best night we ever had was at the Fillmore—the next to the last night, closing weekend. We went onstage around two in the morning, went to about eight in the morning, six hours straight. Finished playing and there was no applause. The place was jam-packed. Not one person clapped. I look out and everybody's got a smile ear to ear. Some guy gets up, opens the door, and

Duane playing his newly acquired tobacco-sunburst Les Paul
on closing night of the Fillmore East, June 27, 1971

the sun comes in. And a New York crowd, they get up and quietly walk out. I remember Duane walking in front of me, dragging his guitar, saying, 'Goddamn! It's like leaving church.'"

The following night, for the very last show at the Fillmore East, Bill Graham decided to add several more acts to the lineup. Along with Albert King and the J. Geils Band, the bill would include Country Joe & the Fish, Mountain, Edgar Winter, and the Beach Boys.

Having the Beach Boys on the bill must have been nostalgic for Duane Allman. Not only were the Allman Brothers helping to wrap up the final night at rock's Mecca, Duane and Gregg would be sharing the stage with the band the Escorts had opened for back in 1965 in Daytona Beach. There was only one hitch: just before show time, the Beach Boys told Graham that they had to be the closing act. Few would dispute that the Beach Boys held an exalted position in rock's pantheon, but in the mind of Bill Graham the Allman Brothers were the single most appropriate act to wrap up the Fillmore East's last stand. In fact, the bad vibrations the Beach Boys were spreading on this historic evening were symptomatic of the reasons that had driven Graham to close the Fillmores East and West in the first place.

Graham's response to this demand was quick and to the point—as far as he was concerned, the Beach Boys could either perform when he told them to perform, or they could pack up their gear and go home. Upon considering their options, they decided to stay and play. And so, on June 27, 1971, the Allman Brothers Band closed the Fillmore East—following the very act that Duane and Gregg had opened for in Florida only six years earlier. The mantle had been passed.

As the Allman Brothers prepared to take the stage, this time the introduction was substantially more than a mumbled "O-*kay*, the Allman Brothers Band." It was Bill Graham himself at the microphone, waxing nostalgic. "Over the years that we've been doing this," he said, "the introductions are usually very short—and this one's going to be short, but longer than usual. The last two days we have had the privilege of working with this particular group, and over the past year or so we've had them on both coasts a number of times. In all that time, I've never heard the kind of music that this group plays. And last night we had the good fortune of having them get onstage about 2:30, 3:00 o'clock, and they walked out of here at 7:00 in the morning. And it's not just that they played quantity. For my amateur ears, in all my life, I've never heard the kind of music that this group plays—the finest contemporary music. We're going to round it off with the best of them all—the Allman Brothers."

Whether the June 26 show actually ended at 7:00 a.m. as Graham said, or an hour later as Butch recalls, is really immaterial. The bottom line is the band had garnered enough respect from the greatest rock promoter of all time to be given the most prized spot in the history of rock's most famous venue.

"The special thing, I think, that will always stand out is the Fillmore experience," Dickey said years later, "when we were all young and we were all pretty naïve and gullible and just really didn't know what the hell we were really into—and not caring. And, at the same time, we knew a hell of a lot more than a lot of people thought we did. And, you know, then the old band was together."

The "old band," of course, being the one led by Duane Allman. It was only a matter of months before the days of the old band would be over.

CHAPTER NINETEEN

Mann & Allman

*"Complexity is the only difference between blues and jazz.
It's all the portrayal of the feelings—and the soul—
in a medium other than words."* — D.A.

John Coltrane and Miles Davis had ranked near the top of Duane's favorite musicians ever since Jaimoe introduced jazz to the guitarist through his record collection, including such albums as Coltrane's *Africa/Brass*, Davis's *Seven Steps to Heaven*, and Tony Williams's *Emergency!* The influences of Coltrane and Davis were apparent in many of Duane's and Dickey's solos, especially when they "stretched out," as evidenced by the tracks recorded at the Fillmore East in March and June 1971. The Tony Williams LP had a lasting effect on the band, too, with its no-holds-barred improvisations featuring John McLaughlin on guitar and Larry Young on organ as well as the leader's potent drumming.

Those who saw the Allman Brothers live or bought their records were, first and foremost, rock fans. The average ABB listener was generally open-minded enough to groove to Duane's improvisational flights in the middle of "You Don't Love Me" or "In Memory of Elizabeth Reed," but it's difficult to gauge what the reaction might have been if the band had suddenly whipped into a twenty-minute version of Davis's "So What" or Coltrane's "Giant Steps"— which is not to say that the idea might not have occurred to Duane Allman.

By the summer of 1971, Duane had been searching for a jazz outlet for some time. He had been excited to meet Joel Dorn, Rahsaan Roland Kirk's producer, and had asked Dorn about working with the iconoclastic multi-instrumentalist. "I actually went to Rahsaan," says Dorn. "He was as much a one-of-a-kind artist as ever existed. He was also a man of gigantic conviction and passions, so I thought Duane would be perfect. I went to him and said, 'There's this guy—you know about the Allmans?' He said, 'Oh, I know about the Allman Brothers.' I said, 'I'd like to do some sessions with you and Duane. I think you could really get something going.' He took it as, 'Oh, now you want to put me with those rock & roll guys so I can make a hit. You're not interested in my music.' I said, 'Nah, it's different. This guy is special, man. He gets the joke. You really ought to. . . .' But he wouldn't do it. So I went back and told Duane. I said, 'I really tried, but you know Rahsaan.' He said, 'Yeah, I know, but it was worth trying.'"

Later, after he met Herbie Mann during Delaney & Bonnie's Central Park concert at the Schaefer Music Festival in August 1970, Duane was ready to take up Mann's offer to play on one of the flutist's future albums. It was just a matter of finding time between Duane's other studio work and the Allman Brothers' constant gigs.

Mann, a Brooklyn native, had been making records since the 1950s. Like Miles—and, to a lesser extent, Coltrane and Williams—Herbie had managed to capture a large enough audience to see several of his albums make it onto the pop charts. He'd even had a genuine hit in 1969 with an album called *Memphis Underground*. Before that, he'd cut an album called *Muscle Shoals Nitty Gritty*, but Eddie Hinton had gotten the guitar slot for that one.

"Duane liked listening to a lot of shit that I'm sure a lot of his contemporaries didn't listen to," says Dorn. "I didn't know the rest of the guys in the band, so I don't have a sense of who was into what. On the other hand, I remember Herbie Mann used to talk about 'In Memory of Elizabeth Reed' all the time. And Herbie never met a good rhythm section he didn't like. If there was a good rhythm section, Herbie was on a plane. He was very smart."

After the closing of the Fillmore East, Duane stayed in New York for his long-awaited sessions with Mann. Cut at Atlantic Recording Studios in only two days (June 30 and July 1), the music that became the album *Push Push* featured an all-star cast including Richard Tee on keyboards; Chuck Rainey, Donald "Duck" Dunn, and Duane's old friend Jerry Jemmott on bass; Bernard Purdie and Al Jackson Jr. on drums; and Ralph McDonald on percussion. Along with Duane, the guitarists were Cornell Dupree and David Spinoza.

Produced by Arif Mardin, *Push Push* turned out to be almost as much Duane's album as it was Herbie's. Allman took the guitar solos on six of the seven tunes including—ironically—"Spirit in the Dark," the title song of an Aretha Franklin album that had featured Duane on a couple of numbers, but not *that* one. *Push Push* wasn't a straight jazz album; Mann and Mardin chose to cover tunes made famous by Aretha, Marvin Gaye, Ray Charles, the Jackson 5, and even the soft-rock group Bread, so no one was going to mistake this LP for the work of Rahsaan Roland Kirk. But it would turn out to be Allman's only real chance to dip a toe into Rahsaan's world. At least the album would be filed in the jazz section at record stores.

Being in New York also gave Allman the chance to get together with Joel Dorn and King Curtis. "When I would be done working and Duane was done and Curtis was done and we'd have some time, you know—like late in the evening—we'd just hang out," Dorn says. "Mostly get high and laugh. That's really what it was about.

"Duane and Curtis and I talked about doing some stuff. Curtis was another guy—I mean, everybody knows him for those solos on that R&B shit he did, but Curtis could *play*. We'd have these reefer conversations and say, 'Yeah, how about if we get this front line together and this rhythm section and do it.' And I would say, 'Well, I can't play nothing, but I'll produce it.' And Curtis would say, '*You* can't produce! Why don't you just sit there and have some lunch or something?' And we would start with that kind of stuff."

As soon as the *Push Push* sessions were over, Duane and the rest of the Allman Brothers Band headed for Newport, Rhode Island, to play at the esteemed Newport Jazz Festival. This would surely be the chance Duane was looking for—an opportunity to play before an appreciative crowd that would allow the band to show off its jazz side in a serious way. Unfortunately, Newport wasn't ready for the crowd that an act like the Allman Brothers would draw. The night before the band was scheduled to perform, thousands of kids waiting outside the festival grounds decided to wait no longer. When they broke down the fence, the Newport police didn't react nearly as kindly as the Atlanta festival promoter had done. The end result was hundreds of hippies in the hospital and the cancellation of the remainder of the Newport Jazz Festival.

Duane had to be more than a little disappointed, but there was no time to fret over what might have been. Within a couple of days the band was in Atlantic City, playing at the Steel Pier for a week. Then they were back on the road, performing in Tampa, Atlanta, and Huntington, New York, followed by two shows in Manhattan's Central Park. The day after the New York concerts, Duane, Gregg, and King Curtis jammed with Delaney & Bonnie & Friends at A&R Recording Studios, and the show was broadcast live on WPLJ-FM. Then the band was off to Virginia Beach, St. Paul, and North Baltimore, Ohio.

At the beginning of August 1971, the Allman Brothers took their first long break from the road since October 1969. Two weeks off was a true anomaly for the band—although Macon had become their adopted home, their real residence was a series of hotel and motel rooms from one end of the country to the other. By this time, Duane had moved from the Big House to 1160 Burton Avenue, where he lived with his new girlfriend, Dixie Lee Meadows. Before his acrimonious split with Donna, Duane had already taken up with Dixie, one of a group of young ladies known to the band and roadies as the Hot 'Lanta Girls.

Dixie would be the inspiration for one of Duane's handful of original compositions. "They were livin' together," Dickey told interviewer Kirsten West. "Duane called her 'Little Martha' . . . his pet name for her." Years later, a rumor started that Allman had named the tune "Little Martha" after one Martha Ellis, a young girl buried at Rose Hill Cemetery, but Betts knew otherwise. "'Little Martha,' for God's sake, is not a baby that died," he told West.

Just as Duane's two-week break was coming to an end, King Curtis was murdered in New York City. On Friday the 13th, Curtis had gone to do some work on a brownstone he owned on West 86th Street. Upon exiting from the side of the building, he heard a man and woman arguing on the front steps. Angered by this disturbance taking place on his property, Curtis confronted the couple. When he did, the young man turned away from the woman, walked down the steps toward Curtis, pulled out a knife, and stabbed the saxophonist in the heart.

"Curtis had a horrible temper," says Joel Dorn. "[Songwriter] Doc Pomus was always telling him, when Curtis would get mad, 'Watch yourself, man.

That temper's gonna kill ya.' And he was right. He ended up dying because he couldn't let shit go. If somebody did something he didn't like, boy, he didn't care who it was."

The day of the funeral, Atlantic Records closed its offices. Held at St. Peter's Lutheran Church in Manhattan, the service was a testament to the music community's admiration for King Curtis. Duane was there, of course, as were Brook Benton, Delaney Bramlett, Ornette Coleman, Aretha Franklin, Dizzy Gillespie, the Isley Brothers, Arthur Prysock, Stevie Wonder, and more than a thousand others. The Reverend C. L. Franklin—Aretha's father—directed the service. Stevie Wonder sang; the Kingpins played "Soul Serenade"; the Reverend Jesse Jackson spoke; and Aretha closed the service with the sadly appropriate gospel song "Never Grow Old." Duane was in no condition to contribute anything musical to the proceedings. He simply sat with the rest of the congregation, crying.

On August 26, Duane was back at A&R—in the same studio where he and King Curtis had played with Delaney & Bonnie just over a month earlier. This time it was the Allman Brothers Band that had been booked for a live gig to be aired over WPLJ. The band whipped through its usual set list: "Statesboro Blues," "Trouble No More," "Don't Keep Me Wonderin'," "Done Somebody Wrong," "One Way Out," "In Memory of Elizabeth Reed," and "Stormy Monday." After they finished the old T-Bone Walker song, Duane stepped up to the microphone and began to reminisce about King Curtis. "Man, that was one of the finest cats there ever was," said Allman. "He was just right on top of gettin' next to the young people, you know? It's a shame."

Less than a week before the Allman Brothers' broadcast, Curtis's latest album, *Live at the Fillmore West,* had been released to rave reviews. "If y'all get a chance," Duane said, "listen to that album he made out at Fillmore West. Boy, it's incredible. It's unbelievable the power and the emotional stature that man had. He was an incredible human being, boy. I hope that—well—that whatever it was that did it knows what he did. It was a terrible thing. At the funeral, Aretha sang and Stevie Wonder played, and, man, they played 'Soul Serenade.'" At this point, Duane picked out the opening line of Curtis's 1964 hit single. "Y'ever hear that? Y'all are prob'ly a little bit young to know it. It's fantastic." As the crowd in the studio applauded in recognition, Allman said, "Yeah, we'll do a little bit of that." He turned to the band and asked, "You wanna do some of that?" Then, softly, as if talking to himself, the guitarist said, "I know where we'll do it."

Then Allman begins playing the intro to "You Don't Love Me." After Gregg sings the first verse, Duane plays his heart out. It's an uptempo solo filled with anger. Gregg comes back for the second verse, followed by Dickey's solo turn, and then Gregg's B-3. After the third verse, Duane enters with another series of rapid licks before holding one long, sustained note until the rest of the band falls out.

As Allman dramatically slows the tempo, there is an occasional drum roll or cymbal fill behind him. After each drawn-out guitar phrase, Oakley answers on his bass. Eventually the drummers and Oakley stop and wait. Both band and audience listen to find out where Duane is going. As the seconds tick by, Duane Allman—alone on the stage—uses his guitar to pour out his grief. Through a series of musical twists and turns, he slowly segues into the introduction to Curtis's "Soul Serenade." Gregg's organ and Berry's bass join in at the perfect moment. Soon the drums are there too, and—like magic—the Allman Brothers have turned into King Curtis's Kingpins, with Duane taking the late saxophonist's part. The audience claps along to the loping beat. Once the statement has been made, the band goes into free time once more as Allman plays a slow gospel dirge. As soon as the last chord is over, he returns to "You Don't Love Me." As always, just before the song comes to its resounding conclusion, Duane's guitar rings out with the melody line of "Joy to the World." The anger, sadness, and grieving are over.

The King is dead. Long live the King.

CHAPTER TWENTY

The Final Tour

"Music is what keeps me together. It's the thing that keeps us all going. God, I've got no idea what I'd do if I wasn't playing. I don't know what would happen." — D.A.

Music industry veteran John Carter—known to everyone in the business as simply "Carter"—was Atlantic's West Coast promo man during Duane's years with the band. "In today's terms, it would probably be called 'artist relations,'" says Carter. Back then, "it was 'underground promotion.'"

Carter's primary responsibility was to get Atlantic's records—and, to a lesser extent, those of its subsidiaries—played on the area's burgeoning FM radio stations. "The West Coast was one of the main areas where those FM stations were, and there were more of them all the time," he says. "Needless to say, in L.A. and San Francisco they were strong. So it was my job to have [radio station personnel] at shows, to get those records played that we weren't going to get played on pop stations. And things were working great. People couldn't believe the number of records the Allman Brothers were selling on what appeared— to the old school—as no airplay. But I knew that the small audience that was listening to those FM stations was religious about it.

"I was always on the road, touring with one of the Atlantic bands that was in my area," Carter recalls. As far as the Allman Brothers Band was concerned, he says, "I'm sure I saw every date they did on the West Coast during the last tour that Duane was with them."

Although the Atlantic execs were clearly proud of their association with Phil Walden, when it came to promotion the emphasis at Atlantic was, understandably, on the acts signed directly to Atlantic. "Let's face it," says Carter. "It was Capricorn. *No* one wanted to work those first two Allman Brothers records. There was no emphasis on those records at the time. They did what they did on their own. I think the Fillmore East record was recognized as a great record, so it took off.

"I was raving at the time that you had to come and see them because, unlike anyone else I'd ever seen, every night was different. It was the same set list, but I'd never seen a band that was so spontaneous and reacted so well to each other. They would let a song stretch because 'it just felt good tonight.' Some nights 'Whipping Post' would be six minutes and some nights 'Whipping Post' would be 15 minutes. And sometimes it'd be 20 minutes. It was all about 'how we're feeling tonight.' I'd never experienced that in show business before.

"Today, with Vari-Lites and stuff, you've got to hit your cue. Every set is rigidly the same. But even in that era, a 45-minute set was 46 minutes tops—except for the Allman Brothers. It was absolutely real and spontaneous and driven by greatness. So I have to say that as far as doing the tour goes, to this day I have never been so blown away by an act.

"Having said that, it was also some of my worst moments—where they were so fucking high that Berry would just fall over. He would fall over during the first song, and they'd drag him offstage. They'd all be cracked up and laughing, and Duane would say, 'Why don't y'all just give us another 30 minutes?' And 30 minutes later they'd come back out and start playing."

By the time of what would turn out to be Duane's final tour with the band, the thought that maybe the road really *does* go on forever was clearly taking its toll. A combination of boredom and chemical recreation led to actions that were simultaneously humorous and horrific. Carter recalls going to "a hotel room someplace, knocking on Duane's door and rolling in. There were four or five guys in the room and a guy sitting at the table who was just as hardcore a hippie as you could possibly be—with that real long little fingernail. The bag was sitting there and I just walked into the room and strutted right over with one finger covering one nostril and the other flared. I got right over it. The guy's just sitting there waiting for me, and as I leaned over, Duane said, 'Cah-tah, that ain't co-caine.' I wheeled around and went right back out of the room,

Two Brothers nearing the end of the road—Berry Oakley and Duane Allman, 1971

and they all started laughing because they knew where I drew the line. Blow? Sure! Heroin? No! But they were doing it all the time."

With little money to show for all of his hard work and success, Duane Allman's outlook was still optimistic—and his Southern sense of humor remained intact. "Duane and I are smoking a joint in a hotel room," recalls Carter, "and we'd been together long enough now that for some reason he's being very philosophical and he says to me, 'Cah-tah, it's a rat race out there—but my rat's winnin'!'"

Unlike the Who and many other bands who had become renowned for their hotel room destruction, the Allman Brothers Band and road crew had devised a much less obvious manner of leaving their mark on their temporary living spaces. "Every hotel room was trashed in a subtle way," says Carter. "They would pull the drawers out of the dresser and throw knives [through the dresser frame], and then put the drawers back in so you didn't see that they had destroyed the fucking wall. A lot of knives—a lot of drugs."

Today's rock stars still get busted occasionally for being caught in possession of one drug or another, but it would seem that modern-day recording artists and their followers don't have quite the same voracious habits as the rock generation of the 1960s and '70s. "It's of the era," Carter says. "I'm sorry to say it, but I was probably as guilty as anyone, using cocaine as a handshake. It was there. I'm saying cocaine, but obviously there were other things around. The drug scene was everywhere: 'I'm one of you. You're one of me. Let's get high.'"

In the handful of interviews Duane gave during his two years and seven months with the Allman Brothers Band, his main thrust was almost always about the music. He would occasionally discuss what he was currently reading (and, of course, there was the unfortunate alcohol-fueled monologue on WABC-FM), but by and large the subject was music: the blues and jazz he loved so much; the sessions he played on as a sideman; putting the Allman Brothers Band together; the thrill of playing with Clapton on the *Layla* album. He seldom spoke out on other subjects. But only two months before his death, he made a chilling statement about why bands sometimes break up: "Drugs is one thing that will do it, and do it quick. I don't allow no shootin' up in this band. . . . I ain't puttin' up with none of that shit. . . . I don't hold drugs against anyone; I just ain't havin' no one shootin' up in this band."

As was the case with Elvis Presley, Allman had apparently created his own set of standards to distinguish "good drugs" from "bad drugs." For Elvis, if a doctor prescribed drugs to him, no matter what size the dosage or how many medications piled up, they qualified as good drugs. But illegal drugs were bad drugs. Duane Allman drew the line quite a bit further down the page: just about everything, including snorted heroin, appeared to be on his "good drugs" list. But the moment a needle came out—as had happened with one of the band's roadies—the line was crossed.

When guitar dealer Kurt Linhof first met Allman in San Antonio in March 1971, he quickly discovered what it was like to live in Duane's world. "I don't remember a whole lot about that night," he says, "except going in the boys' room with Duane and doing some brown powder. Billy Gibbons introduced me to Duane, and Duane introduced me to heroin—all in the same night." But, the guitar dealer confirms, Duane Allman "never, ever shot up."

As Carter points out, drugs were simply a part of the scene. They were one of the identifying factors of a generation of young adults who thought alike. Along with flowered shirts, bell-bottom jeans, and long hair, drugs were one more item on the list that separated the youth from the authority figures that neither "got it" nor wanted to. In 1971, the divide remained wide. The war still raged in Vietnam; Richard Nixon was still in the White House. It didn't take too much chemical enlightenment (if any) to realize that all was not right with the world.

John McEuen, a staunch anti-drug advocate, vividly recalls the era: "I would say that in a time when the body counts were on television, kids were getting murdered on campuses, and the presidents were lying—of course, some things don't change—in that time period, when America was in turmoil, the Allman Brothers, with Duane in the band especially, are one of the reasons that a lot of people in our age group call that time the 'good old days.' The music helped transcend anything that was going on around you."

Although McEuen avoided the drug scene, many of his contemporaries chose to partake. For them, both the music and the drugs were methods of temporary escape from the madness. In Duane's case, although one is left with only conjecture at this point, the causes for his drug use seem to have been multi-layered. When he was sniffing glue and smoking pot as a kid in Daytona Beach—a town with a population of well under 100,000 in those days—Duane might have suffered from the need to avoid the realities of being a bright young man with big dreams trapped in the confines of a small town with its corresponding mentality. "Can you imagine being as talented as he was at a very early age in that small town with no way to get out?" asks Alan Walden.

During his early days on the road with the Allman Joys, working that "garbage circuit of the South" and making $150 a week, Duane would "eat pills and drink" just to keep going. Having little control over the music he was playing during the whole Hour Glass fiasco practically necessitated something to numb the mind and shield him from the miserable reality that he was compromising his talent. And then there was Muscle Shoals—a place so small that Daytona Beach must have seemed like New York City in comparison. "In Muscle Shoals you have a lot of creative people that never do anything beyond that studio," says Walden. "Duane Allman was different in that he wanted to carry his music all over the country. In Muscle Shoals, you had these guys that wrote great songs and played great music, but they were very content sitting there in Muscle Shoals and being session players for the rest of their lives. This man had a dream that went beyond all of that."

During the brief time he lived in his cabin by the lake in Alabama, Duane was as sedate as he would ever be. But he still managed to locate pot and speed—

even in a "dry" county where you had to take a trip over the state line just to buy a beer legally. Later, in Atlanta and Macon, hallucinogens like mushrooms and LSD were easily available. And in Miami during the *Layla* sessions, as Bobby Whitlock admits, "That's when we all started entertaining our own devils."

Perhaps more than anything else, though, it was the never-ending road life that caused band members and roadies alike to turn to harder drugs just to keep going. The great music the Allman Brothers created had gotten them the record deal Duane had dreamed of, which—in turn—gave him the chance to take his music to the people. But taking the music to the people meant the band had to stay on the road. Fans bought records. Fans wanted to see the band. The more fans there were, the more records the band sold. The more records they sold, the more albums had to be recorded to please both the record company and the fans alike. The more albums they recorded, the more fans wanted to see the band. It was a vicious cycle. There was no such thing as MTV or VH1 to keep the group in the public's collective eye while the band rested. The Allman Brothers had no choice but to take their music from town to town. The pace quickened, and the inevitable downward spiral began.

"It burned 'em out," says Johnny Townsend. "Stardom can get to you after a little while. After they had gotten around to doing that *Fillmore East* album—which was just a giant record—they seem to have reached a peak where they were pretty well toasted from being on the road."

From the time the band recorded *At Fillmore East* until mid-October, with just that two-week break in August, the ABB had kept going, playing more than 70 shows, racing from coast to coast and back again. "The last time I saw Duane was at the Atlanta airport in August of '71," says McEuen. "He said, 'John, get out that banjo and pick me a tune.' I said, 'Well, Duane, we're kind of in the middle of the airport, you know.' He said, 'If somebody doesn't like the banjo, they're not American.' So I sat there and played for him for about 20 minutes. I think it helped take him away."

The Allman Brothers leapt from a gig in Tuscaloosa, Alabama, one night to a show in Minneapolis the next. Over the course of three nights, they played in Tennessee, Ohio, and New York. At times their tour schedule appeared to have been put together by a booking agent without a map. It was no wonder that Berry Oakley was falling down. Even without drugs, it's amazing they could even *get* to the stage, much less stand up. But the drugs were undeniably there, and in ridiculous quantities.

"When it comes to your personal habit, you ration yourself according to your stash," explains Carter. "But when you're a big star, people are going to use drugs to get close to you. And the next guy and the next guy and the next guy's gonna get close to you, too. Suddenly you're doing ten times as much as you would if it was just you and your own stash."

A month after Duane had run into John McEuen at the airport, the band was still on the road. "They were playing in Texas," says Kurt Linhof, "so we got together and Duane said, 'Come on the road. I'll pay you $75 a day to be my tech.' I took him up on that. I ended up spending about $125 a day on heroin and cocaine. I remember we spent the night of September 27th in a motel in Austin. Berry was out of drugs and was having a horrible time. I had to get up in the middle of the night and drive to San Antonio to score for him."

By early October, the band knew that a much-needed break was just a few days away. But first there was a gig at the Whisky a Go Go—the very venue where Duane and Gregg had first wowed the West Coast as members of the Hour Glass; the very club where the brothers had first shown many of L.A.'s rock cognoscenti that they were players to be reckoned with in a live setting, if not on the two albums they had done for Liberty Records. And it was the very place the Allman Brothers had been playing less than two years before when their debut album finally landed on the national charts.

There were also two shows in San Francisco. Even after Bill Graham had closed both Fillmores, he continued to book shows at Winterland—a 5,000-seat venue that Pete Townshend of the Who once described to author Robert Greenfield as "the perfect size for a band to play." According to Greenfield, "Bill kept Winterland open because—although he was unwilling to deal with the hassles of flying back and forth from New York to San Francisco [to oversee the operation of Fillmores East and West]—he was not about to stop promoting shows in the Bay Area." But when Graham decided to bring the Allman Brothers Band to Winterland in October 1971, he had unknowingly booked Duane for what would be one of the final concerts of his career.

John Carter was there, as always, for the West Coast leg of the tour. "I must admit that I thought I saw Duane declining—or at least I saw that Dickey

Betts seemed to be taking over the band musically," he says. "I mean, Duane was always the guy that spoke a lot in concerts. He was like the voice of the band. There were so many songs that were based on Duane's guitar work and, of course, they were still great. But I think he was just tired and had been on the road too long."

CHAPTER TWENTY-ONE

A Guitar & a Motorcycle, Part 2

"If you do something, you got to be ready to pay those goddamn dues. I dropped three tabs of good red acid on a motorcycle going a hundred miles an hour down the road—no shoes and no helmet on. And, of course, you've got to pay dues for stuff like that." — D.A.

Heroin use by many in the ABB camp finally reached (or perhaps even surpassed) epic proportions. Duane decided the time had come to either check into rehab or take the chance of watching everything that had taken so long to build up quickly come tumbling down. So, after years of drug and alcohol abuse—around half of his life, in fact—24-year-old Duane Allman (along with two other band members and a couple of roadies) took a trip to Buffalo in the fall of 1971, checking into Linwood and Bryant Hospital to dry out, clean up, and get ready to resume work on the band's next album.

It was an exciting time for both the Allman Brothers and Capricorn Records. On October 25—just as Duane was checking out of rehab—*At Fillmore East* went gold. Meanwhile, Capricorn was building a catalog around the Allman Brothers, releasing a string of albums by acts such as Wet Willie, Jonathan Edwards, Johnny Jenkins, Alex Taylor, Livingston Taylor, and Cowboy, a band that included Duane's old friend Scott Boyer from the 31st of February.

After the demise of the 31st of February, Boyer had teamed up with singer-songwriter-guitarist Tommy Talton. Supported by a fluid lineup of other musicians, the duo formed Cowboy in Jacksonville in 1969. A short time later, Duane heard about Boyer's new group and decided to check them out—in his unique manner. "He pulled up in our driveway about 7 a.m.," recalls Boyer. "He was on his way from Daytona back to Macon. He woke me up and said, 'I hear you got a band.' I said, 'Yeah' and he said, 'Well, play something for me.' So I woke everybody up, and we went down into the music room and played a few songs for Duane. He said, 'Okay, I like your stuff, man. I'm gonna go back and talk to Phil Walden about it.'"

"I don't know what Duane told Walden," says Talton, "but without Phil ever hearing or seeing us, we got publishing, recording, and management contracts in the mail. I've always meant to ask Phil, 'What in the hell did Duane say?' But I don't really need to know. I know what it is—Phil respected Duane and his opinion on music. Apparently it was enough for him that Duane said, 'Man, these cats are doing something you might want to get involved in.'"

Cowboy's first album, *Reach for the Sky*, was produced by Johnny Sandlin and released in February 1971. When the band began work on the follow-up, *5'll Getcha Ten*, Allman decided to help out.

"They were having trouble getting the [Capricorn] studio in Macon to work right, and they had decided to do a redesign," says Boyer. "Johnny Sandlin didn't want to wait to cut our next album, so he talked Phil into buying some time at the Jackson Highway studio [Muscle Shoals Sound], and we went over there and recorded the *5'll Getcha Ten* album. Duane came in a week or so into the project. He flew down from New York City.

"We were in the studio recording 'Please Be with Me,' with Duane playing the dobro, and there was a buzz in the dobro. It was really bothering Johnny Sandlin, so the next day Johnny called somebody—some guitar-tech guy—who came in and fixed the dobro. We re-recorded it without the buzz."

According to Johnny Wyker, there was more than one buzz going on. "On the track that Duane played dobro on, he was snortin' so much coke that—if you listen real close—you can hear him suckin' air up his nose to keep the coke drainage from coming out. His hands were busy playin', so he had to suck it up. We were laughin' our asses off because you could hear him so loud on the track, along with his dobro part. They might have doctored it out of the track, but it happened. I was there."

"When it came time to finish the album," says Boyer, "I went to Johnny and said, 'I really like what Duane did more on the version with the buzz in the dobro, and the buzz doesn't bother me that much.' So I talked him into putting the one I wanted onto the Cowboy album. A few years later, he was put in charge of doing Duane's *Anthology* album, and he called me up and said, 'Look, I want to put 'Please Be with Me' on here, but you've gotta let me use the other version.' I said, 'Fine. Whatever. I'm just flattered to have something on there.'"

Once Duane had completed his stint in rehab, it was almost time to go home. He wanted to get back in time for Linda Oakley's surprise birthday celebration at the Big House, so in preparation for his return he put in a phone call to Grover Sassaman at Harley-Davidson of Macon. His chopper needed new tires. He also decided to order a new helmet.

Duane left the hospital and headed to Manhattan so he could spend some time hanging out with old friends, including John Hammond Jr. "He had just come into New York from Buffalo, where he'd gotten his head together," Hammond told interviewer Jas Obrecht. "He was at the house of a friend named Deering Howe, and I got a call. I went over there, and we had a few beers. When it was time to leave, he came over to my loft on Broadway . . . and we played records and jammed on guitars all night."

Hammond, whom Gregg once described as "Duane's best friend," was looking forward to eventually going back into the studio with Allman. "He and I were talking about making another album together and doing some acoustic stuff. He really admired my slide playing on the National [resonator guitar]— I couldn't believe it, but he did." The next day, Hammond says, "I had to fly out to Newfoundland, and he went home to Macon."

On October 28, Duane flew back to Georgia. Gregg and his new wife, Shelley, were at the airport to meet him. The next day, Dixie Meadows and Candace Oakley baked a cake for Linda Oakley's birthday party while Duane slept in. Later, he got a ride to the Harley-Davidson dealership to pick up his newly re-tired bike.

"Duane's cycle was a Harley-Davidson Sportster," Grover Sassaman told writer John Ogden. "It was a modified chopper with fork legs. He had bought it second-hand from a local kid. The extended forks increase the distance from the handlebars to the shock absorbers on the front wheels and hurt handling at low speeds. All the manufacturers highly discourage them."

As if that modification wasn't dangerous enough, Duane also modified his brand-new helmet. "He climbed on his bike, took the new helmet, and cut the chin strap in two," recalled Sassaman. "I told him that wasn't a good idea, but he just smiled and rode off."

Duane's motorcycle escapades in Macon were the stuff of legend. He had ridden Harleys since his early days in Daytona Beach, and he was notorious for breaking every traffic law in the book. "One night the Macon police caught Duane out riding," Alan Walden says. "He had no tag, no driver's license, no helmet, and he ran a red light. They pulled him over, found out who he was, and escorted him home. They told him, 'Now Duane, you stay home tonight.' They caught his ass about 35 minutes later, running another red light. I don't think they were as kind to him that time."

On October 29, after picking up his bike, Allman rode over to the Big House. Everyone was beginning to gather for Linda's surprise party. Since it was so close to Halloween, Duane spent some time cheerfully carving jack-o-lanterns as he sat on the porch. Phil Walden—who was on vacation in Bimini at the time—would undoubtedly have been more than a little nervous to know that one of the guitar players for the biggest act on his label was whittling away on a pumpkin with a sharp blade. One wrong move and the new album the band had started working on a few weeks earlier could be indefinitely delayed.

It was about half-past five when a small caravan of two cars and a motorcycle got ready to head back to Duane's house to pick up the presents and the cake for a still unsuspecting Linda Oakley. Dixie and Candace were in one car; Berry was in the other. Duane was set to lead the way on his motorcycle.

In the big-screen movie version of Duane Allman's life story, this is the moment when the camera would zoom in on Duane's dog-collared Frye boot kick-starting the Harley. The engine roars to life. The camera pans out to show the guitarist astride his chopper, smiling as he looks back at the folks assembled in front of the Big House. The sliced-in-half straps of his helmet slowly flap in the breeze. As the motorcycle sprays gravel on its way down Vineville Avenue, the camera follows a few feet behind for a block or two before coming to a stop, allowing us to watch the guitarist riding off into the sunset as the familiar introduction to "Statesboro Blues" begins to play. The motorcycle slowly disappears from view as the screen fades to black. Then a paragraph in large white letters—the epitaph from Duane's monument at Rose Hill Cemetery—slowly scrolls up: "I love being alive and I will be the best man I

possibly can. I will take love wherever I find it and offer it to everyone who will take it—seek knowledge from those wiser—and teach those who wish to learn from me."
—Duane Allman.

In the real world, there is no pretty way to tell the story. Duane rode his motorcycle west on Vineville, then turned south onto Pio Nono Avenue. Most drivers would stay on Pio Nono for about a half-mile to Napier Avenue. A right turn on Napier leads straight to Burton Avenue—the street where Duane and Dixie lived. But Allman had resided in Macon for so long that he knew all the back roads and shortcuts. He'd needed that knowledge on those occasions when the local police had to be outrun. Rather than following Pio Nono all the way down to Napier, Allman made a sharp right turn onto Hillcrest Avenue, traveling west once more.

At the intersection of Hillcrest and Bartlett Street, everything went wrong. A truck heading east on Hillcrest began to make a left turn onto Bartlett. Because motorcycles are much less noticeable than four-wheeled vehicles, every seasoned biker is used to having a car, truck, or bus turn left in front of him. Duane was no exception. As always, Allman was going much too fast, but he knew what to do. It was just a matter of swinging to his left, zipping past the truck on the wrong side of the road, and then quickly swerving back into the right lane to avoid any possible oncoming traffic.

What happened in the next few moments is unclear: Duane might have tried—and failed—to squeeze his Harley between the truck and the curb, or he might have decided at the last second to lay the bike down. In any event, there was an impact violent enough to cause his unstrapped helmet to fly off. The bike hit the street so hard that it made holes in the pavement. After one bounce, the big Harley landed right on top of Allman, and then skidded almost a hundred feet down Hillcrest before coming to rest on the curb—its engine still running.

Candace and Dixie, following close behind, got to Duane within a matter of seconds. Candace ran to get help, but she had to go to three different houses before someone finally agreed to let her use their phone to call an ambulance.

When help finally arrived—after what seemed like "forever," according to one account—Duane was unconscious, but his external injuries were no more than a handful of scratches. Dixie thought he had escaped a close call, so it came as a shock to her, as she rode along in the ambulance on the way to the hospital, when Duane stopped breathing. One of the paramedics was able to revive him with mouth-to-mouth resuscitation.

Candace drove on to Duane's house. An oblivious Berry, who had taken the more obvious route to Burton Avenue, was still there waiting. She told the bassist what had happened, and then called Gregg. The younger Allman's apartment was in such close proximity to the Medical Center of Central Georgia that he took off in a dead run to be by his brother's side.

As word spread about Duane's accident, his friends began showing up at the hospital. He was still unconscious, which was not a good sign. Dr. Charles Burton determined that surgery was the only option. Gregg was sent home, and Duane was wheeled into the operating room. Almost exactly three hours after the accident happened, Duane Allman was pronounced dead.

Duane had suffered multiple internal injuries, including a ruptured coronary artery and a severely damaged liver—both presumably caused by the 500-pound Harley landing on top of him.

Red Dog was sent to Gregg's apartment to deliver the tragic news.

Duane's old friend John McEuen was on the road when he found out. "At first I was mad because I wasn't going to see him again," he says. "Then I was mad that I hadn't spent more time around him. The Allman Brothers had been doing well and things were finally starting to happen for them. Hey, what could be better, right? When we heard that he had died it was kind of like you just didn't want to think about it. It just didn't seem fair."

Word of Allman's death soon hit the airwaves. Duane's daughter, Galadrielle, and her mother, Donna, were on a camping trip in the Midwest when Donna was told the news by other campers—campers who had no clue of her relationship to Duane. Donna and Galadrielle immediately made their way to Macon while Geraldine Allman flew up from Daytona Beach.

By the day of the funeral—Monday, November 1—many of the musicians who had been a part of Duane's life had arrived in town to mourn his death. Delaney Bramlett, Thom Doucette, Dr. John, Barry Beckett, Roger Hawkins, David Hood, Jimmy Johnson, and—of course—the five remaining members

Snow's Memorial Chapel, November 1, 1971– (L–R) Berry, Jaimoe, Dickey, Delaney Bramlett, and Butch Trucks performing at Duane Allman's funeral

of the Allman Brothers Band were among the hundreds who filled Snow's Memorial Chapel.

Before the funeral began, road manager Willie Perkins had the difficult job of ushering Duane's family and closest friends into a room adjoining the chapel so they could each see Duane—his casket open—one last time. Just prior to the service, the lid of the casket was finally closed, but not before a Coricidin bottle had been slipped onto his ring finger—and a joint placed in his pocket.

The funeral began at 3:00 in the afternoon. With Duane's guitar case and flower-covered casket in front of them, the Allman Brothers Band with Thom Doucette began the service by playing "The Sky Is Crying." They followed the Elmore James classic with "Key to the Highway," one of the tunes that had featured Duane's slide work on *Layla and Other Assorted Love Songs.* "Stormy Monday" was next—a song Gregg and his brother had played together since the Allman Joys days. Then came "In Memory of Elizabeth Reed."

Delaney Bramlett stepped up to the podium, leading the mourners in the old Carter Family standard "Will the Circle Be Unbroken?" It was a familiar melody that Duane had worked into "Mountain Jam" hundreds of times.

Bramlett closed with "Come On in My Kitchen," the Robert Johnson song on which Duane had played acoustic slide with Delaney & Bonnie less than four months earlier on WPLJ in New York.

Gregg then sat down with an acoustic guitar and sang "Melissa," Duane's favorite of the many songs written by his little brother. "I never much cared for it," said Gregg, "but I'm going to sing it for him."

The band had already done the songs they had planned to perform in the service, but they couldn't seem to quit just yet. Gregg, Berry, Butch, and Jaimoe returned to their instruments while Dickey picked up Duane's Les Paul and launched into Duane's familiar slide intro to "Statesboro Blues."

Jerry Wexler had been asked to give the eulogy. It wasn't an easy task for the man who—not even three months earlier—had attended the memorial service for another close friend. "It was at King Curtis's funeral that I last saw Duane Allman," said Wexler, "and Duane with tears in his eyes told me that Curtis's encouragement and praise was valuable to him in the pursuit of his music and career. They were both gifted, natural musicians with an unlimited ability for truly melodic improvisation. They were both born in the South, and they both learned their music from great black musicians and blues singers. They were both utterly dedicated to their music . . . both intolerant of the false and the meretricious, and they would never permit the incorporation of the commercial compromise to their music—not for love or money."

As he spoke, Wexler unsuccessfully fought back tears. "I remember a magic summer night of music when Duane and Delaney sat on an outdoor patio overlooking the water, both playing acoustic guitars as softly as they possibly could, and both of them singing: Blind Willie Johnson, Robert Johnson, Jimmie Rodgers, and an unforgettable Jimmie Davis song called 'Shackles and Chains.' The music was incredibly pure—completely free of affect—and almost avoided personality as each of them gave himself over to the ineffable beauty of Southern gospel, country, and blues music as only Southern musicians can."

The man who had gotten the call from Rick Hall only three years earlier—the music industry exec who by listening to Duane's guitar playing through the receiver of his phone could recognize greatness—then summed up Duane's too-short life in one concluding paragraph:

"Those of us who were privileged to know Duane will remember him from all the studios, backstage dressing rooms, the Downtowners, the Holiday Inns,

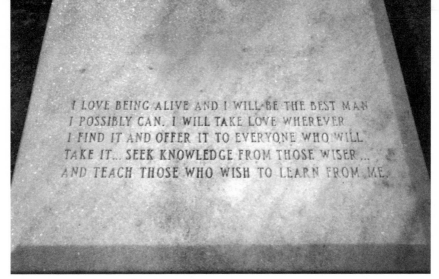

In his own words—Duane Allman's epitaph

the Sheratons, the late nights relaxing after the sessions, the whiskey and the music talk, playing back cassettes until night gave way to dawn, the meals and the pool games, and fishing in Miami and Long Island—this young, beautiful man who we love so dearly, but who is not lost to us, because we have his music—and the music is imperishable."

CHAPTER TWENTY-TWO

Eat a Peach

*"I'm hitting a lick for peace—and every time I'm
in Georgia, I eat a peach for peace." — D.A.*

The funeral was over, and the time had come for the remaining members of the band to make some serious decisions. "We were originally going to take six months off and try to regroup," Butch Trucks said in a conversation with Tom Dowd for *Hittin' the Note* magazine. "There was never any thought of not continuing, because Duane had given us the religion, and we were going to keep playing it."

The Allman Brothers—with their name taking on a figurative sense for the first time—returned to the road. "They went out, without a replacement, as a five-piece band," says keyboardist Chuck Leavell. "That was an emotional time, not only for the members of the Allman Brothers but for all of us that were in the Macon scene. Whether we were connected to Capricorn Records or whatever, it was a very emotional thing to see this great band carry on after such a prominent member had such a tragic demise."

Muscle Shoals-based musician Stephen Foster was there when the five-piece version of the band performed at Auburn University shortly after Duane's death. "The concert was personal and stunning and scary. When the time came for Duane's leads, the band just played rhythm and the crowd started *singing* Duane's leads.

"The band was in tears at times. The entire audience was in tears a lot of the time. Eighteen thousand people singing a slide lead—singing the riffs to 'Statesboro Blues.' It was amazing—almost a religious experience, and a poignant farewell to Duane. It showed clearly how devoted the fans were, and how closely they had paid attention to his musicianship. I was blessed to be there and will never forget it. It gave me a whole new take on Duane's impact."

In late November, the five-piece band played a series of dates in and around New York City, including two shows at Carnegie Hall on the 25th. On the day of the Carnegie Hall concerts—with an unfortunate combination of bad timing and bad taste—the latest issue of *Rolling Stone* hit the newsstands, featuring both a front-page obituary of Duane Allman and what it described as a "candid account" of a week on the road with the Allman Brothers Band. The obituary, written by Jon Landau, told of Duane's death in somber and respectful tones, but the so-called "candid account," written by Grover Lewis, was an unflattering, smarmy piece that portrayed the Allman Brothers as nothing more than a bunch of backwoods rednecks who just happened to be pretty good musicians.

Lewis referred to the band as "Dixie greasers," and the quotes he attributed to Duane and the rest were akin to dialogue from the movie *Deliverance*. "Pretty" became "purty," "thing" became "thang," "tired" became "tahrd," "guitars" became "git-tars," and so on. If the reader is to believe every quote is accurate, almost everyone said "I reckon" at one time or another. Gregg suffered the most, with virtually every quote attributed to him being a mere parroting of whatever his older brother had just said. Lewis also chose to go into great detail about the band's consumption of "piles of coke"—an element of the story that would spell serious trouble for Gregg a few years later.

One person close to the band has suggested that the article was primarily a work of fiction. Whether or not it was an accurate assessment—and despite Lewis's decision to show the band in the worst possible light—there is one phrase that he got exactly right. Throughout the article, Lewis told of various band members and roadies using the expression "hittin' the note."

The phrase's appearance in the *Rolling Stone* piece prompted many an interviewer to ask the members of the original band to define it. Perhaps the best explanation was given by Butch Trucks during an interview with Kevin Spangler and Ron Currens for the magazine that derived its name from the phrase. "Hittin' the note is reaching that point where you can't do any wrong," said

Butch. "With us, when we're playing music, it's where the brain goes away and the body just does what it's supposed to do, and there's no thought and there's no question, and no matter what you do, it's right. It's getting to that spiritual level where the communication is total, but it's not mental.

"Spirituality has to be there or it isn't music. I greatly adhere to the philosophy that what makes us human is that we have a brain and that we need to use it. And we need to not take too much on faith, and we should always be questioning and rational and thinking. Once you quit doing that, you're not human anymore. Then you're like some kind of cattle. What's happened with the great religions and the wars of the world tends to show that to be true. But something happens when you're playing music that kind of bypasses the brain and just goes straight to something else. Now, you have to use your brain to get it going. In order to play what we play, you know, there's thought, there's a *lot* of thought. But once it gets going—once that spark is lit—then everything starts flowing and there's this unity, this spirituality, this communication that happens, and *that's* when you're hittin' the note."

By mid-December, the five-piece Allman Brothers Band was back at Criteria trying to finish their next album. Three numbers—"Blue Sky," "Stand Back," and Duane's instrumental piece, "Little Martha"—were all they had in the can at the time of the guitarist's death. "We knew that this was the last music Duane recorded," says Butch, "and we knew that we had to finish it up so that we could get it out to the people."

Three songs don't make an album, and Gregg and Dickey had only one new work apiece—"Ain't Wastin' Time No More" and "Les Brers in A Minor," respectively—ready to be recorded. Butch recalls, "I talked with Gregg and said that the one song that was Duane's favorite song ever was 'Melissa,' and we had to do that one."

"Melissa," which Gregg had sung at Duane's funeral, was one of the songs that had been recorded during the 31st of February sessions back in the late summer of 1968. Although a 31st of February album with the original version of "Melissa" would eventually be released in late 1972, the Allman Brothers Band's take of the song came out first—and it was far superior to the original.

The group had no problems getting "Melissa" down, but Dickey's new instrumental, "Les Brers in A Minor," was a different matter altogether. While the band had been away from Criteria, a new room—Studio C—had been added to the recording complex. According to Tom Dowd, "When Mac Emmerman—who started and owned Criteria studio here in Miami—built Studio C, it was a copy of the original Atlantic studio we had up in New York." Emmerman built the room based on plans drawn up by Dowd, but there were "a couple of minor changes . . . [and] Mac had lined the walls in shag carpeting." This turned out to be a bad idea.

"It was absolutely the deadest room," says Butch. "We got the intro done, but it was so dead that we had to do something. On 'Les Brers,' there is a noticeable difference in the sound of the instruments from the intro to the meat of the song because we finished it up—after trying about eight times to do it in the other room—in Studio A, which was this big, giant room. I think we got it in one take over there. We literally just picked everything up and dragged it all over to the other studio because we were getting nowhere in that dead room."

A close listen to "Les Brers in A Minor" shows that more than just the ambiance changed when the band moved to Studio A. "There is also a very slight pitch variation between the two parts of that song," recalled Dowd. "Back in those days, the tape machines had a tendency to either run uphill or downhill, depending on where you were on the reel. So if you took something from the beginning of one reel and tried to splice it onto something that was at the end of another reel, you had big problems matching up the speed and the pitch of the instruments." In the end, Dowd decided that the pitch variation was not noticeable enough to require re-recording the intro.

That problem overcome, the band moved on to Gregg's new song, "Ain't Wastin' Time No More." It was a clear statement about his realization that death is an inescapable inevitability—that every day is precious. The relevance to recent events was evident when the band chose the song as the album's opening track.

The Allman Brothers had six songs finished. It was better than three, but a long way from what they needed for an album. Plus, so soon after Duane's death, it was difficult to imagine releasing an album that featured him on only three cuts. The solution was to go back to the live recordings made at the Fillmore East. Tape had been rolling on June 27, when the band had appeared there for the hall's closing night. One highlight from that show was the classic Elmore James/Sonny Boy Williamson song "One Way Out." The band decided to add it to their album-in-progress, along with a version of "Trouble No More" from the March gig.

With just about any other band of that era, and under normal circumstances, an album that was more than half an hour long would have been considered sufficient. But the Allman Brothers weren't just any band, and the circumstances were far from normal. So, after listening to the remaining tapes of their Fillmore East appearances, the group decided to include their ultimate live showpiece: "Mountain Jam."

"The only problem," says Butch, "was there was only one decent recording of it that was good enough to put out, but it was also one of the worst we ever played. We said we had to put that one out because it was Duane playing on it, and we had to use as much of his music as we possibly could at that point. Had Duane not died, *Eat a Peach* would have been just a single album, and not what it ended up being."

When Phil Walden showed Trucks the artwork for the album, he was knocked out by what Jim Flournoy Holmes and David Powell had created, but the title that Capricorn had chosen—*The Kind We Grow in Dixie*—wasn't to his liking at all. "The title sucks!" he told Walden. Then the drummer remembered a quote of Duane's from one of his last interviews. When the writer Ellen Mandel had asked Allman what he was doing to help the revolution, he responded, "I'm hitting a lick for peace—and every time I'm in Georgia, I eat a peach for peace. But you can't help the revolution, because there's just evolution. I understand the need for a lot of changes in the country, but I believe that as soon as everybody can see just a little bit better, and get a little hipper to what's going on, they're going to change it. Everybody will—not just the young people. Everybody is going to say, 'Man, this stinks. I cannot tolerate the smell of this thing anymore. Let's eliminate it and get straight with ourselves.' I believe if everybody does it for themselves, it'll take care of itself."

"Call this thing *Eat a Peach for Peace*," Trucks told Walden. In the end, the title was whittled down to simply *Eat a Peach*.

With that, everything seemed to be in place—but just before the album's release, Phil Walden made a business decision that remains a sore spot with Jerry Wexler to this day. "Phil had an assistant named Frank Fenter," says Wexler. "I had signed the Allman Brothers to a three-year distribution contract. At the

Eat a Peach—*the album's title came from Duane's quote, "Every time I'm in Georgia, I eat a peach for peace"*

termination of that contract, Fenter came up to New York to take them away and get them a different deal with Warner Brothers.

"Somebody once said I didn't want them anymore. Horseshit! Phil pulled the rug out from under me. I never called him on it. But he sent his man up to take them away and sign them to a bigger deal. What apparently was on his mind was that he couldn't get very much on a renewal deal with Atlantic because of our close association. His attitude was, 'Let's go elsewhere where we can really bring the hammer down.' They snatched a jewel, a gem—unconscionably—away from me, without explanation."

Throughout the long career of the Allman Brothers Band—right to the present day—there have been moments when it has seemed that the word "irony" was created just so there would be a way to describe the group's constantly changing fortunes. This was just such a moment.

With the release of *Eat a Peach* in February 1972, the Allman Brothers' popularity surpassed everything that had preceded it. Duane Allman, only four months gone when the double album hit the record stores, was on the verge of having the biggest-selling record of his career. *Eat a Peach* was on the charts by early March, eventually climbing to Number 4—nine spots higher than *At Fillmore East*. But, ironically (there's just no other word to describe it), even *Eat a Peach*—the last album of those released in chronological order to contain tracks that included Duane—would pale when compared to what lay ahead.

CHAPTER TWENTY-THREE

The Allman Brothers Band A.D.

"As soon as we get the money—as soon we get famous and rich and get to be stars—we'll hire some more cats." — D.A.

Eat a Peach brought many new fans into the fold, and the band toured heavily in early 1972. But as the year wore on, Gregg began to seriously consider taking on a solo project. He had always been the band's primary songwriter, but he had begun to compose songs that simply didn't fall into the Allman Brothers' established style.

Before the year was out, Gregg headed into the studio to begin work on the tracks that would eventually make up his first solo album, *Laid Back*. He would call on many of his old friends to play on the recording sessions: Paul Hornsby and Johnny Sandlin from his Hour Glass days, both having worked at Capricorn Studios since 1969; Tommy Talton and Scott Boyer from Cowboy; David Brown from the 31st of February. Gregg also invited Butch Trucks and Jaimoe, along with a host of other players, including—on some songs—a 40-piece orchestra. Another musician who was on hand for the *Laid Back* sessions was the kid who had first heard Gregg singing with the Allman Joys at Fort Brandon Armory in Tuscaloosa.

Chuck Leavell had come a long way since those days. "I am playing piano professionally because of Paul Hornsby," Leavell told John Lynskey. "I was 15 years old when I met Paul, back in Alabama, and he took me under his wing.

He always encouraged me—'Hey kid, you can do this. It's gonna be fine.' He taught me so much about keyboards, and he also encouraged me to sing. I was shy about it, but Paul somehow made me comfortable. I was just a kid, but Paul treated me like an equal. He gave me a break, and that meant a lot to me. I love him for that. When he left for Macon, I was devastated. My big brother, my mentor, was going away. It freaked me out, so the logical solution was to find out where the hell Macon, Georgia, was, and go join him!

"I ended up in a couple of bands that quite often opened concerts for the Allmans. One was with Alex Taylor, James Taylor's elder brother; after that, with Dr. John. I always insisted on an acoustic piano for our sets, and then our equipment would be pulled back and the Allman Brothers would set up and play. Some of the guys in our band would go back to the hotel room or go off to do whatever, but I always liked to hang around and hear the Allmans play. I'd sit there at the piano backstage, and while the Allmans were doing their concert, I'd play along. By doing that, I got familiar with a lot of their tunes."

That familiarity began to pay off for Leavell in late 1972. "I got a call from Johnny Sandlin to come in and play on Gregg Allman's solo album. Johnny was co-producing the album with Gregg. We recorded a couple of songs for *Laid Back*, but sometimes—during the course of the recordings—the rest of the Allman Brothers would come down, and we'd have these jam sessions."

With Gregg in the studio, the band was off the road for once. But the urge to play kept pulling them back together, and the jam sessions were all they needed as an impetus to start working on the next ABB album. However, it was clear that a new direction was necessary. Thanks to the Fillmore tapes as well as the songs that had been recorded before Duane's death, *Eat a Peach* sounded like an album made by the same band that had cut the three previous Allman Brothers albums. But there would be no more contributions from Duane Allman. There was also no possible way to replace him. The time had come for the remaining band members to step up—if the group was to survive, there was no alternative.

The Allman Brothers Band had already seen what happened when key members of other bands had passed away. After the Doors lost Jim Morrison, their recording career was virtually over. On the other hand, the Rolling Stones' greatest successes would come years after original member Brian Jones was found dead in his swimming pool. The situation with Duane was unique. He had been the band's founder and leader; the person who got the band their record deal with Capricorn; the man who spoke between songs onstage; and the guitarist whose incredible musical talent created a genre of Southern music that other musicians and other bands continue to emulate to the present day. Despite all of those things, he had never been the band's "voice." With the exception of "Dimples," Duane wasn't a vocalist during his time with the ABB. That being the case, the remaining members knew there was a chance they could go on, simply because the record-buying public was familiar with the singing voices of Gregg Allman and Dickey Betts. It wasn't like the situation the Doors were in after Morrison died. Duane's role had been different—as Butch said, Duane had given them "the religion." It was the band's mission to keep on proselytizing—spreading the word and adding new converts to the flock.

The band members knew better than to try to replace the messiah of their musical religion. He was gone and there would be no Second Coming. They would simply have to find an alternative—and when Chuck Leavell started jamming with the Allman Brothers during breaks from Gregg's solo album, the light bulb went on.

"One thing led to another, and the sessions started feeling pretty good," recalls Chuck. "Within two weeks, I got a call to go into the offices of Phil Walden. I walked in for this meeting, and there's all the Allman Brothers Band, there's Phil Walden. I'm this kid who was, at the time, barely 20 years old—and next thing I know, I'm asked to be in the Allman Brothers Band. After picking myself up off the floor, I said, 'Yeah! I'd like to do that.'"

For the first time since the band's formation in March 1969, the Allman Brothers had inducted a new member. Logic would seem to have dictated a move more along the lines of Thom Doucette. Much of what Duane had played over the years was so strongly reminiscent of a blues harp's sliding notes that bringing a harmonica player into the lineup could have maintained much of the band's sound without the potential backlash of trying to replace Duane with another slide guitarist. But Chuck's involvement with Gregg's solo session was fortuitous—and the decision to bring him into the fold was a stroke of musical genius.

"Chuck came into the ABB at a very rough, rough time," says Gregg. "As I look back on it now, his coming with the band helped everyone concerned—musically and otherwise."

The band was so excited about the new lineup that Gregg's solo album was set aside for the moment while the Allman Brothers started working on their next record. The sessions began in earnest in October 1972. Once again, Gregg and Dickey had new songs ready to get the project under way. Gregg's latest was called "Wasted Words," while Dickey's new one was the song that would lift the Allman Brothers from the ranks of underground FM bands and carry them the biggest hit of their entire career.

"We were recording every night down there at Capricorn Studios," says Leavell, "and Dickey had 'Ramblin' Man.' We all kind of thought, 'Wow, this is a country tune—but it's a *cool* country tune.' Even so, there was a feeling at first of, 'Does this really belong on the record?'"

Looking back through the mist of the decades that have passed, it's impossible to imagine the Allman Brothers passing up the chance to record the song. It would prove to be the band's biggest hit single, although no one knew that at the time, of course. But it's understandable that the decision to go ahead with "Ramblin' Man" must have seemed like a gamble, as there was nothing they had done before—with the possible exception of "Blue Sky"—that was such a departure from the blues-based works that made up the bulk of the band's repertoire.

"We laid it down," says Leavell, "and with me having just come into the band, a lot of those runs like the intro lick and the lick before the guitar solo—all of a sudden there was a piano playing in those harmonies as well as the guitar."

But something was obviously missing. Even though the decision had already been made to avoid the trap of trying to fill Duane's shoes, the song simply cried out for those familiar twin-guitar lines. "I remember that Dickey felt a little uneasy," says Chuck, "so he wanted to have another guitar."

Dickey knew just the guy. A few weeks earlier, two musicians had arrived in Macon to jam with the Allman Brothers' remaining guitarist. At that time—especially with Gregg working on a solo project—Dickey was thinking about forming a side band to play in when the Allman Brothers weren't in the studio or on the road. (After all, Gregg hadn't called on Dickey to help with his solo project, even though he was using both Jaimoe and Butch.) The two musicians Dickey had jammed with were keyboard player Peter Schless, an old acquaintance of

Dickey's, and guitarist Les Dudek. Betts had been impressed by what he'd heard in Dudek's playing, so when it came time to record "Ramblin' Man," he asked the teenaged guitarist to play on the session.

"So it was two guitars and a piano doing those lines," says Chuck. "We recorded the tune, and I was invited to sing on the choruses—sing a harmony part—so I found my part, and we went in and recorded the harmonies. We had a lot of fun with it."

The band also recorded Gregg's "Wasted Words," which would become the album's opening track. It was early November 1972. There were two songs in the can, and all signs pointed toward a band bouncing back and moving forward. It had been a year since Duane's death, and everyone in the studio was beginning to feel positive about the future of the Allman Brothers Band.

During Duane's days with the band, his leadership had never been challenged. Once he was gone, the burden of being in charge inevitably had to fall on somebody else's shoulders. In many bands, the lead singer is the natural leader—but that had never been the case with Gregg. ("I had never been around a group where the lead singer was so on the side of it all," says John Carter. "He's an amazing vocalist and a fantastic player, but he just hid behind his keyboard.") Like the other members of the Allman Brothers, Gregg had always followed his brother's direction—in fact, he had done that all his life.

Berry Oakley had always been the most organized one of the group. Back in his Jacksonville days, he had acted as manager of the Second Coming. Berry had also been the one who put the jams together at Willow Branch Park, always making sure everything was in order. And he had been very close to Duane since those Jacksonville days—the one Jacksonville guy Duane chose to bring up to Muscle Shoals to play on his solo sessions at Fame.

Although Berry was the youngest member of the band (before Chuck Leavell came on board), the others often looked to him for guidance. After they had moved into the Big House, Berry was the one who organized the meals—no small task for at least half-a-dozen adults and two children. As his sister Candace once put it, Berry was the "master of ceremonies to everyone." After Duane's death, he had even become the band's spokesman onstage. The more time that passed after Duane was gone, the more it became apparent that

Berry was seen by the others as the one to pick up the mantle. It was a great honor for the bass player, but also a heavy burden.

Those who knew Berry well have said that he was incapable of getting over what had happened to Duane. The loss was simply too great for him to bear. Even though he had gotten high enough to fall off the stage on at least one occasion—the kind of thing that some might have taken as a sign to cut back a bit—Berry kept on drinking and drugging.

"Berry started getting really, really messed up," Jaimoe told John Lynskey. "He was having a rough time with himself because he didn't know what to do with the whole situation. It just ate him up, man. We didn't know what was happening with Berry. We didn't know if he was going nuts or what. He was drinking, like, two fifths of vodka a day—crazy stuff like that. He was really disturbed about what was going on, and he missed Duane so much. I remember calling Lamar Williams and telling him how worried I was about Berry and everything that was going on. And then, a couple of weeks later, the accident happened."

The bass player had begun to have nightmares. He immersed himself in the music of delta blues singer Robert Johnson, and was soon telling his wife that there were hellhounds on his trail. Somehow, though, through the haze of drugs and alcohol and mental anguish, Oakley managed to keep his organizational skills intact—to the very end.

Chuck Leavell recalls, "I was living out at Idlewild South with Scott Boyer and David Brown. On the day that Berry died, there was to be this jam session at a place called the Ad Lib in Macon. Berry came out, and as I recall, [roadies] 'Tuffy' Phillips and Kim Payne were with him, and they were pretty lit up, you know. But they were excited, and Berry told us, 'We're going to have the B. O. Jam tonight, and we want y'all to come.'" (The full name of the bass player's local jam session was actually "Berry Oakley's Jive-Ass Revue, featuring the Rowdy Roadies and the Shady Ladies"—understandably shortened to the "B. O. Jam" among the musicians.)

"He invited me and Scott," continues Leavell, "and then he said, 'We're going to have a little rehearsal at the Big House in a couple of hours, so if you want to come, we'll be there,' and then they split. This was exciting news to us, and to me especially, so I said, 'Okay, I'm ready.' A couple of hours later, we got in the car. I had a burgundy '65 Olds Cutlass station wagon, and we drove over to the Big House for the rehearsal."

As Chuck was driving toward the Big House, Berry was on his Triumph 750 motorcycle, going east on Napier Avenue. Kim Payne was riding next to him. They were on their way to the Big House as well. Berry and Kim were playing around on their bikes, one passing a car on the right side while the other passed it on the left. Despite his antics that day, Berry had never been as skilled at riding a motorcycle as some of the other band members and roadies.

The basic principles of riding a motorcycle are relatively simple: accelerate by turning the throttle with the right hand; shift gears by pulling in the clutch with the left hand and pushing down or pulling up the shift lever with the left foot; control the front brake with the right hand; activate the rear brake with the right foot. One of the hardest things to master, though, is making a sharp turn at high speed. The sharper the turn, the more the rider must lean in the direction of the turn. Just leaning isn't enough; in fact, one has to lean while turning the front wheel in the opposite direction—that is, *counter*steering. To cause the bike to turn right, the motorcyclist must turn the front wheel slightly to the left while leaning the bike to the right. Leaning a bike that weighs several hundred pounds while simultaneously countersteering can be pretty unnerving for a novice, because it sometimes feels that the bike might go down on even the slightest of turns.

Going east on Napier Avenue, there is a sharp curve to the right just as one approaches Inverness Avenue. On November 11, 1972, as Berry was nearing Inverness, a city bus was heading west on Napier. The driver saw that the motorcycle was on his side of the road. Even though the bus driver swerved to his right and hit the brakes, Berry failed to lean far enough into the curve to avoid hitting the side of the bus. The impact was so severe that he was thrown almost 60 feet down Inverness. The momentum of the Triumph as it bounced off the side of the bus sent it in the same direction, and it landed right on top of Oakley—precisely what had happened to Duane.

When Kim Payne got to Berry, he found the external damage to be minimal. The bassist's nose was bleeding and his helmet was cracked. Despite the powerful impact of being hit by a bus—or, more accurately, despite the bus being hit by Oakley's motorcycle—Berry was able to stand up. Being less than a mile-and-a-half from the Big House, he decided to catch a ride home rather than go to the hospital.

When Berry got back to the Big House, Scott Boyer reports, "He had a little tiny hole in his forehead. He said, 'I dropped my bike on the way home.'

He was all bummed out about it. But he said, 'Let me go upstairs and change clothes, and we'll go down and jam.'"

A short time later, says Chuck Leavell, "Red Dog and some of the other guys were bringing Berry down the stairs, and he was in obvious agony and pain. The women of the house were all excited, and there was a lot of commotion going on. They told me, 'He's out of his head. We've got to get him to the hospital.' I said, 'Let's go.' We loaded him in my station wagon and got him to the hospital as quickly as we could."

Oakley was admitted to the hospital a few minutes before 3:00 p.m. He was pronounced dead less than an hour later. The cracked helmet, the hole in his forehead, and the nosebleed were all clues to his demise: Berry Oakley had fractured his skull, resulting in hemorrhaging of the brain. Although it didn't make anyone feel any better, the doctors who worked on him would later state that it would have made no difference if Berry had been brought to the hospital sooner. He had been mortally injured the moment the accident happened.

Berry died one year and 13 days after Duane. The two motorcycle accidents had taken place within four blocks of each other. As had been the case with Duane, Berry Oakley was only 24 at the time of his death.

An Anthology— a collection of Duane's finest work both as a session guitarist and as a member of the Allman Brothers Band, released just over a year after his death

Final resting place of Duane Allman and Berry Oakley—Rose Hill Cemetery

The irony of the situation did not stop there. Duane had not yet been laid to rest. Just prior to Berry's accident, Donna had returned to Macon to finally resolve the matter of Duane's burial. Now that Berry was gone as well, the sad solution was obvious. As they had done night after night, sharing a hotel room on the road, Duane Allman and Berry Oakley would lie next to each other once again—this time in Rose Hill Cemetery.

Only a few days after Allman and Oakley were buried, Capricorn Records released the first of two collections featuring the guitar work of Duane Allman. Entitled *An Anthology*, the double album opened with "B.B. King Medley" from the Hour Glass sessions at Fame and included "Goin' Down Slow" from Duane's unreleased solo project, as well as tracks by Clarence Carter, Wilson Pickett, Aretha Franklin, King Curtis, Delaney & Bonnie, Derek & the Dominos, the Allman Brothers Band, and others. More than a year after his death, Duane's popularity was at an all-time high. The record climbed into the Top 30 on the album charts, and before the year was out it had gone gold.

Meanwhile, the Allman Brothers Band played on. Auditions for a new bass player got under way in late 1972, and the five remaining members unanimously chose Jaimoe's old friend Lamar Williams—the man whom Jaimoe had called to express his concerns about Berry only days before the accident. "Wasted Words" and "Ramblin' Man" had already been recorded before Berry's accident, so the

The Allman Brothers Band during the Chuck Leavell/Lamar Williams era

Allman Brothers with Williams on bass cut another song by Gregg—"Come and Go Blues"—and three more by Dickey: "Southbound," "Pony Boy," and a resounding instrumental called "Jessica" that featured Les Dudek on acoustic guitar and an inspired piano solo by Chuck Leavell. The band also recorded a traditional blues called "Jelly Jelly."

As soon as the sessions were over, the band was back on the road playing shows from New Haven, Connecticut, to Ontario, California, and then heading east again, arriving at Watkins Glen, New York, in late July for the biggest single show in rock & roll history to that point. Billed as "a day in the country" with the Allman Brothers Band, the Grateful Dead, and The Band, it drew a crowd that had swelled to some 600,000 people by show time. "Watkins Glen with the Brothers will always stand out as a special moment in time for me," Leavell once said. "It was incredible—not only for the number of people that were there . . . but for the event itself. The Grateful Dead, The Band, the jam with all of us—it was a natural high."

The following month, the new ABB album, *Brothers and Sisters*, was released, as well as a single of "Ramblin' Man." Just as the *Eat a Peach* cover had included the line "Dedicated to a Brother—Duane Allman," the new record included the sadly similar phrase "Dedicated to a Brother—Berry Oakley."

Whatever response the band might have expected, it's doubtful anyone was prepared for the unprecedented success of both the album and the single. Having played to more than half a million people a few weeks earlier no doubt helped to spur sales, but when *Brothers and Sisters* and "Ramblin' Man" hit the stores in August, there seemed to be a race to see which would reach the summit of its respective chart first. The LP won, hitting the Number 1 spot on the Top Pop Albums chart on September 8 and remaining there for an incredible five weeks. On October 13, "Ramblin' Man" peaked at Number 2 on the singles chart, denied the coveted top spot by a 45 called "Half-Breed" recorded by—of all people—Cher.

CHAPTER TWENTY-FOUR

Decline, Fall & Resurrection

"I'm not gonna sit back and watch this whole thing
go down the tubes." — D.A.

After the success of *Brothers and Sisters* and its hit single, "Ramblin' Man," Gregg resumed work on *Laid Back*. Dickey began recording his own solo album as well. In both cases, there was no thought at the time of leaving the group that had gotten them to where they were. Instead, they each had musical points to make outside the confines of the Allman Brothers Band. In Gregg's case, *Laid Back* would even include two songs the band had already recorded: "Midnight Rider" and "Please Call Home." According to Gregg, both songs "were originally written and arranged the way they appear on my solo record." When he had presented them to the ABB, "everyone contributed their own kind of style, their own feel, their own parts"—but on *Laid Back* Gregg was able to record the songs his way. The Allman Brothers' single of "Midnight Rider" had failed to score on the pop charts in 1970, but Gregg's solo take of the song became a genuine hit, reaching the Top 20 in the early weeks of 1974. *Rolling Stone, Billboard, Stereo Review,* and other music magazines raved about *Laid Back*, with most critics agreeing that the new version of "Midnight Rider" was a serious improvement over the original.

Like Gregg's album and *Brothers and Sisters* before it, Dickey's *Highway Call* was co-produced by Johnny Sandlin. Both Allman and Betts included Sandlin,

Tommy Talton, and Chuck Leavell among the players on their solo efforts. But Dickey took a different approach stylistically: while *Laid Back* remained in the R&B/rock & roll/pop vein, Dickey's initial solo project focused on his roots. "Dickey wanted to go in a country direction," says Leavell, "using players like Vassar Clements on fiddle and John Hughey on steel guitar, but with his own personal twist to the music." The album also included a Southern gospel group, the Rambos, on background vocals. The original LP was split in half, with the vocal selections on Side One and the instrumentals on Side Two. Several singles were released, but none of them garnered much airplay. *Highway Call* came out in August 1974 (as did Duane's *An Anthology, Volume II*), and it eventually climbed to Number 19 on *Billboard*'s Top Pop Albums chart. The second Skydog anthology didn't fare as well as the first, peaking at Number 49. As good as it was, critics and record buyers alike felt Duane's finest work had already been presented in the previous two-record set.

Before Dickey's album was released, Gregg had already put together a huge ensemble and begun a tour to promote *Laid Back*, simultaneously recording a live album that would result in his second solo release that October. In an unselfish move not at all typical of the times, *The Gregg Allman Tour* album included two songs by Cowboy, the band that opened the shows. "That tour was just wonderful," recalls Tommy Talton. "We played all the best venues in every large city in the United States. We did 35 gigs in 50 days, from Providence, Rhode Island, to Seattle, San Diego, Chicago, Memphis, Atlanta, Miami, Tampa, Jacksonville, and everywhere in between. Cowboy would start out the show, and we would play for an hour or so. Then we would take a short intermission and come back to support Gregg." Although the album didn't go gold, as its predecessor had done, *The Gregg Allman Tour* sold over 200,000 copies—a respectable number for a live, two-record set.

While Dickey and Gregg were touring, both found themselves obliged to deny rumors that the Allman Brothers had fallen apart. Although it was true that the band was still together, it was on shaky ground. That became obvious in early 1975, when they gathered at Capricorn Studios to work on the next ABB album. They began by recording a Muddy Waters song, "Can't Lose What You Never Had," but then things started going downhill fast.

In a move reminiscent of the days following the demise of the Hour Glass, Gregg took off for Los Angeles. While sitting in with Etta James one night at the Troubadour, he spotted Cher in the audience. Within two days they were dating, and within a matter of months (on June 30, 1975, to be exact), they were married. Gregg stayed in Los Angeles with Cher, recording most of his vocals for the new Allman Brothers album at the Record Plant.

Like *Brothers and Sisters*, the new album was jointly produced by Johnny Sandlin and the Allman Brothers Band. Entitled *Win, Lose or Draw*, it was released in August. Along with the Muddy Waters cover and "Sweet Mama" by Billy Joe Shaver, there were two new songs by Gregg and three by Dickey, including "High Falls," a Betts instrumental that clocked in at more than 14 minutes.

It had been two years since the band's last album. Although the public hadn't forgotten about the Allman Brothers, the long time between releases—and the solo albums by Gregg and Dickey—had unquestionably contributed to a slowing of the band's momentum. In addition, *Win, Lose or Draw* didn't have a single with the catchiness of "Ramblin' Man" or an instrumental with the power of "Jessica." In fact, there would be only one single: "Nevertheless" b/w "Louisiana Lou and Three Card Monty John." Both sides of the 45 would hit the pop singles chart, but neither would come close to making the Top 40. Despite the album's shortcomings—not the least of which was the fact that Gregg's vocals literally sounded more distant than on previous releases—*Win, Lose or Draw* made it to Number 5 on *Billboard*'s Top Pop Albums chart, eventually selling more than half a million copies.

And then the bottom fell out. Thanks in part to Grover Lewis's 1971 *Rolling Stone* article, as well as a *People* magazine piece that described Cher's attempts to keep Gregg off heroin, the federal government had taken an interest in the Allman Brothers' relationship to the men behind the Macon drug scene. In 1975, a local pharmacist, Joe Fuchs, and the band's security director, John "Scooter" Herring, were brought up on charges of conspiracy to distribute narcotics. Fuchs was quick to plead guilty, but Herring decided to fight the charges. When the case went to trial in June 1976, Gregg was brought in to testify against one of his own. Rather than hide behind the Fifth Amendment, he admitted to having purchased drugs from Herring on a number of occasions.

Gregg's decision to testify against a member of the Brotherhood was considered an affront to Dickey, Butch, Jaimoe, and the rest. Duane's 1971 statement that "drugs is one thing [that will break up a band] and do it quick" had turned out to be an eerily accurate prediction of precisely what would happen. Halfway through 1976, the Allman Brothers went their separate ways.

Without its flagship act, Phil Walden's label was in trouble. Walden's solution was to try to re-create the success of *At Fillmore East* by putting together another live, two-record set. The tracks were taken from Allman Brothers concerts ranging from a 1972 New Year's Eve show at the Warehouse in New Orleans to an October 1975 concert at the Oakland Coliseum. Although the recorded sound suffers due to a less-than-stellar mix (in a kind of strange admission, the credits thank Sam Whiteside for his "remixing efforts"), much of the music is surprisingly good—although the band members were not enthusiastic about the release. Jaimoe once said, "When that record came out, I didn't want to hear it. I didn't take the time to listen to it because we were very unhappy that the record company chose to put out an album mostly made up of different versions of songs that had already been released."

Unlike *At Fillmore East*—which had only two songs that had previously appeared on ABB albums (and upon which the live versions were vast improvements over the originals)—the new album was made up *entirely* of songs that had already been on earlier Allman Brothers LPs. "In Memory of Elizabeth Reed" made its third appearance on vinyl although this was only the band's seventh album. And then there was the matter of the album's title: *Wipe the Windows Check the Oil Dollar Gas.* In the history of rock, it has to rank as one of the worst-named records of all time.

Despite its poor mix, repetitive song selection, and inane title, the new album did show off the positive contribution made by the band's revised rhythm section. Jaimoe says, "The record company was just trying to make some quick money, and I ignored the album. A few years later, a friend of mine in Atlanta was talking about the great playing on that album and told me I should really give it a listen. So I finally did, and I was blown away by what I heard. The stuff that Chuck, Lamar, and I were playing—we were out there, man! Despite all the nonsense that was going on, Chuck, Lamar, and I were having a ball. We three were really locking on, and we were basically playing around Dickey, Gregg, and Butch—supporting them—but really playing off each other. It was so much fun, man. There's some damn good playing on there, and if you think about all the stuff that was going on, it's even more amazing that we could play that well. I mean, the walls were coming down, man! I think it's a damn fine record, especially in terms of what Lamar, Chuck, and I were doing."

Unfortunately for the band and its financially strapped label, the fans saw the album for exactly what it was: a semi-desperate attempt by Capricorn to pump out product by a defunct act. After the album was released in late 1976, it crawled to Number 75 on the album charts and then fell off completely after only ten weeks. The label didn't even bother to release a single.

While Gregg and Dickey were now focused on their solo careers, the other former members of the band began to consider their futures. Three of them had already begun playing together apart from the band while the Allman Brothers were still together. "During the years that I was with the Allman Brothers—which would have been '72 through '76—Jaimoe and Lamar Williams and I had a little side band," says Chuck Leavell. "We just loved to play. We'd play all the time. We played at people's parties. We played at Jaimoe's house. We played at my house. We played anywhere we could.

"One time, the Allman Brothers were playing in Boulder, Colorado, and we looked out the hotel window and saw this big field. Jaimoe called up Red Dog and he said, 'Augie'—we used to call him 'Augie Doggie'—he said, 'Augie, go get my drums and get Chuck's keyboard and get Lamar's bass and a couple of amplifiers and as many extension cords as you can and run 'em out in the middle of that field out there. We're gonna go play.' And we did. We would do things like that at the drop of a hat. We were known as We Three. That's what Jaimoe called us—We Three.

"When the Allman Brothers broke up in '76, we sat there in a room and said, 'Why don't we carry on with We Three?' We decided the trio was nice, but it might be good to have a guitar player. So I said, 'I know this guy in Washington, D.C.—Jimmy Nalls. He played with us in Alex Taylor's band.' Jaimoe said, 'Yeah, I remember Jimmy. Let's get him down.' So we got Jimmy. We played and it felt wonderful."

They decided to call the quartet Sea Level—a none-too-subtle wordplay on the keyboardist's name: C. Leavell. "We talked about a producer, and Stewart Levine's name came into play," says Chuck. "Stewart was known at the time for recording all those great Jazz Crusaders records, and we wanted to go in that direction a little bit. So we were fortunate to get Stewart to produce. We made the deal with Capricorn, and that was the first record."

Sea Level was recorded at Capricorn Studios in late 1976. It was released in February of the following year and climbed to Number 43 on the album charts. A jazz-tinged project ("It was more in a fusion direction," says Jaimoe. "Not getting into fusion, but flirting with it"), the album was a great beginning for the band.

After the breakup, Butch was the only former member who decided to get completely away from the madness of the music business. He left Macon and headed back to Florida, re-enrolling at Florida State University and making plans for a future that would no longer revolve around the band that had dominated his life for the last seven years. At least that was his plan.

Dickey Betts, now on his own, decided to leave Phil Walden's record label, management, and publishing company behind. He hired Steve Massarsky as his manager and got himself and his new band, Great Southern, a record deal with Clive Davis's New York-based Arista Records. Along with Dickey on guitar, slide guitar, and lead vocals, the band consisted of "Dangerous" Dan Toler on guitar and background vocals, Ken Tibbets on bass, Tom Broome on keyboards and background vocals, and Jerry Thompson and Doni Sharbono on drums and percussion. It was obvious that the instrumental lineup was identical to that of the original Allman Brothers Band, and their first album—*Dickey Betts & Great Southern*—even included a blues harp player, Topper Price, among the guest artists. Also on hand were Mickey Thomas (lead vocalist on the Elvin Bishop Band's hit "Fooled Around and Fell in Love" and later a member of Jefferson Starship) on background vocals, and a little-known actor named Don Johnson singing background vocals on "Bougainvillea," a song he co-wrote with Betts. The album was produced entirely by Dickey.

Dickey Betts & Great Southern was recorded at the Allman Brothers' old haunt, Criteria Studios in Miami. Singles were released, including "Bougainvillea," but pop radio just didn't seem interested. Even so, Dickey and his new band proved to be a popular live act, and their debut album, released in early 1977, reached Number 31 on the Top Pop Albums chart.

While Dickey was recording in Miami, Gregg was making his next solo album at Warner Brothers' studio in Hollywood with a new group that was now called, simply, the Gregg Allman Band. The musicians were Ricky Hirsch (of Wet Willie fame), Steve Beckmeier, and John Hug on guitars, along with keyboardist Neil Larson, bassist Willie Weeks, and drummer Bill Stewart. Among the host of folks credited as additional musicians on the album was Duane's old friend Mac "Dr. John" Rebennack on piano and clavinet. As he had done on his previous solo albums, Gregg covered an Allman Brothers song—this time it was "Come and Go Blues." Johnny Sandlin was out of the picture for now, so Lenny Waronker and Russ Titelman handled the production duties. Although they were both skilled music men with proven track records, Waronker and Titelman brought a certain slickness to the project that didn't entirely mesh with Gregg's rough-edged vocals. The record, *Playin' Up a Storm*, got mixed reviews when it was released in May 1977. It reached Number 42 on the charts, but the single, "Cryin' Shame," went unnoticed.

When the dust had settled—if it settled at all—in the chart wars, Dickey Betts came out the "winner" among the first batch of post-ABB releases. As one might have expected, none of the former band members' albums made the kind of impression on the public that the Allman Brothers Band's recordings had done. It was a classic case of the sum being greater than its parts.

In the spring of 1977, Gregg and Cher decided to record a duet album. Calling their act Allman and Woman, they cut 11 songs at sessions that took place at the Record Plant and Sunset Sound in Los Angeles. The album was called *Two the Hard Way*, and this time around Johnny Sandlin was back to produce much of the material. Despite what seemed like a highly unlikely mix of vocal styles, *Two the Hard Way* actually worked well musically—especially on Gregg and Cher's version of Michael Smotherman's "Can You Fool." The album, released in the fall, was a combination of familiar classics—from Smokey Robinson's "You've Really Got a Hold on Me" to Leiber & Stoller's "Love Me"—and new songs by writers like Duane and Gregg's old friend Johnny Townsend, among others. The singles were "Move Me" and "You've Really Got a Hold on Me." Neither did anything on the charts. Listening to the album more than two decades later, it seems inexplicable that "Can You Fool" wasn't released as a single. It took country crossover star Glen Campbell's record label to realize the song's potential: Campbell's version of "Can You Fool" became a Top 40 hit a year after Gregg and Cher's version of the song was released as just another album track on *Two the Hard Way*.

Except for some kind words from *Billboard* and a handful of others, the critics lambasted *Two the Hard Way*. Maybe it was hard to get past the album cover photo of a shirtless Gregg draped over a tube-topped Cher in knee-high boots. The supermarket tabloids' constant reportage of their problem-plagued relationship probably didn't help either. The end result was an album stillborn.

Near the end of 1977, Gregg and Cher separated. Around that same time, Dickey Betts was doing a little separating of his own. When he went in to record his second album for Arista, *Atlanta's Burning Down*, all of the original members of Great Southern were gone except for Dan Toler and Doni Sharbono. The new members were Michael Workman on keyboards and vocals, David "Rook" Goldflies on bass, and Dan Toler's brother, David "Frankie" Toler, on drums and percussion. Topper Price was once again among the guest artists, along with Bonnie Bramlett (who by this time had become a solo artist on Capricorn). Reaching all the way back to his Second Coming days, Dickey brought in Reese Wynans to play keyboards on the title track. But even with the help of Bramlett and Wynans—sentimental connections to the Duane Allman days—the new Dickey Betts & Great Southern album failed to live up to the band's previous success.

Nearly a decade would pass before either Dickey or Gregg returned to the studio to record another solo album. Ironically, Sea Level was to become the first of the post-ABB offshoots to actually chalk up a hit album with a hit single. The band's second Capricorn LP, *Cats on the Coast*, featured an expanded lineup: along with the four musicians from the first record, there were saxophonist Randall Bramblett (one of the players on *The Gregg Allman Tour*), guitarist Davis Causey, and drummer/percussionist George Weaver. Released in December, *Cats on the Coast* was momentarily lost among the end-of-year superstar product. But by February 1978, both the album and its single, "That's Your Secret," were on the charts. Granted, the single peaked at Number 50—but the fact that it charted at all meant that it had surpassed the half-dozen singles released by Dickey and Gregg during the previous year.

By 1978, disco ruled the pop music world. On December 16, 1977, the movie *Saturday Night Fever* had been released, and it wasn't long before the Bee Gees and the other artists featured on the film's soundtrack would dominate the charts—along with Andy Gibb, A Taste Of Honey, Donna Summer, Chic, and other disco hitmakers. When the small plane carrying Lynyrd Skynyrd went down near Gillsburg, Mississippi, on October 20, 1977, Southern rock seemed to have crashed along with it. There were still a few bands carrying on the tradition—Marshall Tucker and the Outlaws among them—but for the time being, everybody just wanted to dance.

Then, in the latter half of 1978, a series of events began to unfold that gave hope to fans of the Southern sound. The *Florida Times-Union* out of Jacksonville ran a story reporting that a reunion of the Allman Brothers Band was imminent. Despite the animosity among certain members of the band dating back to the troubles of two years earlier, Gregg was quoted in the article as saying, "Time heals a lot of things."

Gregg and Dickey had run into each other in January 1977 at the inauguration of Jimmy Carter, the former Georgia governor who had gotten strong support from the Southern rock community during his bid for the presidency. Then, during the recording of *Atlanta's Burning Down* some ten months later, Gregg and Phil Walden flew to Miami to begin discussions with Dickey about the possibility of reuniting the Allman Brothers. It would take almost a year, but on August 16, 1978, Gregg, Jaimoe, and Butch appeared onstage in Central Park with Dickey Betts & Great Southern. For the first time since May 4, 1976, the four surviving members of the original Allman Brothers Band played together, and the crowd was in a state of ecstasy. Then, on August 24, Gregg, Dickey, Jaimoe, Butch, Chuck, and Lamar performed together at Capricorn's annual barbeque. It was becoming evident that time had, indeed, healed a lot of things—but not everything.

Phil Walden announced that the band was now back together and getting ready to return to the studio—but there were two major issues standing in the way of Chuck and Lamar's return. One was the growing success of Sea Level; the other was money. Leavell and Williams both felt they had been short-changed in the royalty department, and when it became evident that the issue wasn't going to be resolved anytime soon, they decided to stick with Sea Level—especially since they were halfway through recording their third album. Jaimoe, on the other hand, had already decided to bow out of his former side-project band before work on Sea Level's third album had begun.

By November 1978, there was a new lineup for the Allman Brothers Band: Gregg, Dickey, Jaimoe, Butch, "Dangerous" Dan Toler, and David "Rook" Goldflies—Toler and Goldflies having been recruited from Great Southern. In an effort to make this a genuine reunion in every sense of the word, the band returned to Criteria in Miami—the studio where they had recorded the last ABB tracks with Duane—and chose Tom Dowd to produce the new album. Years later, Butch Trucks would tell Dowd, "The biggest mistake we ever made was thinking we could produce our own albums, and not using you." It would be a mistake they would make again on more than one occasion, but for now Tom Dowd was the man in charge.

Although Gregg had been the one to suggest that the band reunite, this time around it was Dickey who took up the leadership role. He had, after all, given up his own band—something Chuck and Lamar weren't willing to do. He also arrived at the studio with a batch of new songs, including two co-written with his friend Don Johnson. The new album, which would be called *Enlightened Rogues*, had eight songs, with Gregg's sole contribution being "Just Ain't Easy." The near-obligatory blues cover this time around was the Little Willie John classic "Need Your Love So Bad." The rest of the album would belong to Dickey, including the single, "Crazy Love."

Duane Allman's presence can be felt throughout the album. From the very first track, Dickey's slide guitar is a reminder of one of Duane's greatest contributions to the band. And when the harmony guitar parts kick in during the seven-and-a-half minute Betts composition "Pegasus," it is as if the band has found its way back to its glory days. (With "Pegasus," the ABB showed they were finally comfortable with the idea of returning to the original concept of two lead guitarists. Chuck's keyboard contributions had been formidable in the intervening years, but the time had come to allow the spirit of Duane Allman to shine through.) And there's even a hint of the Hour Glass days on "Need Your Love So Bad," where Dickey's bluesy lead guitar intro recalls the way Duane kicked off the "B.B. King Medley" during the Hour Glass's Fame sessions in Muscle Shoals.

The title also recalled the band's original leader. Duane had frequently referred to his band of Brothers as "enlightened rogues." There were more echoes in the promotional campaign: when the album was released in February 1979, full-page ads in various music magazines declared: "The Legend Endures, and the Light Shines On." As *Enlightened Rogues* went gold and "Crazy Love" climbed into the Top 40, it seemed for a time that the light would shine on as brightly as ever—but it was not to be.

Problems were cropping up in abundance for both the band and its label. Lawsuits were flying everywhere. Dickey was suing Capricorn; Dale Betts was suing Dickey; Chuck Leavell was suing the band. When Dickey won an arbitration hearing against Capricorn, the other members realized that they, too, were probably owed enormous amounts of back royalties. Amazingly, the band remained together even as everything fell apart around them.

The disco craze continued to control the radio airwaves in 1979 and 1980, and interest in music by the Allman Brothers and other Southern bands dropped off precipitously. But Dickey still had a great relationship with Arista Records, so the ABB was signed to the label and began work on the first of two albums there—both of which would turn out to be artistic disasters.

The Arista executives decided to push the band in a more "contemporary" direction on their next album. It was a move tantamount to trying to get Michelangelo to paint more like Picasso. Once again Dickey handled most of the songwriting chores, with Gregg contributing two songs he had co-written with Dangerous Dan. But the songs weren't the primary problem—the real issue was a failed attempt to merge the classic with the current. Mike Lawler of the band Lawler & Cobb played synthesizer on some numbers, as did Dickey. Along with his regular drum kit, Butch also brought a syndrum into the mix.

It's impossible, of course, to know where Duane—had he lived—might have taken the band post-1971, but it's a good guess that this wouldn't have been the direction. The spirit of Duane Allman had been more than obvious on *Enlightened Rogues*; this time around, it was gone—unless you counted the album's title, *Reach for the Sky*, which had been the title of the first album by Cowboy, the band Duane had gotten signed to Capricorn back in 1970. ("We went back and forth on the title," recalled Butch, "and somebody said *Reach for the Sky*, so we called it that. We forgot that Cowboy had already done that.")

Tom Dowd's production skills are noticeably absent on the album. One of his many talents was the ability to capture an artist's natural sound, which he did with the Allman Brothers time and again throughout his career. This time, the band co-produced the album with Mike Lawler and Johnny Cobb. Much as had been the case with Gregg's *Playin' Up a Storm*, there is a slickness to the sound that goes against the grain of what the band had always been about.

In the years when Duane had led the group, there had been an ongoing maturation of the Allman Brothers' sound and style. It was easy to hear the natural progression. Even with *Brothers and Sisters*, the band had shown their ability to grow despite the loss of their leader. But with *Reach for the Sky*, they were compromising rather than evolving—and it simply didn't work. Even the advertising campaign was lousy. The magazine ad copy read "The band that opened the game . . . now raises the stakes!" In smaller type was the line "The Allman Brothers Band, making the music of their lives"—a statement that couldn't possibly have been less true.

The band's fan base was still strong enough to sell records, though. The album peaked at Number 27, and its first single, "Angeline," made it as far as Number 58. But the second single, "Mystery Woman," did nothing. And then, as if the release of the Allman Brothers' first truly mediocre album wasn't enough bad news, the band lost another of its founding members.

There are several versions of the story—but, in short, Jaimoe was fired. He discovered this when he arrived at a show to find David "Frankie" Toler's drums set up where his were supposed to be. Jaimoe's unceremonious canning was apparently brought on by his complaints about the band's enormous overhead. According to Jaimoe, he had asked for an audit to get to the bottom of all the unexplained "miscellaneous" expenses. At least one member of the band (Jaimoe's then-wife Candace Oakley says it was Dickey) bristled at the suggestion. In any case, with Jaimoe gone the Allman Brothers Band now had as many players from Great Southern as it did original members.

In March 1981, Gregg, Dickey, Butch, Dan Toler, David Toler, David Goldflies, and Mike Lawler (with his synthesizer collection) went to Nashville, of all places, to record *Brothers of the Road*. Once again, Dickey contributed most the songs—although this time all but one of his compositions had a co-writer. Gregg brought three new tunes. But for the first time ever, there was no instrumental to show off the band's renowned improvisational skills. And finally, there was the death knell: a cover of Elvis Presley's "I Beg of You."

Despite all of the album's shortcomings, it did include a hit single. "Straight from the Heart," written by Dickey Betts and Johnny Cobb, actually reached the Top 40. Although over-produced (this time by John Ryan, who had also produced the Styx hit "Lady"), the song admittedly had a great hook. In fact, it could have been a hit for Styx or any other overblown arena-rock act of the era.

When the Allman Brothers Band appeared on the television show *Solid Gold* to promote their new album, it was one of the more surreal moments in the history of the medium. The show's host was Marilyn McCoo, formerly of the 5th

Dimension, who along with her husband, Billy Davis Jr., had scored hits with songs like "You Don't Have to Be a Star (To Be in My Show)."

"Throughout their long career," McCoo announced dramatically, "our next guests have been through personnel changes and tragedies, but have remained the leaders in Southern rock & roll. They've recorded six gold albums, and their latest, *Brothers of the Road*, is currently on its way to the top of the album charts." (The rhetoric sounded good, but in truth the album would peak some 43 spots below the "top of the album charts.")

The camera then pulled back to show a miserable-looking Gregg Allman standing next to her. "Gregg, I know the band broke up for three years," said McCoo. "Now that you're back together again, is there any difference in your music?" Gregg—who couldn't have possibly looked more bored or sounded less excited—responded, "Yes, we've added a lot of new blood, and we have new players—a synthesizer player—and there's a lot more singing—a lot of excitement." "Good energy, huh?" asked McCoo. "Good energy, yeah," Gregg answered lifelessly.

A few weeks later, on January 23, 1982, the Allman Brothers made another TV appearance—this time on *Saturday Night Live.* They performed "Midnight Rider," "Southbound," and "Leavin'." And leave they did. Once again, the Allman Brothers decided to go their separate ways.

Sadly, former ABB and Sea Level bassist Lamar Williams passed away less than a year later at the age of 34. The cause of death was lung cancer, which his doctors believed might have been brought on by his exposure to Agent Orange while in Vietnam.

Over the next several years, Gregg and Dickey each formed bands and played gigs. Neither of them released any albums during that time, but the two bands began touring together in March 1986. Dickey's band would open, Gregg's band would follow, and then the two bands would get together and play Allman Brothers songs. On a couple of occasions that year, the Allman Brothers Band—despite all their past differences—actually regrouped in the form of Gregg, Dickey, Butch, Jaimoe, Chuck Leavell, Dan Toler, and Bruce Waibel on bass; they played at Charlie Daniels's Volunteer Jam XII and at the "Crackdown on Crack" concert at Madison Square Garden.

During 1987 and 1988, Gregg's recording career once again caught fire. The Gregg Allman Band signed with Epic Records and scored a huge hit single with "I'm No Angel." The album by that title and its follow-up, *Just Before the Bullets Fly,* both hit the charts. *I'm No Angel* even went gold, becoming Gregg's best-selling record since *Laid Back.* In 1988, the Dickey Betts Band's *Pattern Disruptive* charted as well.

The following year, PolyGram Records released a four-CD boxed set entitled *Dreams.* The collection featured plenty of Allman Brothers tracks, but also included selections by the Allman Joys, the Hour Glass, the 31st of February, and the Second Coming, along with "Goin' Down Slow" from Duane's aborted album project, solo recordings by Gregg and Dickey, cuts by Dickey with Great Southern, and even "Can You Fool" by Gregg and Cher. It was all the band needed to bring them back together again.

With Gregg and Dickey both on Epic Records, the Allman Brothers were also signed to the label. Over the next decade, the revitalized band would record a half-dozen albums for Epic: *Seven Turns, Shades of Two Worlds, An Evening with the Allman Brothers Band, Where It All Begins, 2nd Set,* and *Peakin' at the Beacon.* On all but the last one, guitarist Warren Haynes and bassist Allen Woody were part of the lineup. Tom Dowd was back, too.

The band's first Epic record was hailed by the critics as the Allman Brothers' "comeback album"—and the second CD proved that it wasn't a fluke. It also showed that the band was willing to expand both musically and in terms of additional personnel. "After we did *Seven Turns,*" said Tom Dowd, "we next went to Memphis and did *Shades of Two Worlds,* which is where they picked up [percussionist] Marc Quinones. Butch had heard him at a Spyro Gyra concert and said, 'We gotta get this kid,' because we were talking about adding percussion to the album. . . . They said, 'All right, we'll try him.'" Not only did they try him—they kept him.

Following the success of the two studio albums, the Allman Brothers decided it was time to record live again, to capture what Duane had always referred to as the band's "natural fire." The initial plan was to make the album in Macon. It seemed like a good idea—to everyone but the producer. "That was bizarre," Dowd said. "We talked about it and I said, 'Are you guys sure you want to go back to Macon? I mean, it's like 20 years later. You're all family men. Old girlfriends and every other goddamn person is going to show up.' They got back there and it was Nostalgia Trip Number 1. . . . They took turns getting drunk, getting high, or just being dumb. The second night when we decided we were going to play 'Good Clean Fun,' everybody is ready to play. Gregg gets up there and he's got a goddamn notice on his organ sitting there in, like, ten-inch letters saying 'Good Clean Fun' and he says, 'Now here's a song from our latest album,' and he starts singing something off *his* last album. Three of the guys are playing downbeats to 'Good Clean Fun.' Everybody looks across at each other and goes, 'Oh, shit!' It was deplorable."

With nothing salvageable from the Macon shows, the band moved on to Boston and New York, using tracks from performances recorded in those two cities to create *An Evening with the Allman Brothers Band*, released in March 1992. The album was a collection of songs from every era of the band's career, including "Dreams," "Revival," "Blue Sky," and the more recent "End of the Line" and "Get on with Your Life."

"Before we started recording the next album," Dowd said, "we had to find a studio. We wanted to get into Criteria, but it was booked for two months. Butch, who lives in South Florida, knew of Burt Reynolds's place, and he went by to check it out since he knew there was a soundstage for filming. He then called me to go take a look, so I drove up and inspected it, and it seemed like we could make something work there."

"We set up the amp line and the drums just like onstage . . . except we used half-rigs," Betts told Kevin Ransom in a *Guitar Player* interview. "Me and Warren each played one guitar, and we would change pickup settings or turn the volume up or down, just like live, with the whole band playing at once. We rehearsed for three weeks and then cut the entire album in a week. Tom Dowd is such a genius at miking; he uses the bleed-over in a way that creates a sort of reverb. I don't know how the hell he does it." The album they cut, *Where It All Begins*, featured several songs the band still performs today, including Haynes's composition "Soulshine." It also became the best-selling album of the Allman Brothers' Epic years.

Surprisingly, the band decided to follow that album with yet another live recording. Although the idea might have seemed like overkill at the time, the critics loved it, with one writer calling *2nd Set* "a high-water mark in their Epic Records catalog." Insiders in the music business loved it, too, singling out "Jessica" for a Grammy as 1995's Best Rock Instrumental Performance. It was their second notable honor of the year: on January 12, the original six-member lineup of the Allman Brothers Band was inducted into the Rock and Roll Hall of Fame,

The Allman Brothers Band in 2006—(L–R) Gregg, Butch, Jaimoe, Derek Trucks, Warren Haynes, Oteil Burbridge, and Marc Quinones

with Willie Nelson (whose many hits include "Midnight Rider") making the presentation.

After *2nd Set*, the band went five years without making another album. Some might say they should have waited even longer. In the interim between *2nd Set* and *Peakin' at the Beacon*, Warren Haynes and Allen Woody left to form the band Gov't Mule with drummer Matt Abts. They were replaced by guitarist Jack Pearson and bassist Oteil Burbridge, whose playing recalled the melodic skills of Berry Oakley more than any of the band's other post-Oakley bass players. In mid-1999, Butch's nephew, Derek Trucks—a prodigy of the slide guitar—came on board to replace Jack Pearson. But the personnel changes didn't end there.

After 31 years, Dickey Betts parted ways with the other original members of the band. The chemistry—and the chemicals—had changed. On October 29, 1996—the 25th anniversary of Duane's death—Gregg had gone on the wagon. Four years later, a clean and sober Gregg Allman didn't like what he was hearing. After the release of yet *another* live album—the muddy-sounding *Peakin' at the Beacon*—Dickey Betts was fired. One of the stories regarding Dickey's dismissal recalled an unfortunate onstage incident: When, upon kicking off a song, it was evident that something was going terribly wrong, Dickey is said to have turned to one of the other musicians and asked, "What song are we playing?" To which the other player responded, "You mean me or you?"

In the fall of 2000, the film *Almost Famous* was released. Written and directed by Cameron Crowe, the movie was a thinly disguised fictional account of Crowe's days on the road with the Allman Brothers, covering the band for a piece in *Rolling Stone*. In the film, the band was called Stillwater, with Billy Crudup—looking practically identical to a young Dickey Betts—playing the part of the group's lead guitarist. The soundtrack album, which included the ABB's "One Way Out," went on to win the Grammy as Best Compilation Album for a Motion Picture.

For a while in 2000, Jimmy Herring replaced Dickey Betts in the ABB lineup. That August, the band's former bass player, Allen Woody, was found dead in a motel room in Queens. In March of the following year, Warren Haynes returned to the Allman Brothers, creating the lineup that has remained in place to 2008: Gregg, Butch, Jaimoe, Derek, Warren, Oteil, and Marc.

In 2003, the band released *Hittin' the Note* on their own label, Peach, and some critics once again hailed it the Allman Brothers' great comeback album. At this point, the band seemed to be rivaling Muhammad Ali in the comeback department. In several interviews, Gregg called *Hittin' the Note* the band's best album since *Eat a Peach*—and he might very well have been right. With Tom Dowd's passing in 2002, the band had turned to Michael Barbiero to produce the record, and his work was practically an homage to Dowd.

In September 2003, Bruce Waibel—the bassist who had played on Gregg's albums *I'm No Angel* and *Just Before the Bullets Fly*, as well as with the ABB for a short time—was found dead at his home in Florida. Incredibly, between 1972 and 2003, four of the band's six bassists had passed away.

When the Allman Brothers had gotten back together in 1989, their New York venue of choice was the Beacon Theater. Although they could have sold out much larger halls in Manhattan, the band loved the vibe in the old building at the corner of 74th and Broadway. Gregg has said it reminds him of the old Fillmore East. From 1996 to 2007, the band has played a series of shows there every March—the yearly event now referred to by fans as "March Madness."

In March 2004, the Allman Brothers released a two-CD set of live recordings made at the Beacon the previous year. Entitled *One Way Out*, it was a vast improvement over *Peakin' at the Beacon*. The review in the *All Music Guide* reads: "Pair this with *Hittin' the Note*, the studio album from 2003, and you have the sound of a band that has no peers. *One Way Out* is essential for anyone interested in rock & roll. Period." The 18 tracks on *One Way Out* feature songs from the band's entire career, including "Trouble No More"—the very first song that Duane, Gregg, and the rest of the original Allman Brothers Band played together back in Jacksonville, Florida, all those years ago.

Still Peakin' at the Beacon

*"One night at the Beacon I looked down and realized
I was the only one left on the front line." — GREGG ALLMAN*

It's a Friday night in New York City. In the tradition of more than 150 previous Allman Brothers Band shows at the Beacon Theater, the joint is packed tighter than a subway car at rush hour. This is a ritual that shows absolutely no signs of losing its decade-and-a-half-long head of steam.

Throughout the week, the band has been giving the crowd exactly what they've come for: exemplary musicianship, a light show straight out of another era, an impressive array of guest musicians sitting in night after night, and classic songs from the Allman Brothers Band's 35-year career. In fact, on this night— March 26, 2004—the band and audience are celebrating *exactly* 35 years of Allman Brothers history.

The first half of the show includes plenty of the old chestnuts—"Statesboro Blues," "Can't Lose What You Never Had," "One Way Out" (with guest guitarist Lee Roy Parnell sharing slide duties with Derek Trucks and Warren Haynes)—as well as "Rockin' Horse" and the heart-wrenching "Old Before My Time," both from *Hittin' the Note*, the band's well-received album of the previous year.

As if that weren't powerful enough, after the intermission there is a seismic shift upward in the energy level as the band opens the second set with "Mountain

Jam." All of us behind the stage—grizzled road warriors, music industry veterans, various ABB family members, assorted friends and associates—are struck by the stepped-up intensity. The backstage chatter stops. We inch forward, ignoring the white stripe painted on the floor that both the fire marshal and tour manager Kirk West have already pointed out as the line not to be crossed under *any* circumstances (excluding, presumably, fire). The "Mountain Jam" drum solo has begun. The other band members drift offstage. Whether or not he's conscious of the anniversary date at this moment, Jaimoe has figuratively caught fire. The years fall away as the trade-offs between Jaimoe and Butch seem to conjure the same magic they had at the Fillmore East more than three decades ago. The only difference is the addition of Marc Quinones on percussion, bringing congas, timbales, and cymbal crashes into the mix.

After the drummers have done their thing, the rest of the band returns to the stage—but instead of resuming "Mountain Jam" they segue into "I Walk on Gilded Splinters." The song was originally written and recorded by Dr. John, but the version that comes to my mind tonight is Johnny Jenkins's 1970 rendition with Duane Allman on dobro.

Duane stays on my mind as Gregg Allman begins to sing "Ain't Wastin' Time No More," the song he wrote immediately after his brother's death. The historic night ends with encores of the Otis Redding ballad "I've Got Dreams to Remember" and "Southbound" from *Brothers and Sisters*—the first Allman Brothers album without Duane.

Watching the band walk past me as they head offstage and into the night, I wonder if the set list for the second half of the show was intended as a tribute to Duane Allman, or if it was simply a selection of great songs that worked well together in that sequence. I also think back to the show of three nights earlier and a rather unsettling moment that has stuck in my head.

At the Tuesday night Beacon show, the band's pre-encore closer was "No One to Run With," one of the standouts from their 1995 album, *Where It All Begins*. The lyrics tell the story of a man whose friends have all left town. As Gregg sang, the screen above him was filled with images of musicians now gone. The New York crowd, many of whom probably weren't even born at the time of Duane Allman's death, had virtually no reaction as flickering images of Duane appeared on the giant backdrop. Footage of Berry Oakley was met with the same eerie silence. A few cheers could be heard when pictures of former ABB bassist Allen Woody came up, but when Jerry Garcia's face splashed across the screen, the crowd erupted in a loud roar.

Garcia's voluminous contributions to American music and culture notwithstanding, observing the audience's reaction—or lack thereof, with respect to Duane and Berry—was nothing short of disconcerting to me. I couldn't help but wonder if Duane Allman has begun to fade from the public's collective memory—even from the memories of many fans of the very band that bears his name. A year earlier, the Allman Brothers had added "Layla" to the set list—an overt tribute to Duane. Did the audiences who attended Allman Brothers concerts that year really grasp the connection, or were they simply cheering the band's decision to cover an old Eric Clapton record?

In September 2003, *Rolling Stone* published its list of the "100 Greatest Guitarists of All Time," placing Duane at Number 2, just behind Jimi Hendrix. "I thought it was a very wonderful gesture," Gregg told *Hittin' the Note*'s John Lynskey. "And I thought, 'You made your mark, man. You didn't make any money, but you made your mark.'" Rounding out the top five on *Rolling Stone*'s roster were B.B. King, Eric Clapton, and Robert Johnson—pretty impressive company for a kid from the South who didn't even live to see his 25th birthday.

• • •

March 2005: It has now been almost exactly a year since I was last in New York to see the Allman Brothers at the Beacon. As had been the case in 2004, every seat at every show is filled. A tenth night has even been added as a benefit concert for the Big House Foundation, a nonprofit organization created for the purpose of turning the Allman Brothers' old home in Macon into an ABB museum. For this special night, Chuck Leavell is coming back to sit in with the band.

During the past year, there have been indications that a Southern rock resurgence is stirring. The Grammy awards show presented a tribute during its annual telecast, featuring a collection of modern-day country acts performing with Dickey Betts and the remnants of Lynyrd Skynyrd. CMT—the Country Music Television network—has been running a documentary entitled "American Revolutions: Southern Rock" several times a week. Both Chuck Leavell and former Allman Brothers road manager Willie Perkins have published autobiographies. The Black Crowes—second-generation Southern rockers—have gotten back together. Cingular Wireless has run an ad campaign using Gregg's

"Melissa" as its theme music. KFC has done the same with Lynyrd Skynyrd's "Sweet Home Alabama," and Duane's seven-note lick from "Layla" could be heard in commercials for SBC.

It's difficult to imagine what Duane would have thought about the use of "Layla" to plug a telecommunications company, but it's certain that he would have been proud to know that along with Muddy Waters's "Hoochie Coochie Man" and John Coltrane's *Giant Steps*, the Library of Congress has chosen *At Fillmore East* as one of the selections added to its National Recording Registry this year. The genre jump-started by Duane Allman seems to have gained a whole new life, along with a whole new audience.

The 2005 shows at the Beacon retain much of the old magic. Kirk West is still there telling those standing backstage to stay behind the white line. The light show continues to flicker on the giant screen behind the band. Special guests, including blues legend Little Milton (in what would turn out to be one of his last performances), sit in with the band. Even basketball star Bill Walton—famous not only for his days on the court but also for attending more than 650 Grateful Dead concerts—is in the house.

On Tuesday, March 15, I spend some time with Percy Sledge. The singer who recorded "When a Man Loves a Woman" in Muscle Shoals back in 1966 is in Manhattan, having been inducted into the Rock and Roll Hall of Fame the previous night. He talks to me about the days when Jaimoe—whom he still refers to as Johnny—was playing drums for him. Percy can't remember exactly when Jaimoe was in his rhythm section, so I tell him it has to have been at least 37 years ago, since the Allman Brothers Band is on the verge of celebrating its 36th anniversary. Percy stares at me in amazement. "Oh my God, Randy," he whispers, "could it really have been that long ago?"

• • •

March 2006: Yet another year has come and gone. This Beacon Run—March 9 to March 26—marks another anniversary. It has been 35 years since the recording of *At Fillmore East*. On March 13, the Allman Brothers perform the entire album, in sequence. There is bedlam at the Beacon. If the Second Coming is going to happen tonight, Jesus would be well advised to wait until the band has finished "Whipping Post."

As the concerts wind through the month of March, the guest musicians continue to flow in: Taj Mahal, Cornell Dupree, Jerry Jemmott, Gary Rossington, Hubert Sumlin, Roy Haynes, and many others—all contributing their talents to the festivities. But it is on Sunday, March 26, at the final show, when everything comes full circle. Finally, almost 35 years after Duane Allman passed on, the Allman Brothers get the chance to play straight-ahead jazz. The song is "Afro-Blue," popularized by John Coltrane on his 1963 album *Live at Birdland*. Sitting in with the band are John Coltrane's son, Ravi, on saxophone, and the man who played drums on Miles Davis's *Kind of Blue*, Jimmy Cobb.

After the intermission, a gray-haired gentleman comes out on the stage, alone. With nothing but an acoustic guitar and a harmonica, he begins to play and sing an old blues song called "My Mind Is Ramblin'." Derek Trucks comes out to join the singer for his next number, "Stone Pony Blues," and then the whole band returns to the stage to accompany him on "Shake for Me." The bluesman is John Hammond Jr.—the guy the Muscle Shoals Sound rhythm section wasn't sure about until Duane showed up to express his admiration; the man Gregg has called "Duane's best friend"; the musician who stayed up all night with Duane in New York City, playing records and jamming on guitars, just before Skydog made that final journey back to Macon.

On more than one occasion, Butch Trucks—who grew up in the Southern Baptist church—has referred to playing music in the band's early days as a "religious experience." Not long before Tom Dowd passed away in 2002, Trucks and Dowd had a conversation in which the drummer explained why the band chose to continue playing after the passing of their leader: "Duane had given us the religion," he said, "and we were going to keep playing it."

After wandering for years in the wilderness, with the formation of the Allman Brothers Band Duane could deliver the musical message he had been carrying in his soul. He had spent a lifetime—short though it was—trying to create the sound he heard in his head and felt in his heart. It was his calling, and he had struggled at every turn to achieve his dream.

The three complete Allman Brothers albums Duane played on were recorded at the end of one decade and the beginning of another. Duane and his band arrived at the perfect moment to play music for the generation Otis

Redding had referred to as the "Love Crowd." And just like Otis, Duane Allman passed away before the Love Crowd would be swallowed up by a world not nearly so loving.

In his book *Fear and Loathing in Las Vegas*, Hunter S. Thompson referred to living in that era as being akin to "riding the crest of a high and beautiful wave"—a wave that, in less than half a decade, had broken and receded. Duane Allman didn't live to see the power of the Love Crowd rapidly fading away. It would have been, no doubt, a painful experience for him.

In my conversations with Rick Hall, the record producer frequently referred to Allman as being "ahead of his time." Although this was certainly the case as far as his early days in Muscle Shoals were concerned, from 1969 to 1971 Duane Allman was very much a man *of* his time. He rode right on the crest of the wave.

On October 29, 1971, Duane Allman's ride came to an end, but his music did not—and neither did the Brotherhood. The band's name was always more than a reference to Duane and Gregg's relationship; it was *truly* a brotherhood. But the Brotherhood didn't exist just among the members of the band and their roadies. It existed—and continues to exist—among the fans as well. It is also a community specific to neither age nor gender. Gregg Allman has spoken of seeing audiences that included the children and grandchildren of folks who had attended Allman Brothers gigs two and three decades earlier.

The Allman Brothers have more in common with the Grateful Dead than just Bill Walton. There is a bond among those who listen to the band's music. The spirit of community—even of family—goes on. Skydog's musical vision was the catalyst, but the spirit will remain long after the last note of that inevitable final concert fades away.

And some day—many years from now—a young boy and his sister will stand on the pier at Daytona Beach, listening to a slide guitarist as he plays an old, old song by the Allman Brothers Band. It will be a sound the young boy will never forget.

Afterword

*I was doin' a cat a favor. That's all—but I'm sure glad
I was around for it. – JOEL DORN*

Those were the closing comments Joel Dorn made about his production
of the track "Please Call Home" for the Allman Brothers' *Idlewild South*
album in my March 2006 interview with him, for the original hardcover
edition of *Skydog*. They were the last words I would ever hear him say. On
December 17, 2007, Joel Dorn died of a heart attack. He was 65 years old.

Sadly, Joel Dorn has not been the only loss to the Brotherhood. In the
course of only three months during the last quarter of 2007, four other important figures in the ABB camp passed away. Mike Callahan—Berry Oakley's
old friend who drove the bus for the Roemans and later became the Allman
Brothers Band's first soundman—died on September 26 at the age of 62.
Steve Massarsky, who became the manager for Dickey Betts & Great Southern
in 1976 (and took over management of the Allman Brothers Band two years
later), succumbed to cancer at the age of 59 on October 5. On October 14,
John Meeks, drummer for the Second Coming, was killed in a house fire. The
following month, John "Scooter" Herring—whose federal drug case in June
of 1976 led to the first breakup of the band—passed away on November 10.

Indeed, much has happened in the world of the Allman Brothers Band since
the initial release of *Skydog* in the fall of 2006, but not all of the news is tragic.

In May of 2006, Derek Trucks joined Eric Clapton's touring band. Clapton and Trucks kept the spirit of Duane Allman alive as the band traveled around the world, playing a set list that included "Layla"—featuring Derek on slide guitar.

Not wanting Trucks to miss out on the opportunity to tour with Duane's old friend, the ABB worked their schedule around Clapton's gigs throughout the rest of the year.

Reminiscent of Duane's hectic schedule back in the days when the guitarist would play on sessions in New York, Muscle Shoals, Macon, or Miami between gigs with the Allman Brothers Band, Derek had very few days off once Clapton's tour got underway. In one three-week stretch, Trucks played a show with Clapton in London on June 10, flew to the U.S. to play a dozen gigs with the ABB between June 16 and July 2, and then returned to Europe to meet back up with Clapton on July 7 for a show in Italy.

Trucks left the Clapton tour in early 2007 to regroup with the Allman Brothers Band for their annual Beacon shows that March.

On December 19, 2007, the Big House Foundation announced its purchase of the house at 2321 Vineville Avenue in Macon, following through with its plans to turn the former home of the band into a museum filled with ABB memorabilia.

On February 24, 2008, the Macon Film Festival hosted a sold-out showing of *Please Call Home: The Big House Documentary*. The film includes in-depth interviews with Gregg, Butch, Jaimoe, Linda Oakley, Chuck Leavell, Red Dog Campbell, Kim Payne, Tuffy Phillips, Alan Walden, and others who were part of the Macon scene during the band's years there.

The documentary captures a very special moment in time, showing that the Allman Brothers Band was much more than just a group of excellent musicians who happened to spend a brief period of time under the same roof.

In other motion picture–related developments, the long-rumored filming of the second Atlanta International Pop Festival has turned out not to be a rumor at all. A documentary consisting of performances by a number of bands at the festival—including the Allman Brothers—is being produced, finally giving Duane's fans the opportunity to see him perform on film in an extended live setting. Taking place less than a year after the original Woodstock festival, the communal spirit of the era was clearly still going strong in Atlanta during those three days in July of 1970.

Duane Allman's dream of perpetuating that communal spirit would eventually become a global reality, due in great part to the advent of the Internet. Today, thanks to the band's official Web site—allmanbrothersband.com—thousands of ABB enthusiasts from all over the world have the opportunity to stay in contact with each other through the site's forums and chat rooms. Many fans who had previously only met through the Web site have gotten the opportunity to meet in person when they've gathered at the Beacon and other venues to see the band perform.

When I finished writing the first edition of *Skydog* in mid-2006, the Web site youtube.com was still in its infancy. All of my research pertaining to Duane Allman on film and video had been done by purchasing or borrowing bootlegged, multigenerational VHS tapes and DVDs, usually showing very grainy footage of Duane and the band in action. Now all one has to do is go to youtube.com to find a host of great archival moments of the ABB during Duane's time with the band. Another Web site— WolfgangsVault.com—features the audio portion of entire sets of Duane with the Brothers.

As is the case with many books written during the Internet age, the Web site skydogbook.com was created when the original hardback was published. Included on the site is an e-mail link that has resulted in my receiving hundreds of messages from Duane Allman fans worldwide. Many people wrote to tell me that the book had caused them to dig through their old vinyl and CDs, in search of recordings featuring Duane.

Some shared with me their experiences of having seen the Allman Brothers Band live at the Fillmore East, the Fillmore West, the Warehouse, the Roxy, the Cosmic Carnival, Love Valley, Ludlow Garage, and dozens of other places where Duane and the band performed. Some wrote to tell me of seeing the guitarist when he appeared with Derek & the Dominos in Tampa, Florida. Others told me of seeing Duane with D&D in Syracuse, New York.

A few folks even wrote to tell me about errors I had made in the original text. (In those cases where I was able to verify inaccuracies, corrections have been made for this edition.)

But to me, the most fascinating result of the e-mail link has been my receipt of numerous messages from people who actually knew Duane, jammed with Duane, or even played in early bands with Duane back in Daytona Beach.

Shortly after the hardcover edition of *Skydog* was released, I was asked to do a reading and book signing at Book Soup, an ultra-hip bookstore on Sunset Boulevard in Los Angeles. Those in attendance included Billy Gibbons (ZZ Top member and this book's foreword writer), Mike Johnstone, and Johnny Townsend. It was a magic moment to have three of Duane's old friends together in the same room for the first time.

The next day I began a book-signing tour of the Southeast, with stops in Muscle Shoals, Jacksonville, Atlanta, and other cities where I met many more of Allman's old friends who were happy to share their "Duane stories" with me.

The highlight of the trip was a book-signing party at the Big House, graciously organized by Kirk and Kirsten West. That night, Kirk put me up in what had been Duane's bedroom. As I sat on the bed, checking e-mails on my laptop, I saw a message from a familiar name—Deering Howe. Duane had been at his friend Deering's place on his last night in New York City before that final trip back to Macon in late October of 1971.

In his e-mail, Deering Howe wrote, "You captured Duane, his love of life, his love of music, and his love of people. He was one hell of a man and one hell of a musician. I miss him a lot. Thanks for portraying him as he truly was, warts and all."

For many years, one of the catchphrases for the Allman Brothers Band's annual series of shows at the Beacon Theater has been "March Madness." In 2008, the concert dates were moved from March to May. Without missing a beat, the band's Web site splashed the news under the headline "Mayhem in Manhattan."

But it was not to be. Rumors about Gregg Allman's health had already been swirling around for months when the band released a statement, on March 27, announcing that the Beacon shows had been postponed indefinitely due to Gregg's ongoing treatment for Hepatitis C. In the press release, Gregg stated, "I'm getting better, but I'm still tired. I need to be at 110 percent to do the shows the way we do them. I can't tell you how much I appreciate the support and understanding my Brothers and our fans have given me."

A few weeks later there was another press release, this one announcing that the Beacon shows had been cancelled. "New York's a second home to us," said Gregg. "We love playing there and are as disappointed as anybody not to be able to get there this time."

• • •

March 15, 2008: It's the annual SXSW Music Conference and Festival in Austin, Texas. Former Derek & the Dominos member Bobby Whitlock, along with his wife CoCo Carmel, take the stage at the Cedar Door, supported by a stellar lineup that includes guitarists Stephen Bruton and David Grissom. The show consists primarily of songs from Bobby and CoCo's album, *Lovers*, which was released a few weeks earlier.

Near the end of the set, though, Whitlock begins to reminisce about his days with Derek & the Dominos, and the recording of the classic song for which the group would always be best remembered.

"Most people don't realize that it was Duane Allman who brought us those seven notes," says Whitock, "the seven greatest notes in the history of rock." And then Bobby, CoCo, and the band break into an absolutely riveting version of "Layla." When the last note ends some seven minutes later, the applause seems to go on almost as long as the song itself.

As the concert comes to a close and the crowd begins to file out, I think back to the final words of Jerry Wexler's eulogy for Duane: "We have his music—and the music is imperishable."

The road goes on. . . .

Acknowledgments

There is no way I can properly express my gratitude to all of the people who contributed their knowledge and time to this project, other than to say thanks so much to everyone who took my calls, answered my e-mails, dug through their photo collections, gave me words of encouragement, listened to my late-night dramatic readings, corrected my grammar and punctuation, etc.

In writing about a person who died so young—and so many years ago—the only way to tell the story is by calling upon the memories of those who were actually there as events unfolded, and by researching existing books, magazine articles, liner notes, and many other materials. While working on *Skydog*, as well as other projects about Southern music, I conducted interviews with dozens of people who knew Duane Allman. Most of those interviews were specifically for this book. Others were for projects such as a United Airlines audio channel show on Southern rock, the liner notes for a CD called *The Muscle Shoals Sound*, and magazine articles about various Southern musicians. Some of the interviews not originally done for this biography took place as far back as the 1970s. When I began this project almost 30 years later, I returned to several of those same interviewees, only to find that their memories of events remained unchanged. But, as Jerry Jemmott said to me recently, "Everybody wants to put their spin on the story so they can have a little piece of the legacy."

In those cases where the spin didn't fit the story told by others who were there, I went with what the majority told me. In other cases, I told several versions of the same story, believing that the truth exists somewhere therein. Reese Wynans laughingly warned me at one point that some of what I would hear would be "35-year-old stories told by musicians of various repute." In the end, I found that those I talked to were very intent on telling me their Duane Allman stories as accurately as possible—and several came back to me later to revise dates and names or offer other corrections.

My special thanks go to the following people who contributed their knowledge over the phone, in person, on tape, or via e-mail: Gregg Allman, Al Aronowitz, Joe Bell, Derek Bowers, Scott Boyer, Bob Brozman, Don Butler, Pete Carr, John Carter, Walter Carter, Dan Coleman, Bill Connell, Dick Cooper, Swamp Dogg, Joel Dorn, Jimmie Fadden, Matt Ferguson, Stephen Foster, Rick Hall, Rodney Hall, Jeff Hanna, Van Harrison, Frank Hartley, Lee Hazen, Jim Henke, Lamar Hill, David Hood, Paul Hornsby, Jerry Jemmott, Jimmy Johnson, Mike Johnstone, Chuck Leavell, Peter Leinheiser, Kurt Linhof, John D. Loudermilk, Brian Mayes, John McEuen, Eddie Reeves, Mike Reilly, Michael Buffalo Smith, Tommy Talton, Bill Thames, Johnny Townsend, Jim Wagner, Alan Walden, Louis Washburn, Sylvan Wells, Jerry Wexler, Ray White, Bobby Whitlock, Johnny Wyker, and Reese Wynans.

From the beginning of this project, I have received much-appreciated support from Joe Bell, Bill Ector, and John Lynskey of *Hittin' the Note* magazine. This book simply could not have been written without them, or without reference to many articles that have appeared in *HTN* over the years—particularly Bill's massive interview with Tom Dowd, as well as interviews with Gregg Allman, Dickey Betts, Butch Trucks, and Jaimoe conducted by John Lynskey, Kirsten West, Ron Currens, Kevin Spangler, Alan Paul, and others.

Dave Kyle was kind enough to provide me with access to interviews he had conducted with a number of the principals, including a previously unpublished interview with Delaney Bramlett. He also allowed me to use several photographs he had taken, for which I am extremely grateful.

Thanks to Jeff Sacharow for introducing me to Jay Rosenthal. Jay, Gerald Weiner, Bert Holman, and Kirk West were all helpful in the "all access" department—allowing me the opportunity to see the band live on a number of occasions, both in New York and Los Angeles.

Richard Johnston and Kevin Becketti of Backbeat Books have been supportive from Day One of this project. Richard's many suggestions throughout the writing process were monumentally helpful and constructive.

Although my name is on the cover, my editor, Jim Roberts, took what I had written and—through a host of suggested changes, corrections, additions, and deletions—helped turn *Skydog* into the book that it is.

Designer Rich Leeds patiently listened to my numerous requests and suggestions, coming up with exactly what I wanted for the book's cover.

Thanks to all of the other fine folks at Backbeat who have been so helpful in the creation of *Skydog*.

I was pleased to receive an e-mail from Galadrielle Allman in May 2004. Galadrielle is working on her own book about her father, so she politely declined to be involved with mine. She also wrote these words: "I believe there is room for many different books about his life and music. So, although I will be focusing on my own project, I wish you the best of luck with yours."

Billy F Gibbons is not only one of the finest guitar players and songwriters on the planet—he also has a way with prose. Thanks, Billy, for your poetic foreword, and thanks to Tom Vickers for the hook-up.

Thanks also to Clinton Ashton, Roger Deitz, Robert Greenfield, Peter Guralnick, David Ritz, Jerry Schilling, and everyone else who gave advice and counsel during the two years I was writing *Skydog*.

Finally—and most important—thanks from the bottom of my heart to my wife, Mina, and to my son, Riley, for your patience and understanding during my many late nights at the computer.

Farther on Up the Road

Many of Duane Allman's friends and associates would go on to have successful careers in the music business. Here's a quick look at what happened to some of them in the years after Duane's death, along with a sampling of their memories of Duane.

Johnny Townsend

As a member of Dirty John & the Nightcaps, Townsend was greatly impressed with the professionalism and musicianship of the Allman Joys. He would eventually join forces with Ed Sanford to become the Sanford/Townsend Band and record the 1977 Top 10 hit "Smoke from a Distant Fire," produced by Jerry Wexler and Barry Beckett at Muscle Shoals Sound Studios.

"Duane had the patience of Job," says Townsend. "I once saw him coaching Tippy Armstrong. Tippy was always cautious about not wanting to steal any of Duane's licks, but Duane took him aside and showed him some methods and modes and things that he could play around in, to come up with his own stuff. Duane Allman improved the quality of life for a lot of people around him."

Paul Hornsby

Hornsby's many Southern rock production credits include albums by the Marshall Tucker Band and the Charlie Daniels Band. He produced Tucker's hits "Can't You See," "Fire on the Mountain," and "Heard It in a Love Song," and Daniels's "Long Haired Country Boy" and "The South's Gonna Do It Again."

In 2005, Hornsby and several of his old friends got together to (re-)form the Capricorn Rhythm Section. Playing gigs that frequently include special guests such as Bonnie Bramlett and Lee Roy Parnell, the band is made up of Hornsby on keyboards, Johnny Sandlin on bass, Scott Boyer and Tommy Talton on guitars and vocals, and Bill Stewart on drums.

"During the Hour Glass days, Duane was visually the focus of the band," says Hornsby. "He was *the* commanding personality. When there's somebody like that in a group, you realize, 'Well, hey, we gotta do what this guy says because he's the stuff,' you know? He's the first person I ever saw that looked that way, acted that way, talked that way, played that way. He was really an American original."

Johnny Sandlin

Another former member of the Hour Glass, Sandlin would produce not only "Ramblin' Man" and other works by the Allman Brothers, as well as solo projects by Gregg and Dickey, but also a host of other acts, including Cowboy, Wet Willie, Elvin Bishop, Bonnie Bramlett, the Outlaws, the Dixie Dregs, and Widespread Panic.

"Duane was one of the most interesting, exciting, and alive people that I ever knew," Sandlin said in a *Gritz* magazine interview. "He was one of the most intelligent as well. Most of the time he was great to be around, and he was so dedicated to music. Whenever anyone played with Duane, he would bring out the best in them. . . . He was an inspiration. He was one of the best that there ever was."

John McEuen

McEuen and his fellow Nitty Gritty Dirt Band members were at the onset of a critically acclaimed and commercially successful career when they met Duane and Gregg in 1967. In early 1971, the NGDB scored a Top 10 hit with "Mr. Bojangles." The following year, the band single-handedly ushered in the Americana music scene with the release of their platinum-selling, Grammy-nominated three-record set, *Will the Circle Be Unbroken*. In May 2006, the Dirt Band celebrated its 40th anniversary—one of the few bands that have been around even longer than the Allman Brothers.

"Being a bandleader—being somebody that other people rally around and get behind—is not an easy thing," says McEuen. "Most often, somebody has to be a strong person to have people believe in them. With Duane, you're talking about a great bandleader."

Reese Wynans

After his days with Boz Scaggs, former Second Coming member Wynans went on to play keyboards with Stevie Ray Vaughan & Double Trouble until Vaughan's tragic death in a helicopter crash on August 27, 1990. Wynans continues to be one of the most sought-after keyboard players around, having recorded with Carole King, Joe Ely, Lee Roy Parnell, Kenny Wayne Shepherd, Buddy Guy, Brooks & Dunn, Montgomery Gentry, Johnny Winter, and Los Lonely Boys.

"Duane entered a room and you just wanted to go over there and say hello to him," Reese recalls. "He had a lot of enthusiasm and charisma. And you could just *hear* the passion in Duane's playing. His playing would soar. It would take me to places that I had never been."

David Brown

After his time with the 31st of February, Brown went to San Francisco with Reese Wynans to play bass in Boz Scaggs's band. He remained with Scaggs for several years, appearing on the albums *Moments, Boz Scaggs & Band*, and *My Time*. He also played on Gregg's *Laid Back* LP, as well as recordings by Bonnie Bramlett and Elvin Bishop.

Scott Boyer

In addition to his work with Tommy Talton in Cowboy, Boyer also played on albums by Gregg, Dickey, Wet Willie, Bonnie Bramlett, Sailcat, and others. His composition "Please Be with Me"—on which Duane played dobro for the original Cowboy recording—was covered by Eric Clapton on his classic 1974 Tom Dowd–produced album, *461 Ocean Boulevard.*

"Duane was a very humble guy in that he looked to find something good in every musician he played with," says Boyer. "He wanted to add to what you did. In a musical situation, he never put himself above anybody else."

Johnny Wyker

Still a mainstay of the Southern music scene today, Wyker formed Sailcat in the early 1970s and had a hit with "Motorcycle Mama" in 1972. He continues to promote the catalog of the late Eddie Hinton—the studio guitarist, songwriter, recording artist, and record producer who was the inspiration for Duane's move to Muscle Shoals in 1968. Wyker is also the mastermind behind the Alabama-based Mighty Field of Vision Web Radio and Foundation. The radio format focuses on (primarily Southern) independent music, while the foundation was created to provide emergency charitable assistance to indigent and disabled musicians.

Pete Carr

Former Hour Glass bassist Carr, who produced the *Motorcycle Mama* album for Sailcat, went on to become one of the greatest studio guitarists of his time. His playing can be heard on Bob Seger's "Main Street" and "Fire Lake," Paul Simon's "Kodachrome" and "St. Judy's Comet," Luther Ingram's "(If Loving You Is Wrong) I Don't Want to Be Right," Barbra Streisand's "Woman in Love," and the biggest hit of Rod Stewart's career, "Tonight's the Night." He has also played on recordings by Bobby Womack, Percy Sledge, Willie Nelson, Hank Williams Jr., Cat Stevens, Wilson Pickett, and Joe Cocker.

In 1977 Carr joined forces with singer Lenny LeBlanc; as LeBlanc & Carr, they had a Top 15 hit that same year with "Falling." LeBlanc & Carr were on tour with Lynyrd Skynyrd when Skynyrd's plane crashed on October 20, 1977, killing band members Ronnie Van Zant, Steve Gaines, and Steve's sister, background vocalist Cassie Gaines. Fortunately, Carr and his partner were not on the plane.

Alan Walden

After a parting of the ways with his brother Phil in 1970, Alan continued to work in the R&B and rock worlds, eventually managing Lynyrd Skynyrd and the Outlaws. In 2003 he was inducted into the Georgia Music Hall of Fame.

"Duane was the undisputed leader of the Allman Brothers," he says. "Gregg and everybody had to take note when Duane spoke his mind. In Lynyrd Skynyrd, Ronnie Van Zant was the undisputed leader. His word was law. In the Allman Brothers, Duane was the one that everybody had to look up to."

Phil Walden

Phil Walden was inducted into the Georgia Music Hall of Fame in 1986. As if managing Otis Redding and founding Capricorn Records weren't enough, he also helped to finance Jimmy Carter's successful bid for the presidency in 1976 through a series of fund-raising concerts performed by Capricorn artists. Walden's monumental successes and equally monumental failures are far too many to enumerate here. He lived life on a grand scale and is worthy of his own book-length biography. Phil Walden passed away on April 23, 2006, at the age of 66. He, too, is buried at Rose Hill Cemetery in Macon.

He once observed, "If I had to say who I thought was the most important contemporary figure in rock music as far as the launching of what became known as Southern rock music is concerned, it would be Duane Allman."

Chuck Leavell

After his days with the Allman Brothers and Sea Level, Leavell went on to become one of rock's best-known keyboard men. The artists he has recorded with include the Fabulous Thunderbirds, the Black Crowes, Blues Traveler, Linda Ronstadt, Richard Ashcroft, Lee Ann Womack, Gov't Mule, and Widespread Panic. He has toured with George Harrison and Eric Clapton, and has recorded three albums with Clapton, including the guitarist's multi-million-selling *Unplugged*. As if all of that weren't impressive enough, since 1982 Leavell has handled keyboard duties for the Rolling Stones. He has played on all of their albums from *Undercover* to the present, as well as having toured with the band for more than 25 years, serving as both keyboardist and musical director.

And a Final Word from Gregg Allman

"My brother was a real pistol," the younger Allman brother once said. "He was a hell of a musician, but he was a hell of a person, too. People forget that sometimes. . . .

"He taught me to stick to my guns. 'Stand up for what you believe in and don't let anyone tell you what to play'—that's how Duane put it to me, and I've never forgotten it. That's how he lived, so it wasn't a hard lesson to learn."

Duane Allman– A Discography

Unlike the cases of Jimi Hendrix, Bob Marley, Jerry Garcia, and Tupac Shakur, there has not been a wave of previously unreleased Duane Allman recordings flooding the marketplace in the years since his death (although there are a number of bootlegs circulating with Allman Brothers live performances and unreleased studio sides from the Duane era, as well as several of the tracks from Allman's aborted solo album).

This discography does not include bootlegs, samplers, imports, flexi-discs, singles on which both sides appear on an album already listed, soundtrack albums featuring recordings that previously appeared on other releases, or many of the seemingly endless "greatest hits" collections by the Allman Brothers Band and other artists on whose recordings Duane played. In the case of certain recordings Allman is *alleged* to have played on—but for which he is credited neither on session sheets, the albums themselves, nor by any other currently verifiable means—such tracks have not been included. One record producer has said the guitarist had a habit of unexpectedly showing up and sitting in on sessions, playing on a number of recordings for which he has received no credit to the present day—thus making a complete discography of Duane Allman virtually impossible.

The extremely observant will notice that the two King Curtis tracks from Atco's *Soul Christmas* LP do not appear in this discography. Despite the fact that Duane was credited as the guitarist on "The Christmas Song" and "What are You Doing on New Year's Eve?" on Rhino Record's reissue of *Soul Christmas*, it would seem to be a chronological impossibility. Aside from the fact that the guitarist doesn't sound like Allman (but does sound an awful lot like Eric Gale), the two songs in question were cut in New York at Atlantic Recording Studios several weeks prior to Duane becoming a sideman on Atlantic sessions. In addition, both of the Curtis sides were produced by Tom Dowd, who said in a number of interviews that he didn't know about Duane until he heard Allman's guitar work on Wilson Pickett's version of "Hey Jude" (which wasn't recorded until the King Curtis Christmas tracks had already been released).

Many of the recordings listed here first came out on vinyl; have since gone in and out of print on both vinyl and CD; and have returned on CD again with bonus tracks, remixed, remastered, resequenced, etc. Therefore, I have chosen to reference the original domestic album or single made by the artist listed, as well as the original label.

With regard to recordings made by the Allman Brothers Band, for obvious reasons I have listed only those albums from the years during which Duane was a member. I have also listed the ABB albums in the order they were released, as opposed to the chronological order in which they were recorded (which is why, for example, the April 1970 recording of *Live at Ludlow Garage* appears prior to *Fillmore East: February 1970*).

For an extremely detailed account of the Allman Brothers' recordings through the year 2000, check out Dean Reynolds's beautifully illustrated *The Complete Allman Brothers Band Discography*.

I am extremely grateful to Stuart Krause—Duane Allman discographer extraordinaire—who made me aware of some of the recordings D.A. played on that weren't a part of this discography in the first edition of *Skydog*.

Recordings By Bands Featuring Duane Allman

Allman Joys
"Spoonful"/"You Deserve Each Other" (Dial) 1966—Duane Allman's first commercially released record, the A-side featuring an uptempo, fuzz-heavy version of Willie Dixon's "Spoonful." Produced by legendary Nashville songwriter John D. Loudermilk at Bradley's Barn recording studio in Mt. Juliet, Tennessee.

Early Allman, Featuring Duane and Gregg Allman (Dial) 1973—These 12 tracks include the A-side of the Allman Joys' first single, as well as seven songs written or co-written by Gregg. According to Duane, after Dial owner Buddy Killen heard these tapes in 1966 he advised the band to go "look for a day gig."

Hour Glass

Hour Glass (Liberty) 1967—The debut album by the group Duane later called "a good damn band of misled cats."

Power of Love (Liberty) 1968—The band's much-improved second (and last) album, including the excellent "Down in Texas," written by Muscle Shoals–based songwriters Eddie Hinton and Marlin Greene. The title song, by fellow Shoals songwriters Dan Penn and Spooner Oldham, is another highlight.

31st of February

Duane & Greg [sic] *Allman* (Bold) 1972—Although the 31st of February released its debut album on Vanguard, that LP predated Duane and Gregg's involvement with the band. The songs on *Duane & Greg Allman* were recorded in 1968 by the 31st of February's five-member lineup (Duane, Gregg, Butch Trucks, Scott Boyer, and David Brown). As was the case with the Allman Joys album, these recordings were not released until after Duane Allman's death. Duane's slide playing is captured on tape for the first time here, on Gregg's song "Melissa."

The Allman Brothers Band

The Allman Brothers Band (Atco/Capricorn Records Series) 1969—The band's debut album, recorded in New York in only six days, featuring three of Gregg Allman's finest compositions: "It's Not My Cross to Bear," "Dreams," and "Whipping Post."

Idlewild South (Atco/Capricorn Records Series) 1970—Dickey Betts's first songwriting contributions to the band are here: the classic instrumental "In Memory of Elizabeth Reed" and the album's single, "Revival." The latter song would tap the bottom of the Top 100 Singles chart for three weeks. It was as close as the band would get to a hit single during Duane's lifetime. Incredibly, the 45 of "Midnight Rider"—which would later be a solo hit for Gregg and other artists—failed to make it onto the charts at all.

At Fillmore East (Capricorn) 1971—The masterpiece. Considered by many to be the greatest live recording ever ("Play all night!"), this double album is the ultimate testament to Duane Allman's talent as a guitarist, bandleader, and musical visionary. From "Statesboro Blues" (the first cut on Side One) to "Whipping Post" (which takes up all of Side Four), the band is nothing short of flawless. Absolutely essential.

Eat a Peach (Capricorn) 1972—Unfinished at the time of Duane's death, this second double album includes Duane's acoustic instrumental "Little Martha," Dickey's beautiful "Blue Sky," Gregg's "Melissa," and a 33-minute version of "Mountain Jam"—one of the album's three tracks culled from the remaining Fillmore East recordings of March and June 1971.

Dreams (PolyGram) 1989—The boxed set that brought the band back together. Over the course of four CDs, *Dreams* chronicles not only the ABB's well-known works but previously unreleased recordings by the Allman Joys, the Hour Glass, and the Allman Brothers, as well as Duane's heartfelt tribute to King Curtis, "You Don't Love Me"/"Soul Serenade," and the first non-bootleg release of "Little Martha" that includes Oakley's bass guitar (which was mixed out of the *Eat a Peach* version).

Live at Ludlow Garage 1970 (Polydor) 1990—Proof positive that the band was already a hot live act by April 1970. This two-CD set includes a rare "I'm Gonna Move to the Outskirts of Town" and an even more mountainous take of "Mountain Jam" than the one on *Eat a Peach*—this version clocking in at 44 minutes. Of particular interest is Duane's lead vocal on "Dimples."

The Fillmore Concerts (Polydor) 1992—An interesting two-CD "parallel universe" version of *At Fillmore East* and the live tracks from *Eat a Peach*, including some alternate takes, all transferred to digital format and remixed (and, in some cases, re-edited by splicing together two different versions of the same song) by Tom Dowd.

Fillmore East: February 1970 (Grateful Dead Records) 1997—These recordings were made by the Grateful Dead's Owsley Stanley during the run of Fillmore shows in which the Allman Brothers opened for the Dead. Long out of print, this one's now a highly-sought-after collectible.

American University 12/13/70 (Allman Brothers Band Recording Company) 2002—Taken from two sets performed at Leonard Gym on the American University campus in Washington, D.C., this CD was released as the first in a series of historic live recordings on the band's own label.

SUNY at Stony Brook 9/19/71 (Allman Brothers Band Recording Company) 2003—Second in the series of historic live recordings, this two-CD set was recorded on ¼-inch tape at 7½ inches per second (and it sounds like it). Despite the bootleg-ish sonic quality, the spirit is there. The second disc includes near-20-minute versions of "Dreams" and "In Memory of Elizabeth Reed." It is also notable because it marks one of Duane's last performances with the band.

Live at the Atlanta International Pop Festival: July 3 & 5, 1970 (Epic/Legacy) 2003—The Allman Brothers opened and closed this three-day Woodstock South. Five of the same songs appear in both the July 3rd and July 5th shows, but there's still plenty of variety. Thom Doucette's harmonica abounds throughout much of the proceedings, and Johnny Winter steps in to play along on the July 5th performance of "Mountain Jam."

At Fillmore East: Deluxe Edition (Mercury) 2003—One more time, but *this* collection consists of the entire original album, the live tracks from *Eat a Peach*, the Fillmore East recordings that first appeared on the two Duane Allman anthologies, and the Fillmore East recording of "Drunken Hearted Boy" that first appeared in the *Dreams* boxed set.

Eat a Peach: Deluxe Edition (Mercury) 2006—Another two-CD set, with the original *Eat a Peach* album on disc one. Disc two is the revelation of this collection, consisting of the final Fillmore East concert from June 27, 1971. "One Way Out" is included on the second disc (even though it also appears on disc one), as well as "Midnight Rider," which made its debut on *An Anthology, Volume II*. The remaining tracks that make up disc two are all previously unreleased, providing fans with seven "new" recordings of the ABB in its prime.

Boston Common 8/17/71 (Allman Brothers Band Recording Company) 2007—The third in a series of live recordings of the ABB during Duane's tenure with the band, this CD captures the first of two shows performed that day. It's the usual set list from the era ("Statesboro Blues," "Trouble No More," "Whipping Post," etc.), the highlight being a scorching, 26-minute take on "You Don't Love Me."

Duane Allman's Session Work (in alphabetical order)

The Bleus
"Milk and Honey"/"Leavin' Lisa" (Amy single) 1968; "Julianna's Gone"/ "Mystery Smoke" (Bell single) 1969—Two 45s recorded by this "blue-eyed soul" band from Gadsden, Alabama, with Duane playing guitar on "Milk and Honey" and "Julianna's Gone" and bringing out his slide for "Leavin' Lisa."

Ella Brown
"A Woman Left Lonely"/"Touch Me" (Lanor single) 1971—Recorded at Capricorn Studios in Macon, Duane Allman played on both sides of this soulful 45. Ella Brown, wife of Jackie Avery (the man responsible for bringing Duane and Jaimoe together), went on to become a member of the Williettes, Wet Willie's all-female group of background singers.

James Carr
"These Ain't Raindrops"/"To Love Somebody" (Goldwax single) 1969—The vast majority of recordings by this greatly underrated soul singer were cut in Memphis, including the A-side of this 45. "To Love Somebody" was recorded at Fame Studios in Muscle Shoals, with Allman and Jimmy Johnson sharing guitar duties.

Clarence Carter
The Dynamic Clarence Carter (Atlantic) 1969—This album consists of some of Duane's earliest recordings as a sideman in Muscle Shoals, including his spectacular slide playing on "The Road of Love."

Coleman-Hinton Project
Lost and Found (Breathe Easy Music) 1995—Recorded from 1969–1971, this collection was cut in Muscle Shoals by Jim Coleman and studio guitarist Eddie Hinton. Hinton wanted Duane to play on the whole album, but Coleman preferred Tippy Armstrong (who would later become lead guitarist for Muscle Shoals Sound's rhythm section). Duane ended up playing on one song, "What Goes On," which also featured a soprano sax solo by King Curtis.

Arthur Conley

More Sweet Soul (Atco) 1969—Following in the footsteps of Wilson Pickett, Conley (of "Sweet Soul Music" fame) covers the Beatles. This time it's "Ob-La-Di, Ob-La-Da," a charting single—although not nearly as successful as Pickett's recording of "Hey Jude." Duane has a field day here on "Stuff You Gotta Watch."

Cowboy

5'll Getcha Ten (Capricorn) 1971—Among the best of the Capricorn artists, Cowboy was also among the least successful sales-wise. Duane plays dobro on Scott Boyer's ballad "Please Be with Me," later covered by Eric Clapton.

Delaney & Bonnie (& Friends)

To Bonnie From Delaney (Atco) 1970—Duane's dobro is featured on the medley of "Come On in My Kitchen"/"Mama, He Treats Your Daughter Mean"/"Going Down the Road Feeling Bad." Allman plays guitar on several tracks, including the hit single "Soul Shake," but he truly shines on the uptempo rocker "Living on the Open Road."

Motel Shot (Atco) 1971—Duane is back to play dobro on a full-length version of "Come On in My Kitchen" on this primarily acoustic affair. Bonnie Bramlett recalls Allman handling the rhythm parts for some songs by beating on a briefcase. Duane plays slide on the album's best number, "Sing My Way Home."

D&B Together (Columbia) 1972—Released after Duane's death. His guitar work appears on "A Good Thing (I'm on Fire)."

Derek & the Dominos

Layla and Other Assorted Love Songs (Atco) 1970—If Duane Allman had played on no other album but this one, he would still deserve "legend" status. Appearing on 11 of the 14 cuts, Allman matches musical wits with Eric Clapton on one of the finest rock albums ever made. His slide work over the piano track at the end of "Layla" helped to create an FM radio staple that continues to receive steady airplay to the present day—and his "birdcalls" that conclude the song would be emulated by Lynyrd Skynyrd on "Free Bird," their anthem dedicated to the guitarist.

The Layla Sessions: 20th Anniversary Edition (Polydor) 1990—A three-CD celebration of the original album with alternate takes, Duane's duet with Eric on "Mean

Old World," and five different jams—including one with both Allman brothers, Clapton, Bobby Whitlock, Dickey Betts, Berry Oakley, and Butch Trucks.

The Duck & the Bear

"Goin' Up to Country"/"Hand Jive" (Atlantic single) 1969—A one-off single featuring Duane on slide and Eddie Hinton on lead. Screwed-up title and all, this is the two guitarists' instrumental spin on Canned Heat's "Goin' Up the Country."

Doris Duke

I'm a Loser (Canyon) 1969—A year after the demise of the Hour Glass, Duane and Pete Carr got back together to play guitars on one of the best Southern soul albums of the era. According to Swamp Dogg, the album's producer, "Duane came in the studio one morning immediately after arriving from a tour and said he wanted to sit in. As a result he played on several of the tracks in conjunction with Pete."

Eric Quincy Tate

Eric Quincy Tate (Rhino Handmade) 2006—As with Lynyrd Skynyrd and the Marshall Tucker Band, no one in the group was actually named Eric Quincy Tate. EQT's debut was released on the Cotillion label in 1971. When Rhino Handmade reissued the band's first album on CD in 2006, seven bonus tracks were added, including a demo of "Comin' Down," featuring slide work by Duane.

Aretha Franklin

This Girl's in Love with You (Atlantic) 1970—This album scored five hit singles including "The Weight," with the funkiest slide playing of Duane's career. *This Girl's in Love with You* also includes some of the earliest work of Allman and King Curtis together, on both "The Weight" and Ronnie Miller's "It Ain't Fair."

Spirit in the Dark (Atlantic) 1970—Duane can barely be heard playing acoustic guitar on "Pullin'," but the one other track he's on, "When the Battle Is Over," is a virtual guitar-fest, featuring Allman, Eddie Hinton, and Jimmy Johnson.

Barry Goldberg . . . and

Two Jews Blues (Buddah) 1969—A solo album from the former Electric Flag member, featuring Duane's guitar work on "Twice a Man."

John Hammond

Southern Fried (Atlantic) 1970—Hammond was having a difficult time trying to get the Muscle Shoals Sound rhythm section into his blues groove until Allman showed up out of nowhere to save the day. Duane plays on "Shake for Me," "I'm Leavin' You," "Cryin' for My Baby," and "You'll Be Mine."

Ronnie Hawkins

Ronnie Hawkins (Cotillion) 1970—Features Duane on the single "Down in the Alley," as well as "Forty Days," Who Do You Love," and "Matchbox"—the last song including Hawkins's exclamation, "Go Skydog!"

The Hawk (Cotillion) 1971—Allman plays on almost every track, and even does a bit of vocalizing on "Drinkin' Wine Spo-Dee-O-Dee."

Johnny Jenkins

Ton-Ton Macoute! (Atco/Capricorn Records Series) 1970—Produced by Johnny Sandlin, this album has a stellar cast of musicians including Allman Brothers Band members Duane, Berry, Butch, and Jaimoe, as well as former Hour Glass members Paul Hornsby, Pete Carr, and Sandlin. "Down Along the Cove"—a track from Duane's aborted Fame solo album—gets a second life here with Jenkins's vocal replacing Allman's.

King Curtis

Instant Groove (Atco) 1969—Allman performs on four songs, including the Grammy-winning "Games People Play." It's evident his stature as a sideman was growing by this time, as there is a separate credit for him on the back cover. (None of the other musicians, except Curtis himself, are listed.)

Laura Lee

Love More Than Pride (Chess) 1972—Laura Lee and her label mate, Etta James, made some of their finest records under the tutelage of producer Rick Hall at Fame Studios. Duane, Rick's "go-to guy," played on the Laura Lee tracks "It Ain't What You Do (But How You Do It)" and "It's How You Make It Good."

The Lovelles

"I'm Comin' Today"/"Pretending Dear" (Atco single) 1969—Duane played on both sides of this single produced by Dave Crawford and Roy Lee Johnson.

With a slight lineup change, the Lovelles would go on to have a series of R&B hits under the name Faith, Hope & Charity.

Lulu
New Routes (Atco) 1969—Recorded by the "To Sir with Love" singer in Muscle Shoals. Duane kicks off the album with his slide playing on "Marley Purt Drive" and also plays on "Dirty Old Man," "Sweep Around Your Own Back Door," and the song first made famous by his old friends in the Nitty Gritty Dirt Band, "Mr. Bojangles."

Herbie Mann
Push Push (Embryo) 1971—Duane finally gets his chance to show that he can more than hold his own in the world of jazz-funk. When the album was re-issued in 1989, it included an additional track and the credit "Featuring Duane Allman" on the back of the CD.

Judy Mayhan
Moments (Atco) 1970—Mayhan's debut album on Atco, including Allman on "Everlovin' Ways."

The New Rock Band
"Rock Steady"/"Little David" (Scott single) 1968—The New Rock Band consisted primarily of session players at the same studio where Duane and Gregg recorded with the 31st of February. Duane sat in on both sides of this single.

Laura Nyro
Christmas and the Beads of Sweat (Columbia) 1971—Appearing only on "Beads of Sweat," Allman once again gets his own separate credit on the back of the album.

Wilson Pickett
Hey Jude (Atlantic) 1969—Duane's lead guitar work on the title track brought him to the attention of Jerry Wexler and Phil Walden, resulting in Allman's signing with Capricorn Records. Despite his now-legendary playing on several of the album's 11 songs, the original credits listed him as "David" Allman.

Otis Rush
Mourning in the Morning (Cotillion) 1969—Produced by Mike Bloomfield and Nick Gravenites at Fame Studios, this one has a standout performance by Duane

on "Reap What You Sow"—the song that includes the phrase from which the album's title was derived.

Sam Samudio

Sam: Hard and Heavy (Atlantic) 1971—Best known as leader of Sam the Sham & the Pharaohs (remember "Wooly Bully"?), Samudio was produced by Tom Dowd on this solo album, which includes Allman's dobro work on the John Lee Hooker song "Goin' Upstairs."

"Key to the Highway"/ "Me and Bobby McGee" (Atlantic single) 1971—Duane played dobro on "Me and Bobby McGee," a track that did not appear on the *Hard and Heavy* album.

Boz Scaggs

Boz Scaggs (Atlantic) 1969—Long before his string of hits for Columbia, Scaggs cut this album at Muscle Shoals Sound Studios. Fenton Robinson's "Loan Me a Dime," with its long guitar solo by Duane, is a classic. The record also includes Duane's dobro playing on the Jimmie Rodgers standard "Waiting for a Train."

Soul Survivors

Take Another Look (Atco) 1969—Blue-eyed soul from the "Expressway to Your Heart" hitmakers. Duane takes a fine slide solo on "Darkness."

Irma Thomas

In Between Tears (Fungus) 1973—As with Doris Duke's *I'm a Loser*, this album features Duane Allman and Pete Carr back together again in the studio.

Willie Walker

"A Lucky Loser"/"Warm to Cool to Cold" (Checker single) 1968—Walker recorded this 45 for Chess Records subsidiary, Checker. The A-side is one of the great "lost" singles of the era, tastefully filled with Duane's trademark licks.

Spencer Wiggins

"I Never Loved a Woman (the Way I Love You)"/"Soul City USA" (Goldwax single) 1969—Horn-laden Southern soul, this is Wiggins's gender-reversed take on Aretha's hit with Duane Allman's call-and-response guitar work throughout.

The Duane Allman Compilations

An Anthology (Capricorn) 1972—Released the year after his death, this 19-track double album captures many of the highlights of Duane Allman's life in music. Beginning with the "B.B. King Medley" from the ill-fated Hour Glass sessions at Fame and ending with Duane's own "Little Martha" from *Eat a Peach*, the first LP includes Wilson Pickett's "Hey Jude"—the recording that led Duane out of the wilderness and into the Promised Land; Clarence Carter's "The Road of Love"—with its incendiary slide solo; "Goin' Down Slow"—from Duane's aborted solo project; "Games People Play"—King Curtis's Grammy-winning single; and the 13-minute "Loan Me a Dime" from Boz Scaggs's debut album. The second disc includes the alternate take of Cowboy's "Please Be with Me"—featuring Duane's beautiful dobro work; "Mean Old World"—a previously unreleased duet by Duane and Eric Clapton; five recordings by the ABB; and Derek & the Dominos' epic, the full-length version of "Layla."

Dialogs (Capricorn) 1972—This promotional-only album was shipped to radio stations to coincide with the release of *An Anthology*. It includes Ed Shane's 1970 interview with Duane, as well as Shane's then-current interviews with Jerry Wexler of Atlantic Records and Jon Landau of *Rolling Stone*. Also on the LP is the insightful "Duane Allman Radio Hour"—a one-time event hosted by Allman on Atlanta's WPLO-FM in 1970—that gave Duane the opportunity to discuss some of his musical influences, including John Coltrane and Miles Davis.

An Anthology, Volume II (Capricorn) 1974—Twenty-one additional great moments from Duane's work as a sideman and with the Allman Brothers. This second two-record set includes "Happily Married Man" and "No Money Down"—two more songs from Allman's unfinished solo album; Herbie Mann's "Push Push"—Duane's foray into jazz; Delaney & Bonnie's "Come On in My Kitchen"—a live recording with Duane on acoustic slide guitar; and "Dimples"—the only song featuring Duane on lead vocals during his days with the Allman Brothers Band.

The Best of Duane Allman (Capricorn) 1979—This ten-song collection brings together some of the finest moments from the two *Anthology* albums.

The Guitars of
Duane Allman

n bars, rehearsal spaces, dorm rooms, all-night diners, and numerous guitar forums across the Internet, stories about Duane Allman's guitars continually abound among musicians and fans—some of which might actually be true. Attempting to discern fact from fiction is no easy task when it comes to tracking down specific instruments played by Allman from around 1960 until his death in late 1971.

The following information is based on photographs; the memories of musicians in Duane's circle during his lifetime; Allman's guitars currently on loan to the Rock and Roll Hall of Fame and Museum; conversations with Walter Carter, historian for the Gibson Guitar Corp.; interviews with Lee Hazen, Kirk West, and Delaney Bramlett conducted by Dave Kyle; and information from other guitar experts, including Kurt Linhof, Bob Brozman, Don Butler, Jim Wagner, Brian Mayes, Matt Ferguson, Mike Reilly, Peter Leinheiser, and Derek Bowers.

This is not intended to be an exhaustive inventory of every guitar Duane Allman ever played or owned. Furthermore, having listed those who were helpful in assembling this information, I should point out that any possible inaccuracies about the instruments discussed here are entirely my responsibility.

• • •

Duane Allman's first electric guitar was a double-cutaway 1959 Gibson Les Paul Junior. It was owned for several years by Delaney Bramlett, later sold to a San Francisco collector, and now belongs to a collector in Japan. Bramlett told Dave Kyle how he came to acquire the instrument: "I was somewhere—Atlanta, I think. When we were traveling—doing shows—I would wake up early and go out to pawn shops. I saw this little Junior, and I believe I picked it up for 60 bucks. I brought it back to the hotel—no case or anything. Duane was sitting there, and he kept looking over at me. Then he would look at the floor—then back at me. Finally he said, 'Would you look at the back of that and see if there is a gouge that looks like a thumbnail scratched it?' I turned it over and said, 'Yeah, boy, there it is.' He said, 'Damn it! That's where I hocked that thing!' He had gotten drunk and pawned it and forgot where. He said, 'That's my first electric guitar. Can I have it back?'" Bramlett laughed and told Allman, "No way!"

Gregg Allman told *Guitar Player* magazine in October 1981 that he got his first electric guitar, a Fender Musicmaster, in 1960. "By this time, Duane had to have one," Gregg said. "Mom got him an electric. It was a Les Paul Junior—one of those old purple ones with a real thin body and just one pickup." It actually would have been cherry red, but the mahogany body of the guitar might have caused it to appear purple (at least to Gregg). Walter Carter points out that the guitar has been altered. "It would have originally had a wraparound bridge/tailpiece rather than the Tune-o-matic and stopbar."

Another of Allman's early guitars, a '56 or '57 Fender Stratocaster, originally belonged to Daytona Beach recording enthusiast Lee Hazen. Hazen told Dave Kyle: "I had rewired it and put some special features on it. It had a rotary switch with 11 positions—11 different capacitors in the tone-control circuit. I had modified the selector switch to five positions by filing extra notches in the little detent. Then I put two phase switches on it for the second pickup. I put another switch that would connect the first and third pickups, so you could get any combination of the three pickups in any combination of phase. You could get all of these weird sounds." Duane's friend Sylvan Wells confirms the modifications, saying the Strat had "little switches that Lee had put in, and nobody knew what they were for."

In an early promotional photo of the Allman Joys, Duane is seen holding a mid-1960s Gibson ES-335 with block inlays and a Bigsby vibrato tailpiece. (According to Peter Leinheiser, the "Bigsby was optional on the 335 during that time.") Allman owned this guitar when he was in the Escorts. He can be seen playing it in photos of the April 17, 1965, concert when the Escorts and the Nightcrawlers opened for the Beach Boys.

Gregg says that while Duane was still in the Allman Joys—and also during his Hour Glass days—he played a Fender Telecaster with a Stratocaster neck. According to Pete Carr, Duane came back from a series of Allman Joys gigs in Greenwich Village with a "white/yellowish Telecaster with a silver metal Vox fuzz distortion

Duane at Fame playing a Fender Stratocaster

box mounted on it." In a May 1973 *Guitar Player* article, Richard Albero wrote: "In those days, Duane was playing through a very early model blonde Fender Telecaster with Fender's 150 Rock and Roll strings. He used Vox Super Beatle amps, a very popular model at the time with six ten-inch speakers and two horns. He had a distortion device somewhat like a fuzz tone that he actually attached on a little bracket connected to the volume and treble knobs. He also had an Echoplex tape delay unit." In the same *GP* article, Albero wrote: "The first [Hour Glass] album was cut with his Fender Telecaster played through Vox amplifiers while the second was through [a] Fender Twin Reverb."

When Allman became a studio musician in Muscle Shoals, his guitar of choice was a Stratocaster. "Mainly at the time," recalls Jimmy Johnson, "Duane used a Strat and a Fender Twin amp with JBLs. He had one gadget—a Fuzz

Face—and that was it. He was going through it all the time, although he might not have always had it kicked in. He used a lot of feedback . . . between the pickups and the speakers—incredible stuff! Sustain for the world. And the thing about his Fuzz Face was when he'd pop that 9-volt battery in there, a new one wouldn't suit him. He would actually—some way—get batteries that were almost worn out, because the Fuzz Face had a special sound just for so many hours with the batteries at a certain strength. He was into weak batteries."

Along with the Stratocaster he used in his early session days, Allman had at least two more Strats in his arsenal. The Hard Rock Café now owns one of them, while another was in Delaney Bramlett's collection for a number of years. When Dave Kyle asked Bramlett how he came to own Duane's three-tone sunburst, rosewood fretboard '61 Strat, he said: "I begged and begged and begged! He finally got sick of me begging. He knew I loved it. Every time he would join me on the road or whatever, I would make him play my guitar and I would play his Stratocaster.

"We were somewhere and he had to get back to Macon for some reason. He used to climb up the vines outside my window to my balcony and come into my bedroom and wake me up. I told him I was tired that night and I wanted to go to sleep. I locked the window—so he couldn't get in—and went to bed. I heard this 'Bam! Bam! Bam!' I just figured he wanted me to get up and go to town or something, so I didn't get up. He was trying to wake me to get a ride to the airport.

"So he went over and knocked on my brother Johnny's door to get a ride. He wrote a note and left it on the guitar: 'Wear it in good health. I know you love it. Duane.' He told my brother, 'Give this to Delaney. I know he loves it so much.' I woke up the next morning and Johnny said, 'Duane left you a present.' It's all scratched up because he had a leather string around the neck, and he would just hang it from a nail on the wall."

Duane's primary resonator guitar was a 14-fret National Duolian. Bob Brozman, the author of *The History & Artistry of National Resonator Instruments*, says Duane's Duolian was made between 1937 and 1939. Brozman characterizes the model Allman owned as "bottom of the line, preferred by many blues players."

Among Allman's other acoustic instruments was a Gibson L-00, which

Walter Carter describes as "Gibson's most popular acoustic of the pre-World War II era." He says Duane's L-00 was made in the late 1930s or early 1940s.

The first of Allman's Gibson Les Pauls was his 1957 goldtop, serial number 7-3312. He bought the guitar early in the Allman Brothers Band era and can be seen playing it in photos from the Atlanta International Pop Festival in July 1970. Duane played this guitar throughout the recording of *Idlewild South*—and, maybe more significantly, it was used on *Layla*, according to Don Butler.

According to a number of sources, Duane traded his goldtop for a '58 (or later) cherry sunburst Les Paul on September 16, 1970, after jamming with a band called the Stone Balloon in Daytona Beach. As the story goes, Duane agreed to pay the band's guitar player a few hundred dollars as part of the trade.

Allman with his Gibson L-00 pre-war acoustic guitar

Duane took the guitarist with him to get the money, but not before (allegedly) he surreptitiously instructed roadies Red Dog and Joe Dan Petty (or Kim Payne, depending on who's telling the story) to switch the pickups on the two guitars. Don Butler says, "I'm inclined to believe it's a '58. The top's plainer than [that on] a '59 or '60."

On Wednesday, July 21, 1971, the Allman Brothers Band played two shows at the Schaefer Music Festival in Central Park. The place must have been packed with photographers, as more pictures of Duane seem to have been taken on that day than at any other event in his career. Because of the many photos of Duane in Central Park that have appeared in many publications, one could get the impression that the guitar he was playing that day was his main instrument. In fact, on the ABB albums recorded and released during his lifetime, he was usually playing one of the aforementioned Les Pauls—and therein lies one of the mysteries surrounding the guitar Allman used to play slide at the Schaefer Music Festival.

As Gibson guitar buffs are well aware, the Les Paul underwent a radical design change in the early 1960s. From 1961 through late 1963, the double-

Duane in the studio with his 1957 Gibson Les Paul goldtop

cutaway body style known today as the SG was called a Les Paul Standard and Les Paul's name was inscribed on the truss-rod cover. After 1963, the Les Paul name was dropped. This happened, says Walter Carter, because "Gibson's agreement [temporarily] ended with Les Paul in 1963." After that, the double-cutway guitar became the SG Standard, and the truss-rod cover was blank.

In some of the photos of Allman at Central Park, the blank truss-rod cover can clearly be seen. So, from reviewing the photographic evidence, it initially appeared that Duane was playing an SG from late 1963 or thereafter. The instrument's pickguard is another clue: "The small pickguard was used only through 1965," Walter Carter says, "so that would be the latest that this guitar could be."

The guitar in question is currently on loan to the Rock and Roll Hall of Fame and Museum. After my initial conversation with Walter Carter, Jim Henke, chief curator of the museum, informed me that its serial number is 15263. Upon receiving this information, Carter checked the Gibson files and discovered that the guitar was "entered into the ledger books on April 26,

Duane Allman with the cherry sunburst Les Paul

1961." Therefore, the instrument Duane used to play slide at the Schaefer Music Festival was not a 1963 SG Standard, as has been reported—it was a 1961 Les Paul Standard. But what about that blank truss-rod cover? "If the factory ran out of the Les Paul covers," says Carter, "they would have used plain ones rather than hold up production."

The most obvious modification to the guitar is its missing tailpiece. A vibrato was standard equipment on this model, according to Carter. "There were two types of vibratos and tailpieces during that era," he says, "a complicated side-to-side mechanism that didn't work well at all, and a standard up-and-down-action vibrato that was basically a U-shaped spring. Both vibratos had the long cover plate with engraved lyre." Jim Henke states that there are still four screw holes on the body of the guitar where the tailpiece was once attached.

Because the SG continues to be manufactured by Gibson to the present day, and due to the fact that the name "Les Paul Standard" applied to the model

*Duane in Central Park
playing his 1961 Les Paul
(SG) Standard*

for such a brief time, all of the Gibson guitars of this design—even those from 1961 through 1963—are usually referred to as SGs.

Don Butler states that the SG/Les Paul in question had been purchased by Dickey Betts in 1970. "He had a fairly new Gibson ES-345 before that, which had the trapeze tailpiece instead of the stop tailpiece," explains Butler. "He liked the SG better but really wanted a Les Paul goldtop. Duane bought the SG from Dickey so Dickey could buy a goldtop. Duane tuned the SG to open *E* and used it for slide."

After Duane's death, the guitar ended up with Gerry Groom. "He was sort of Duane's protégé," says Butler. "There was a guy by the name of Gerry Groom," Kirk West told Dave Kyle, "who was a kind of precocious little guitar player from Miami. Duane took a shine to him in 1969 or '70. Gerry was—how would you put it?—fond of himself. Nobody else was very fond of him, except Duane. But he was around a lot. Apparently somewhere along the line, Duane had said to Gerry, 'If anything ever happens to me, I want you to have this guitar.' So he got the guitar early in '72."

Later, when Groom needed money for an operation, he sold the guitar to Graham Nash's wife, who wanted to give it to her husband as a Christmas present, according to Kirk West. It was sold with the condition that it could not be sold again unless it went back to Gerry Groom, his family, or somebody in the Allman Brothers' organization. "Gerry died in a scuba diving accident before he could buy it back," says Butler.

Among the more rarely seen Allman guitars is the dot-neck Gibson ES-335 he used at the Cosmic Carnival in Atlanta on June 13, 1970. "It [dates to] anywhere from 1958 to mid-1962, when the block inlay came in," says Walter Carter. "Nothing else changed during that period except the pickguard." And, of course, the pickguard is missing. "The tuners should be Klusons with plastic tulip-shape buttons, like the '59 Les Pauls," adds Carter. "It looks like metal tuner buttons on Duane's." On close inspection, it can be seen that the body of the 335 is discolored below the stopbar, so it appears to have previously had a Bigsby tailpiece.

Finally—and perhaps best known to guitar aficionados—there is Allman's tobacco sunburst Les Paul. Nicknamed "Hot 'Lanta" (although *not* the guitar he used to record the song of that name), this beautiful instrument was acquired by Duane in June 1971 from vintage guitar dealer Kurt Linhof. "We met through Billy Gibbons," says Linhof, "who introduced me as 'the best guitar finder in Texas.'" Duane was in search of a tobacco sunburst Les Paul, and Linhof agreed to locate one for him.

Among the many stories that have circulated about this guitar is that it once belonged to Christopher Cross of "Ride Like the Wind" fame. Although there is a connection of sorts, here's the real story, straight from the man who found the guitar and later delivered it to Duane Allman: "This high school buddy of Chris Cross's found the guitar. He had paid a guy 80 bucks for it, with the peghead broken off—[and then] paid 80 bucks to have the head fixed. He called me up and said, 'Do you want a sunburst Les Paul?' I said, 'Well, yeah. Bring it over.' He brought it over, and it was what Duane had asked for. I said, 'Sure, I'll take it. What do you want?' He said, 'Well, I need another guitar.' The only thing I had that I was willing to part with was a stripped '54 Stratocaster. I paid him the $160 he had in it, cash, plus the Stratocaster that I probably had $100 in. I delivered the guitar on the afternoon of the first of the last Fillmore shows [June 25, 1971], along with a load of tweed Fender Bassman amps and a '60 Fender Jazz Bass for Berry. I swapped the pickups on the guitar and put the strong one in the bridge [position]."

Linhof says the guitar's name came later. "[The song] 'Hot 'Lanta' was in the can already, so the guitar was probably named by Twiggs [Lyndon] while he owned it, or, if not, by some dilettante on the Les Paul Forum [on the Internet] who thought it needed a name. It was certainly not named by Duane—or Gregg. I referred to it as 'the Tiger' for the awesome tiger-flame maple used [for the top], and Duane used that in conversation at the time. But he wasn't the kind of guy to name a guitar."

The guitar's model year remains something of a mystery. Derek Bowers at Gibson Guitar Corp. says, "There is no serial number on the guitar, and without a serial number there is no way to say for sure what year the guitar was made." Linhof, who says he can determine the year of any Les Paul by feeling its neck, believes that it was probably made in late 1959, but adds that "since I never touched the neck, it could have been anything."

Regarding the "tobacco sunburst" description, Walter Carter points out that "all of the finish color names that we use today—darkburst, faded cherry sunburst, heritage cherry sunburst, and so on—are modern delineations. In 1958, '59, and '60, they were all cherry sunburst. The cherry part usually fades on the originals."

One other unique feature of the guitar is its back. Kurt West told Dave Kyle that at some point after Duane's death, Twiggs Lyndon had the guitar refretted. "Twiggs inlaid Duane's name with the old frets," said West. "He didn't want to discard anything [from Allman's guitar], so he took the old frets and spelled Duane's name on the back."

Sadly, Twiggs was killed in a skydiving accident in November 1979 (ironically, in the town of Duanesburg, New York). In the months prior to his death, he had been the tour manager for the Dixie Dregs. With the permission of Lyndon's brothers, Dregs guitarist Steve Morse later used the guitar on a number of the band's records. In a 1982 interview with Jas Obrecht of *Guitar Player*, Morse talked about playing the Les Paul on the recording of "Ridin' High": "Since it wasn't my guitar, I couldn't jack up the action, which was so low the slide would touch the frets. So I stuck a toothpick under the first fret. This raised the action just a little bit, and it also meant I couldn't tune up without holding the slide on the 12th fret. Unless you are playing an open string—which I didn't do at all—you never hear the toothpick since the fulcrum is between the slide and the bridge. Every string was totally dead, except the one I was playing. I damped everything behind the slide, which was on my third finger, and I damped the strings I wasn't playing with the heel of my hand and my left-hand pinkie. The key thing was plucking with my fingers rather than using a pick. I always believed that's the way Duane Allman got that sound and had that control."

When Gibson Guitar Corp. acquired the rights to create its Duane Allman Signature Edition Les Paul, this was the guitar they based it on. The instrument was eventually given to Duane's daughter, Galadrielle, and is currently on loan to the Rock and Roll Hall of Fame and Museum. (This is the guitar Duane is playing on page 189—also pictured on the cover.)

Duane Allman played through a number of different amplifiers during his career, beginning with the aforementioned Vox models and Fender Twins. With the Allman Brothers, says Don Butler, "Duane's Marshall rig was two 50-watt

Front and back of Gibson's Duane Allman Signature Edition Les Paul

Marshall bass heads with two Marshall Bass 100 cabs. The cabs were loaded with a combination of Celestions and Cerwin-Vega ER-123 speakers. The ER-123s were Cerwin-Vega's answer to JBL's D-120s. Duane used three 'Y' cables: the first one was right from his cord, which split the signal to the other two, [each of which] went to an amp head. Duane used both channels of his Marshall heads at the same time. Using both channels, he could get both halves of the first tube, which drove the rest of the amp. By using both halves, he got more gain, which gave him more distortion. Duane wanted all the gain he could get going right into the amp, and he got it by using the 'Y' cables."

For the recording of *Layla and Other Assorted Love Songs*, Allman went in the opposite direction. As Tom Dowd told interviewer Bill Ector, "Duane and Eric were playing on Fender Champs—and the biggest thing that they had was a Princeton. Of course, Duane was used to playing *loud*, so that was certainly a step down." On the album, Clapton and Allman both proved that sometimes size really *doesn't* matter. With close miking of the small but cranked-up amps in the confines of Criteria Studio, both guitarists were able to re-create the sound of their stage amps.

References

Books

The Allman Brothers Band: The Definitive Collection for Guitar, Volume I. Milwaukee: Hal Leonard Corporation, 1995.

The Allman Brothers Band: The Definitive Collection for Guitar, Volume II. Milwaukee: Hal Leonard Corporation, 1995.

The Allman Brothers Band: The Definitive Collection for Guitar, Volume III. Milwaukee: Hal Leonard Corporation, 1995.

Andrews, Walter G., with Najaat Black and Mehmet Kalpakli, ed. *Ottoman Lyric Poetry: An Anthology.* Austin: University of Texas Press, 1997.

Bonds, Ray, ed. *The Illustrated Directory of Guitars.* New York: Barnes & Noble Books, 2004.

Bradley, Jeff. *Moon Handbooks: Tennessee, Third Edition.* Emeryville: Avalon Travel Publishing, 2002.

Brant, Marley. *Freebirds: The Lynyrd Skynyrd Story.* New York: Billboard Books, 2002.

—. *Southern Rockers: The Roots and Legacy of Southern Rock.* New York: Billboard Books, 1999.

Brozman, Bob with Dr. John Dopyera Jr., Richard R. Smith, and Gary Atkinson. *The History & Artistry of National Resonator Instruments.* Anaheim Hills: Centerstream Publishing, 1998.

Campbell, Joseph L. "Red Dog". *A Book of Tails: My Life and Travels on the Road*, 2001.

Carter, Walter. *Gibson Guitars: 100 Years of an American Icon.* Los Angeles: General Publishing Group, 1994.

Crow, Bill. *Jazz Anecdotes.* New York: Oxford University Press, 1990.

Derek and the Dominos: Layla and Other Assorted Love Songs, Guitar Recorded Versions. Milwaukee: Hal Leonard Corporation, 1993.

Editors of *Rolling Stone. Rolling Stone Rock Almanac: The Chronicles of Rock & Roll.* New York: Rolling Stone Press, 1983.

Freeman, Scott. *Midnight Riders: The Story of the Allman Brothers Band.* Boston: Little, Brown and Company, 1995.

Gordon, Robert. *Can't Be Satisfied: The Life and Times of Muddy Waters.* Boston: Little, Brown and Company, 2002.

Graham, Bill and Robert Greenfield. *Bill Graham Presents: My Life Inside Rock and Out.* New York: Da Capo Press, 2004.

Guralnick, Peter. *Sweet Soul Music: Rhythm and Blues and the Southern Dream of Freedom.* New York: Harper & Row, 1986.

Handy, W.C. *Father of the Blues: An Autobiography.* New York: Da Capo Press, 1991.

Kahn, Ashley. *A Love Supreme: The Story of John Coltrane's Signature Album.* New York: Penguin Books, 2003.

Leavell, Chuck with J. Marshall Craig. *Between Rock and a Home Place.* Macon: Mercer University Press, 2004.

McNally, Dennis. *A Long Strange Trip: The Inside History of the Grateful Dead.* New York: Broadway Books, 2002.

McStravick, Summer and John Roos. *Blues-Rock Explosion.* Mission Viejo: Old Goat Publishing, 2001.

Miller, Jim, ed. *The Rolling Stone Illustrated History of Rock & Roll.* New York: Random House/Rolling Stone Press, 1980.

Newquist, HP and Rich Maloof. *The Blues-Rock Masters.* San Francisco: Backbeat Books, 2003.

Obrecht, Jas, ed. *Rollin' and Tumblin': The Postwar Blues Guitarists*. San Francisco: Miller Freeman Books, 2000.

Odom, Gene with Frank Dorman. *Lynyrd Skynyrd: Remembering the Free Birds of Southern Rock*. New York: Broadway Books, 2002.

Oliver, Paul, Max Harrison, and William Bolcom. *The New Grove Gospel, Blues and Jazz*. New York: W.W. Norton and Company, 1986.

Perkins, Willie. *No Saints, No Saviors: My Years with the Allman Brothers Band*. Macon: Mercer University Press, 2005.

Reynolds, Dean. *The Complete Allman Brothers Band Discography*. Cincinnati: Berman Printing Company, 2000.

Roberty, Marc. *Eric Clapton: The Complete Recording Sessions, 1963–1992*. New York: St. Martin's Press, 1993.

Ruppli, Michel. *Atlantic Records: A Discography, Volume 2*. Westport: Greenwood Press, 1979.

—. *Atlantic Records: A Discography, Volume 3*. Westport: Greenwood Press, 1979.

Schumacher, Michael. *Crossroads: The Life and Music of Eric Clapton*. New York: Citadel Press, 2003.

Thomas, J.C. *Chasin' the Trane*. New York: Da Capo Press, 1976.

Ward, Ed with Geoffrey Stokes and Ken Tucker. *Rock of Ages: The Rolling Stone History of Rock & Roll*. New York: Rolling Stone Press/Summit Books, 1986.

Wardlow, Gayle Dean. *Chasin' That Devil Music: Searching for the Blues*. San Francisco: Miller Freeman Books, 1998.

Wexler, Jerry and David Ritz. *Rhythm and the Blues: A Life in American Music*. New York: Alfred A. Knopf, 1993.

Whitburn, Joel. *Billboard's Top 10 Charts: 1958–1988*. Menomonee Falls: Record Research, Inc., 1988.

—. *Joel Whitburn's Top Pop Albums: 1955–1996*. Menomonee Falls: Record Research, Inc., 1996.

—. *Joel Whitburn's Top Pop Singles: 1955–1993*. Menomonee Falls: Record Research, Inc., 1994.

—. *Joel Whitburn's Top R&B Singles: 1942–1995*. Menomonee Falls: Record Research, Inc., 1996.

Zimmerman, Keith and Kent. *Sing My Way Home: Voices of the New American Roots Rock*. San Francisco: Backbeat Books, 2004.

Articles & Liner Notes

Abram, Malcolm X. "Byron Pop, 1970: Woodstock, Middle Georgia Style." *Hittin' the Note*, Issue 29.

Andrietsch, Meg and Sara Thrift. "On the Road with the Brothers' Road Crew." *Hittin' the Note*, Issue 15.

Bangs, Lester. "Duane Allman in Perspective: Session Cat to Star." *Rolling Stone*, February 1, 1973.

Brooks, Michael. "Meet Dick Betts." *Guitar Player*, October 1972.

Crowe, Cameron. "The Allman Brothers Story." *Rolling Stone*, December 6, 1973.

Curatolo, Robbie. "Watkins Glen: Then & Now." *Hittin' the Note*, Issue 39.

Dann, Laurel. "Pure Attitude." *Guitar World*, November 1991.

Dubro, Alec. "Them Vino-Lovin' Allman Brothers." *Rolling Stone*, March 4, 1971.

Ector, Bill "In Honor and in Tribute—To Brother Duane and B. O." *Hittin' the Note*, Issue 31.

—. "Tom Dowd—In His Own Words." *Hittin' the Note*, Issue 9.

—. "An Interview with John Hammond." *Hittin' the Note*, Issue 1.

—. "At Fillmore East . . . Again!" *Hittin' the Note*, Issue 16.

Edmonds, Ben. "The Hour Glass." United Artists Records, 1973.

Fisher, Ben. "Delaney Bramlett (& Friends)!" *Guitar Player*, March 1996.

Glover, Tony. "Dedicated to a Brother." *Rolling Stone*, April 13, 1972.

—. *An Anthology*. Capricorn Records, 1972.

Hall, Russell. "Capricorn Records: The Story of Phil Walden & the South's Most Famous Record Label." *Gritz*, Spring 2004.

Hare, Sam. "Slowhand Remembers Skydog—Eric Clapton Comments on Duane Allman." *Hittin' the Note*, Issue 26.

Hoover, Tim. "Soul Serenade: The Life and Times of King Curtis." *Hittin' the Note*, Issue 35.

Knap, Joe. "Weekend with Dickey Betts at the Rock and Roll Hall of Fame and Museum." *Hittin' the Note*, Issue 15.

Krause, Stuart. "Duane Allman: The Studio Recordings." *Discoveries*, November 2005.

Kyle, Dave. "Gregg Allman: The First Guitar-Playing Allman." *Vintage Guitar*, July 1, 1996.

—. "Remembering Duane Allman." *Vintage Guitar*, January 1997.

Landau, Jon. "Bandleader Duane Allman Dies in Bike Crash." *Rolling Stone*, November 25, 1971.

Leavell, Chuck. "Memories of Berry." *Hittin' the Note*, Issue 22.

Lewis, Grover. "Hitting the Note with the Allman Brothers Band." *Rolling Stone*, November 25, 1971.

Lynskey, John. "Reflections—The World According to Jaimoe." *Hittin' the Note*, Issue 21.

—. "Reflections, Part 2—The World According to Jaimoe." *Hittin' the Note*, Issue 22.

—. "Reflections, Part 3—The World According to Jaimoe." *Hittin' the Note*, Issue 23.

—. "Gregg Allman: Simplicity Found." *Hittin' the Note*, Issue 19.

—. "Lamar Williams: Out of the Shadows." *Hittin' the Note*, Issue 17.

—. "Greens & Blues Forever: Chuck Leavell's World of Trees and Keys." *Hittin' the Note*, Issue 30.

—. "Memories of Atlanta Pop." *Hittin' the Note*, Issue 40.

—. "Gregg Allman: Trouble No More." *Hittin' the Note*, Issue 45.

Mandel, Ellen. "The Georgia Peach." *Guitar World*, November 1991.

Meeks, John. "A Tale of the Second Coming." *Hittin' the Note*, Issue 21.

Oakley, Candace. "Memories of a Brother." *Hittin' the Note*, Issue 3.

Obrecht, Jas. "Duane Allman: 1946–1971." *Guitar Player*, October 1981.

—. "John Hammond." *Guitar Player*, July 1991.

Ogden, John. "First There Is a Mountain." *Hittin' the Note*, Issue 22.

—. "The Hoochie Coochie Man." *Hittin' the Note*, Issue 22.

Paul, Alan. "Low Down and Dirty: Shades of Dickey Betts." *Hittin' the Note*, Issue 22.

—. "Low Down and Dirty: Gregg Allman: Looking Back . . . Looking Forward." *Hittin' the Note*, Issue 26.

—. "Gregg Allman: A Brother Off the Road." *Hittin' the Note*, Issue 31.

—. "A Conversation with Warren Haynes." *Hittin' the Note*, Issue 28.

Santoro, Gene. *Derek & the Dominos: The Layla Sessions, 20th Anniversary Edition*. Polydor Records, 1990.

Shapiro, Harry. "The Price of Love . . . Or How the Recording of *Layla*, Clapton's Ode to Forbidden Love, Made Victims of Derek & the Dominos." *Mojo*, January 2001.

Smith, Michael Buffalo. "The Duck & the Goat: Johnny Sandlin." *Gritz*, Spring 2004.

Spangler, Kevin and Ron Currens. "Butch Trucks, the Different Drummer." *Hittin' the Note*, Issue 15.

Swenson, John. *The Allman Brothers Band: Dreams*. PolyGram Records, 1989.

"Twiggs Lyndon Booked for Murder." *Rolling Stone*, May 28, 1970.

West, Kirsten. "Big News for the Big House." *Hittin' the Note*, Issue 5.

—. "Inside the Elusive Mr. Betts." *Hittin' the Note*, Issue 10.

Whitney, Rick. "The Allman Brothers Band: Architectural Heritage—A Tale of Two Houses." *Hittin' the Note*, Issue 26.

—. "'1979: The First Reunion': The Return of the Allman Brothers Band." *Hittin' the Note*, Issue 17.

Winkles, Stuart. "Duane Allman: Skydog's Sessions, '68–'71." Goldmine, April 11, 1986.

DVDs

The Allman Brothers Band—Live at the Beacon Theater. Sanctuary, 2003.

The Best of the Allman Brothers Band. Hal Leonard, 2002.

Legends of Bottleneck Blues Guitar. Vestapol, 2002.

Tom Dowd & the Language of Music. Palm Pictures, 2003.

Web sites

www.abbdiscography.com

www.allmanbrothersband.com

www.allmanbrothers.info/daresources.htm

www.BigHouseFoundation.com

www.hittinthenote.com

www.WolfgangsVault.com

www.youtube.com

About the Author

Grammy nominee Randy Poe was born in Fayette, Alabama, and raised in Muscle Shoals. He moved to New York City in 1980, where he became executive director of the Songwriters' Hall of Fame. In 1985 he was named president of Leiber & Stoller Music Publishing. Poe has written two other books, dozens of articles for various music magazines, and the liner notes to over 100 albums. A recipient of the ASCAP-Deems Taylor Award for excellence in music journalism, Poe lives in Los Angeles with his wife, Mina, and son, Riley.

Photo Credits

Index